Douglass in His Own Time

WRITERS IN THEIR OWN TIME

Joel Myerson, *series editor*

DOUGLASS

in His Own Time

A Biographical Chronicle of His Life, Drawn from Recollections, Interviews, and Memoirs by Family, Friends, and Associates

EDITED BY

John Ernest

University of Iowa Press,
Iowa City

University of Iowa Press, Iowa City 52242

www.uiowapress.org
Printed in the United States of America

The University of Iowa Press is a member of Green Press Initiative
and is committed to preserving natural resources.

Printed on acid-free paper

Library of Congress Cataloging-in-Publication Data
Douglass in his own time: a biographical chronicle of his life, drawn from recollections, interviews, and memoirs by family, friends, and associates / edited by John Ernest.
pages cm.—(Writers in their own time)

Includes bibliographical references and index.
ISBN 978-1-60938-280-3 (pbk)
ISBN 978-1-60938-289-6 (ebk)
1. Douglass, Frederick, 1818–1895. 2. Douglass, Frederick, 1818–1895—Friends and associates. 3. African American abolitionists—Biography. 4. Abolitionists—United States—Biography. I. Ernest, John, editor.
E449.D75D687 2014
973.8092—dc23
[B] 2014010229

Contents

Introduction

ONE OF THE MOST incredible stories in American history is that of Frederick Douglass, the man who escaped from slavery and rose to become one of the most celebrated and eloquent orators, writers, and public figures in the world. His story was, in fact, so incredible—it strained credulity to such an extent—that early in his career many doubted that the powerful orator before them had ever experienced slavery. But when Douglass committed his story to writing, in his 1845 autobiography *Narrative of the Life of Frederick Douglass, an American Slave*, with the important phrase *Written by Himself* included in the title, he answered the doubters and gave the world a glimpse into his remarkable determination and abilities. Over the course of his life, Douglass would expand on his story considerably—in two other autobiographies: *My Bondage and My Freedom* (1855) and *Life and Times of Frederick Douglass* (1881), followed by a revised edition in 1882 and a revised and expanded edition in 1893. He would also write innumerable newspaper articles and editorials, countless orations, and a novella, writings that helped establish him as the most prominent and influential African American of his time and one of America's greatest writers. In spite of all his writing, what has stood out most for readers from his own time to ours has been the simple story of his life as he first related it in 1845. One might even say that Douglass is not merely celebrated for his story; he is also contained by it, reduced to the confines of a heroic struggle against slavery and his attainment of a glorious freedom through which he continued his antislavery work. Less a living presence than an inspiring tale to relate during Black History Month, Frederick Douglass remains relatively unknown even to many of those who celebrate his achievements.

Douglass in His Own Time offers an introduction to Douglass the man by those who knew him—but even in these writings Douglass can seem elusive, shadowed by the fame that enters every room before him. Even those who knew him felt compelled to tell again and again the main features of the story he related in the most famous of his autobiographies, the 1845 *Narrative.* In fact, in selecting pieces to include in this volume, I have excluded those from a number of important writers, both black and white, whom one might well expect to encounter here—among them, Harriet Beecher Stowe, author of *Uncle Tom's Cabin*; antislavery activist and fellow editor Lydia Maria Child; author and editor Pauline Hopkins; historian George Washington Williams; and biographer of the race William J. Simmons. Each of these writers honored Douglass in print, but each of them felt compelled to follow the outlines and details of the story the great man told in his first autobiography. Even in the selections included, one will encounter the main narrative of Douglass's story again and again, as well as a handful of legendary tales told about him through the years. If all of the writings on and biographies of Douglass could be included here, readers would be justified in asking whether, after reading so much about Douglass, they were getting any closer to an understanding of the man behind the story.

To be sure, Douglass's life is a story worth telling. Born in slavery in Maryland in 1818, the son of a slave woman, Harriet Bailey, and a white man, Douglass came to define the African American experience of the nineteenth century. Most biographical sketches of Douglass focus on the process by which he came to awareness of his situation, his acquisition of basic literacy while still enslaved, his heroic struggle with a slave breaker that signaled his determination to resist enslavement, and then, in 1838, his escape to nominal freedom in the North. With the help of a free black woman who would later join him in the North, where they were married, Douglass disguised himself as a free black sailor and with borrowed identification boarded a train and traveled north from Baltimore to New York City. Within three years, Douglass joined William Lloyd Garrison's antislavery organization and became a full-time lecturer and one of the most justly famous orators in American history. Following the publication of his *Narrative*, Douglass traveled to England to escape those who, following the trail of his book and of his fame, would have tried to re-enslave him. For twenty months, Douglass lectured in England, Ireland, and Scotland, returning to the United States with the funds and the determination to publish his own newspaper, the *North Star*, initially published in concert with another prominent black abolitionist, Martin Delany. Douglass's own career, his increasing prominence and independence, and his changing views on the proper path of abolitionist activism led to a split with the Garrisonian factions of the antislavery movement. Douglass once again had to leave his home (which, since his return to the United States, had been Rochester, New York), this time for Canada, when he was suspected of playing a role in John Brown's 1859 raid on Harpers Ferry, though he had turned down Brown's request that he be part of that failed attempt to overturn the system of slavery. Douglass was active throughout the Civil War—most prominently, by encouraging Lincoln to recruit African Americans for the Union army—and after, when he was appointed to various political offices that had not before been offered to any African American: president of the ill-fated Freedman's Savings and Trust Company (1874), U.S. marshal of the District of Columbia (1877), recorder of deeds for the District of Columbia (1881), consul general to Haiti (1888), and chargé d'affaires for Santo Domingo (1889). Small wonder that Douglass has been as prominent since the nineteenth century as he was through his long and active life—the subject of numerous biographies and often the sole representative in American classrooms of African American life, thought, and literary genius before the Civil War.

When related in such broad strokes, what this story doesn't reveal is the man behind these many achievements. Few Americans—President Obama prominent among them—are in a position to appreciate the private challenges behind this public story. No African American had risen to anything like Douglass's prominence before him, so he had no models to follow, and he lived in a time when the force of racism (and the assumption of white supremacy) was ubiquitous, unashamed, and sometimes violent. Douglass often found himself in situations that no black American had experienced before, and he was almost always treated as an exceptional representative of his race—that is, considered exceptional in his achievements but representative all the same of black Americans everywhere. Any misstep on Douglass's part was treated with special scrutiny; any ideological or social position he took was examined for its potential to disrupt the social order; any achievement he managed was explained away (for example, by referring to his mixed-blood ancestry and attributing his successes to his white blood). Throughout his accomplished life, Douglass was alone in ways that very few people have the mixed fortune of experiencing, with the broad world open before him and untold numbers of land mines awaiting every step.

Such a life yields many stories, the most interesting and revealing of which would be the ones not immediately available to the public. The full story of Douglass's life would include numerous behind-the-scenes revelations on the role of racial prejudice and assumptions in American political, economic, religious, and social life. Imagine if President Obama were completely free to speak, without consequences, of his experiences as the first African American to hold the highest office in the country. What might we learn about the racially charged operations of American society, business, politics, and government—all things we should have figured out long ago. Similarly, Douglass found himself in situations that no African American had seen before, and he fought his way into the backrooms of power to which no African American had before gained access. It is almost strange that so many published sketches of Douglass largely repeat the story he first told in 1845, for the many stories that followed are likely to be among the most fascinating and revealing tales of his life. But his struggles during his first twenty years continue to dominate our understanding of Douglass, largely because of the success of his *Narrative*, a great work of literature as well as an important eyewitness account of slavery and the struggle for freedom. So influential has the *Narrative* been that many readers have not looked beyond it for testimony about slavery. As Deborah E. McDowell, one of the most cogent commentators on the scholarship on African American history, has noted, both scholars and lay historians alike have considered Douglass to be not only a representative man but also "the part that stands for the whole," the story that keeps us from looking further. McDowell notes that scholars and teachers have "privileged and mystified Douglass's narrative" and in doing so have twice distorted Douglass's purposes into a kind of "double duty: not only does it make slavery intelligible, but the 'black experience' as well."[1] The story Douglass told in 1845 has become, it seems, rather too easy to tell, and it has come to obscure as much as it reveals.

When his *Narrative* is examined carefully, the various racial tensions that characterized Douglass's life become clear, though too often the only tensions readers see are between black slaves and white slaveholders, a simple morality tale that was eventually resolved, or so the story goes, by way of civil war. The *Narrative* was published under the auspices of the antislavery society in Boston, and in that publication Douglass's own telling of his life is preceded by comments from two of the most prominent white abolitionists of the time—in a preface written by William Lloyd Garrison and a letter by Wendell Phillips, the white lawyer known for his antislavery work and one of the most celebrated orators of his day. Both prefatory pieces are resounding in their admiration for Douglass, but both carry the marked rhetoric of the presumption of authority and perhaps more than a hint of patronage and benevolent condescension. Literary scholar Robert B. Stepto has noted that Garrison's "Preface" to Douglass's *Narrative* indicates that, rather than introduce the reader to Douglass's writing, "Garrison is far more interested in writing history . . . and recording his own place in it" and that, accordingly, "we might be tempted to see Garrison's 'Preface' at war with Douglass's tale for authorial control of the narrative as a whole."[2] For Stepto, "that tension is stunted by Garrison's enthusiasm for Douglass's tale";[3] but for literary scholar William L. Andrews and others, the tension persists, becoming clear to Douglass when later he broke from the Garrisonians and thereby "gained a perspective that allowed him to see signs of 'oppression' in the very 'form' of the fugitive slave narrative that he had written in 1845."[4] When Douglass returned to the story of his life in his 1855 autobiography, *My Bondage and My Freedom*, as Andrews argues, Douglass's approach to his story becomes a declaration of independence not only from the paternal authority of Garrison and the Garrisonian mode of antislavery activism but also from the narrative conventions that determined the history that Douglass could draw from his life in 1845. Revealingly, the preface to the 1855 autobiography was written by a black colleague, James McCune Smith.

As many of the memoirs, newspaper articles, biographical sketches, and letters that follow indicate, Douglass's break with his 1845 allies was quite public and pronounced, and the tensions revealed by those breaks extended to virtually all areas of Douglass's life. In the pages that follow, readers will encounter many signs of the turbulence that characterized Douglass's life. There were many causes for these troubles, but we can generally group them under three headings: race, politics, and religion. Of course, Douglass's status as a black man, and the inability of those around him to recognize a black man's equal authority in matters social, political, and religious, played a prominent role in all of these struggles. But those struggles often came to a head in instances of simple racism (or in limiting and belittling racial assumptions), in disagreements over political goals and methods, and in reactions to Douglass's independent and seemingly iconoclastic religious beliefs.

Consider, for example, the racial attitudes even of Douglass's closest white allies. Leon Litwack has noted that "when the *Colored American* reviewed the economic plight of the Negro in the wake of the Panic of 1837, it noted that not one local abolitionist had placed a Negro in any conspicuous position in his business establishment; in fact, it could not even find a Negro in the offices of the New York Anti-Slavery Society."[5] The situation did not change dramatically in later years. Indeed, as William H. and Jane H. Pease have noted, much of what white abolitionists said and did "betrayed an implicit and at times explicit belief in [black] racial inferiority."[6] Edmund Quincy, for example, "lashed out in a letter to Caroline Weston in 1846 at 'Wendell's nigger,' whom he held responsible for botching an Anti-slavery Report," and "as late as 1860 Theodore Parker, a backer of John Brown, observed [in a letter published in 1860] that 'the Anglo-Saxon with common sense does not like this Africanization of America; he wishes the superior race to multiply rather than the inferior.'"[7] These were not isolated examples, as Frederick Douglass emphasized in his commentary on a letter from the Reverend Samuel Ringgold Ward published in *Frederick Douglass' Paper* on April 13, 1855. Noting that "we look upon the past as a precedent for the future," Douglass supports Ward's public declaration of frustration with white antislavery allies:

> Our oppressed people are wholly ignored, in one sense, in the generalship of the movement to effect our Redemption. Nothing is done—no, nothing, as our friend Ward asserts, to inspire us with the Idea of our Equality with the whites. We are a poor, pitiful, dependent and servile class of Negroes, "*unable to keep pace*" with the movement, to which we have adverted—not even capable of "*perceiving what are its demands, or understanding the philosophy of its operations!*" Of course, if we are "unable to keep pace" with our white brethren, in their vivid perception of the demands of our cause, those who assume the leadership of the Anti-Slavery Movement; if it is regarded as having "*transcended our ability*," we cannot consistently expect to receive from those who indulge in this opinion, a *practical recognition of our Equality.* This is what we are contending for. It is what we have never received. It is what we must receive to inspire us with confidence in the self-appointed generals of the Anti-Slavery host, the Euclids who are *theoretically* working out the almost insoluble problem of our future destiny.[8]

Douglass put it even more plainly in 1856, in an article entitled "The Unholy Alliance of Negro Hate and Anti-Slavery": "Opposing slavery and hating its victims has come to be a very common form of Abolitionism."[9]

The selective vision of white antislavery reformers simply didn't recognize the systemic realities that restricted opportunities and economic access for their black colleagues—but this recognition was fundamental to the African American communities, motivating the establishment of various institutions, from churches to "mutual benefit" societies, devoted to black collective self-determination.

I do not mean to undervalue the extent to which white and black men and women alike overcame their prejudices and hesitations about one another to work together under the abolitionist cause, for such alliances were both many and strong. They were, however, always complicated, and it can be too easy to overlook the challenge of managing such alliances at a time when African Americans were denied even fundamental access to education, political self-representation, and economic opportunity. When even walking publicly with a white man or woman might cause a stir, working across racial lines required ongoing and reciprocal negotiations to build mutual trust, often at some risk to the personal safety and social acceptance of those involved.

Complicated, too, was the question of how to address this world of demonstrable wrongs and systemic inequalities—and on political goals and methods Douglass often differed dramatically from his colleagues, both white and black. Douglass was first embraced and recruited by William Lloyd Garrison, editor of the *Liberator* and the most prominent and formidable abolitionist of the nineteenth century, and Douglass considered Garrison both a friend and mentor. But Douglass was insatiable in his intellectual curiosity and restless when confronted with settled views, and he soon found himself differing from Garrison on the methods by which the abolition of slavery might be achieved. Garrison advocated moral suasion as the means to the abolition of slavery. Believing the U.S. Constitution to be a proslavery document and the political system inherently corrupted by slavery, he advocated moral reform as the only suitable way to address the sinfulness inherent in the system of slavery. Certainly, Douglass shared Garrison's moral stance against slavery, though he believed that American churches and the institution of religion itself were themselves corrupted by slavery, and Douglass came to believe that the abolition of slavery could be accomplished by political means, the process by which ideal ends and compromised means are reconciled over time.

Douglass's turn to political strategies, joined with his formation of his own paper—first called the *North Star* and later renamed *Frederick Douglass' Paper*—constituted a dramatic break from Garrisonian abolitionism and from Garrison himself, and the tensions between the two men (and those associated with both) were heated. Both men were proud, stubborn, and righteous in their convictions, and both were constitutionally unable to present their differences in the form of a civil disagreement. The break became especially public in 1853 through a series of editorial battles between Douglass, Garrison, and others, and it continued for many years. In an 1860 letter to fellow white abolitionist Samuel J. May, Garrison noted his inability to attend an event at which Douglass was also expected, and he noted,

> But, were I "in speaking order," the fact that Frederick Douglass is to be present at the celebration, and to participate therein, would powerfully repel me from attending. I regard him as thoroughly base and selfish, and I know that his hostility to the American Anti-Slavery Society and its leading advocates is unmitigated and unceasing. He has just attended Stephen S. Foster's Political Convention at Worcester, and made it an occasion for fresh misrepresentation of the Society, and fresh sneers at its friends. His contemptuous treatment of George Thompson, during his late visit to England, was unprovoked and outrageous. In fact, he reveals himself more and more to me as destitute of every principle of honor, ungrateful to the last degree and malevolent in spirit. He is not worthy of respect, confidence, or countenance.[10]

Garrison's lingering scorn would continue many more years, as would Douglass's—and even at Garrison's death, Douglass's clear expressions of admiration and love for his former mentor and friend carried the traces of their former dispute, war wounds still capable of causing aches and pains in old age.

The third great cause of Douglass's struggles stemmed from his independent and principled views on religion at a time when the church was at the center of virtually all social and cultural life. Douglass's Christian beliefs had always been important to him, and they remained so throughout his life, though sometimes in forms that other Christians could not recognize or appreciate. While still enslaved, he had taken "leadership roles in clandestine religious institutions designed to teach slaves to read the Bible."[11] Although the slaveholders broke up these Sabbath schools, his experience in them remained important to Douglass. Commenting on the schools in

My Bondage and My Freedom, he observed, "I have had various employments during my short life; but I look back to *none* with more satisfaction, than to that afforded by my Sunday school."[12] In New Bedford, where he first settled after his escape from slavery, following a disappointing experience with the first church he attended (which required separate communion for black and white congregants), he turned to the African Methodist Episcopal Zion (AMEZ) Church and continued his personal ministry, earning a license to work as a local preacher by 1839. Many years later, he would similarly reflect on valued experiences, noting in 1894, "My connection with the little church continued long after I was in the antislavery field. I look back to the days I spent in little Zion, New Bedford, in the several capacities of sexton, steward, class leader, clerk, and local preacher, as among the happiest days of my life."[13] Clearly, the Christianity that had inspired him when he was enslaved remained a central presence in Douglass's life in freedom.

It wasn't long, though, before Douglass came to the conclusion that all American churches, even those emerging from and serving black communities, were implicated in sustaining the system of slavery. Of his beloved AMEZ Church, he concluded, "I could not see it to be my duty to remain with that body, when I found that it consented to the same spirit which held my brethren in chains."[14] Of churches generally, he was more severe. "I assert most unhesitatingly," he states in an appendix to his 1845 *Narrative* devoted to the subject of religion, "that the religion of the south is a mere covering for the most horrid crimes,—a justifier of the most appalling barbarity,—a sanctifier of the most hateful frauds,—and a dark shelter, under which the darkest, foulest, grossest, and most infernal deeds of slaveholders find the strongest protection."[15] He was direct as well in his belief, stated in an 1849 speech, that "the Slaveholder has no earthly right—I believe that he is not born of Heaven—he is no mortal—he is a monster."[16] Moreover, he was consistently clear that his denunciations of slaveholding religion were not limited to southern churches. "The church in America is," he stated in an 1847 speech, "beyond all question, the chief refuge of slavery. When we attack it [slavery] in the state, it runs into the street, to the mob; when we attack it in the mob, it flies to the church; and, sir, it is a melancholy fact, that it finds a better, safer, and more secure protection from the shafts of abolitionism within the sacred enclosure of the Christian temple than from any other quarter whatever."[17]

In itself, such statements were radical but not singular, for many in the antislavery movement were highly critical of churches that did not take a strong antislavery stand, and Douglass himself simply echoes even harsher statements against American churches passed as resolutions at the 1843 National Convention of Colored Citizens, held at Buffalo. Beginning with an affirmation of the delegates' belief "in the true Church of Christ," which "will stand while time endures," the first resolution states that any true church "will evince its spirit by its opposition to all sins, and especially to the sin of slavery, which is a compound of all others." "The great mass of American sects, falsely called churches," this resolution continues, "which apologize for slavery and prejudice, or practice slaveholding, are in truth no churches, but Synagogues of Satan." The second of the resolutions emphasizes this last point, identifying "slaveholding and prejudice sustaining ministers and churches (falsely so called)" as "the greatest enemies to Christ and to civil and religious liberty in the world." The resolutions that follow call upon "the colored people in the free States" to resist these churches, participation in which makes them "guilty of enslaving themselves and others."[18] Douglass was involved in framing and voting on these resolutions in Buffalo, and when he later echoed them in his *Narrative*, he did so with the assurance of a supportive community.

What distinguished Douglass's religious views for many, and what drew the ire of even his black admirers, was his emphasis on human activism, often explicitly in place of faith in the providence of God. "There is another religion," he stated in 1847, a religion that "takes off fetters instead of binding them on," and "the Anti-Slavery platform is based on this kind of religion." "This," he stated proudly, "is Anti-Slavery—this is Christianity."[19] For Douglass, the antislavery cause was fundamentally devoted to the reform and reinvigoration of Christianity, work that remained long after the antislavery mission was seemingly complete. The problem, Douglass argued in 1849, is that "we think that religion is the entertainment of hope." "I know there is a hope in religion," Douglass acknowledged; "I know there is faith and I know there is prayer about religion and necessary to it, but God is most glorified when there is peace on earth and good will towards men." Douglass presented this ideal as the promise delivered by angels "when our Saviour came into the world," and he presented it as the primary test of any religion, and any individual, claiming the authority of Christianity.[20] Believing that "there can be no virtue without freedom" and that "there can be no obedience to the Bible without freedom," Douglass found his beliefs most fully realized when men and women did the work necessary for social reform. "When we see men binding up the wounds of those who fall among thieves," he observed in 1849, "administering to the necessities of the down-trodden, and breaking off the chains of the bondsmen, it is evidence enough that their works are of God, and, whatever may be their abstract notions, Christ himself lives within them; for this was his spirit."[21] Years later, in 1870, he would echo this statement, exclaiming, "I want to express my love to God and gratitude to God, by thanking those faithful men and women, who have devoted the great energies of their souls to the welfare of mankind. It is only through such men and such women that I can get any glimpses of God anywhere."[22]

For some, this statement that could be read as praise for the power of a community of believers was seen instead as placing men above God, and Douglass himself above all. Moreover, Douglass was consistently clear that his denunciations of slaveholding religion were not limited to southern churches, and his consistent attacks upon churches were often noted by the black press. Like other African American leaders, Douglass was sometimes very critical of black ministers who placed religious passion above an educated and thoughtful approach to religion. During Douglass's tenure, beginning in 1870, as owner and editor of the *New National Era*, a weekly newspaper in Washington, D.C., Douglass sometimes drew the ire of the chief organ of the A.M.E. Church, the *Christian Recorder*. One brief note, published in the July 15, 1872, issue of that paper, complained, "We have it on good authority that Frederick Douglass, when in Jackson, Miss., made the remark in the presence of quite a large assembly, 'If you want to put a Methodist preacher to sleep, put a book in his hand.' Of course, then, they could not read the New Era. Will these sleepy preachers stay awake long enough, to note the fact, and guide themselves accordingly?" The following month, the *Christian Recorder* urged its readers not to support Douglass's paper, explaining that "Frederick Douglass is not at all anxious that any Methodists should take the New National Era. If he were, he would not insult them by speaking foolishly and falsely of them and their religion. Till he comes to his right mind, we hope all of our people will let him and his paper severely alone."[23] But Douglass's late-career critiques were of a piece with his early ones. Once the refuge of slavery, Douglass believed, the church had been and continued to be the refuge of ignorance.

Of course, these various statements would have little force if Douglass were dismissive of Christianity altogether, and in fact he viewed Christianity as vital to antislavery efforts. Following a parody of a slaveholding sermon, a frequent segment in his speeches, Douglass explains his sense of the importance of faith in his antislavery work and draws from the Bible (James 3:17) to testify to his personal beliefs. "I dwell mostly upon the religious aspects," he states, "because I believe it is the religious people who are to be relied on in this Anti-Slavery movement. Do not misunderstand my railing—do not class me with those who despise religion—do not identify me with the infidel. I love the religion of Christianity—which cometh from above—which is pure, peaceable, gentle, easy to be entreated, full of good fruits, and without hypocrisy."[24] Presenting the battle against slavery as a struggle of biblical proportions between Christian "votaries" and the religion of the "Priest and Levite," Douglass expresses his hope for a Christian revival.[25] This was the battle he faced when enslaved, and he holds to the faith that encouraged his initial resistance to slavery. "The masters won't have the Bible among their slaves," he noted in 1847, "because it teaches them their right to liberty."[26] "It is idle to make the Bible and Slavery go hand in hand," Douglass stated in 1849, though he knew full well that the Bible was used regularly not only to support slavery but also to discourage or moderate antislavery efforts. For Douglass, the antislavery movement was, among other things, a theological movement—involving not only contrasting interpretations of the Bible but also the challenge of providing liberating doctrine to those who were denied both the ability to read and the freedom to act upon their readings.[27] For many, though, the theological reforms Douglass envisioned were too radical a challenge to the authority of the religious community.

These struggles—over racial prejudices and assumptions, over political methods and goals, and over the nature of belief and the requirements of religious observance—characterized Douglass's long career in the public eye, but all of these struggles emphasize the fundamental and definitive characteristic of Douglass's life, his independence. Having escaped from slavery, Douglass was determined to be free in his views and actions; and having educated himself without the benefit of formal schooling, Douglass was insatiable in his intellectual curiosity and freedom of thought. He did not claim to be always right, and he was never fully free from the influences around him, but he was determined to think for himself and to go his own way.

That independent spirit comes through in the various documents that make up *Douglass in His Own Time*, a collection of writings about Douglass by those who knew him—including those who knew him only from a distance, as a public figure. In almost all of the documents that follow, we confront again and again the very public life that Douglass lived, with few sustained glimpses into his private realms. As you read the pages that follow, you will encounter many writers—some good friends, some respectful antagonists, and some distant hecklers—contending with, repeating the terms of, manipulating, and otherwise negotiating with the force of Douglass's public presence.

Douglass in His Own Time includes a broad range of writings—some intended for public viewing and some private correspondence, all of which contend with the force of Douglass's overwhelming presence. We begin, in fact, with an instructive example of that force—a piece designed to comment not on Douglass but rather on the mansion of his original owners, the Lloyds. In many ways a conventional piece that surveys the legends and ancestry associated with the great house, it is presented as a chapter in a book on great mansions, and its author realizes that he can hardly discuss the house without mentioning that Douglass was associated with it. But once Douglass enters the narrative of this great house, the author barely knows what to do with him, and the narrative veers off on a tangent from which it never recovers, concluding finally with a mention of Douglass's association with John Brown, arguably a strange way to end a narrative about Douglass, and by any measure an even stranger ending to a chapter about the Wye House of Talbot County, Maryland. In the subsequent writings, we follow at least loosely the chronology of Douglass's life, and we encounter many more disrupted narratives along the way. Quite simply, Douglass enriched and complicated every story of which he constituted a part.

Among the subjects covered by the various writings that follow, one in particular deserves special notice, a gathering of documents I have grouped under the heading "The Great Controversy." They all have to do with the very public disputes that followed Douglass's break with the Garrisonians, his establishment of his own newspaper, and his criticism of the American Anti-Slavery Society (AASS). Most of the pieces included in this section are from 1853, the year that saw the most direct and scathing public exchanges, but the controversy had its roots in earlier years, and its effects continued for many years more. After Douglass returned from England to the United States in 1847, he relocated to Rochester and established his own paper, the *North Star.* Garrison viewed the paper as unnecessary competition to his own *Liberator*, and especially so as Douglass's views on the antislavery movement and its strategies began to change. By 1853, Douglass's critique of Garrisonian abolitionism was explicit, and Garrison's response was itself direct and forceful. Almost immediately, the attacks became personal on both sides, and they involved a number of allies in the movement, black and white. These exchanges (of the many published) reveal Douglass's own temperament at the time and also how others dealt with his legendary presence in the movement.

In this exchange of attacks, one especially personal charge against Douglass concerned his association with the white woman who had followed him from England to help with the *North Star*, Julia Griffiths. Garrison more than intimated that Douglass was involved in an extramarital affair with Griffiths. Douglass responded, but especially notable was a letter sent to Garrison for publication in the *Liberator* from Douglass's wife, Anna Murray Douglass, the black woman who had helped Douglass escape from slavery and then had moved north to marry him after his successful journey to freedom. Together the couple had five children, and in response to Garrison's charge, Anna's letter stated, "SIR—It is not true, that the presence of a certain person in the office of Frederick Douglass causes unhappiness in his family. Please insert this in your next paper."[28] But there is more to this story, as to most stories. Susan B. Anthony, a friend of the Douglasses, later wrote to Garrison, "We were all surprised & shocked at the appearance of Anna Douglass' letter in the Liberator. *Anna did not*, to my certain knowledge, intend that letter to cover all the *essentials* of the Liberator's charge—for she declared to Amy Post, who happened to call there about the time, it was concocted by Frederic [*sic*] & Julia; that she would never *sign* a paper that said, Julia had not *made her trouble.* She said, *Garrison is right*—it is Julia that has made Frederic hate all his old friends. Said she, I don't care anything about her being in the *office*—but I won't have her in my house."[29] Like many male celebrities, Douglass found his privacy most challenged, and his public career made most vulnerable, by his conduct with women.

Douglass's relationship with his wife was, like other aspects of his life, complicated. Anna, the woman he met when he was enslaved, was illiterate, and his attempts to educate her largely failed. Although he had in her a faithful companion, Anna was unprepared to follow her husband's astounding growth into an unprecedented public role as one of the great orators and intellectuals of his day, a man of insatiable intellectual and cultural appetites. A couple of years after Garrison's public charge and Anna's contested letter denying Douglass's infidelity, Douglass offered a revealing glimpse into his marriage in an 1857 letter to a friend, Mrs. Lydia Dennett: "I am sad to say that she [Anna] is by no means well—and if I should write down all her complaints there would be no room even to put my name at the bottom, although the world will have it that I am actually at the bottom of it all." Sounding not at all like a great leader and more like a stereotypical husband, Douglass continued, "She has suffered in every member except one. She still seems able to use with great ease and fluency her powers of speech, and by the time I am at home a week or two longer, I shall have pretty fully learned in how many points there are needs of improvement in my temper and disposition as a husband and father, the head of a family! Amid all the vicissitudes, however, I am happy to say that my wife gives me an excellent loaf of bread, and keeps a neat house, and has moments of marked amiability, of all of which good things, I do not fail to take due advantage."[30]

Unsurprisingly, then, the public exposure of his relationship with Griffiths was not the only time when Douglass's interactions with white women created a stir. Douglass was attacked when walking with two white British women in New York City in 1849, for such close associations were enough to lead many to associate abolitionism with what would later be called miscegenation (a term coined for a political pamphlet in 1864 and designed to inspire fears over the "blending of the races"). Douglass proved quite willing to both feed and challenge such fears. Though he remained with Anna until her death in 1882, rumors of his infidelity were not uncommon, as in the case of Garrison's charge. In addition to his intimate friendship with Griffiths, who helped him with his writing, his finances, and his career generally, Douglass for many years was engaged in an intimate relationship with Ottilie Assing, a German journalist. The heart of the relationship involved intellectual exchange and cultural interests, but Assing committed suicide when, following Anna's death, Douglass married his white secretary, Helen Pitts, a woman twenty years his junior. Assing had been diagnosed with breast cancer, a disease even more difficult to face at that time than in ours, and she faced other personal difficulties as well, so her suicide was not necessarily provoked by Douglass's choice, though her despondence at Douglass's decision is undeniable. Douglass's marriage to a white woman was met with public denouncements and private rejections. A few friends proved true, but many could not accept this crossing of the demanding racial lines of the time.

Although Douglass's public ideological and political disputes are important, and although his intimate relations with white women are unavoidably of interest, the great majority of the writings that follow are concerned with finding the language and a narrative capable of doing justice to Douglass's amazing and influential career. As noted, I have not included several biographical sketches authored by some of the most important white and black writers of the time, largely to avoid tasking the reader with endless retellings of the story Douglass relates in his 1845 autobiography. But even those who extended their biographical sketches beyond the outlines and details of Douglass's original self-presentation find themselves challenged to account for Douglass while also accounting for Douglass's world. Some find Douglass's accomplishments simply unaccountable; others look to account for his life by accepting Douglass's own speculation, in his *Narrative* when trying to account for his great fortune in being sent to Baltimore as a young slave, that he was favored by Providence. Booker T. Washington, among others, accepted this reading and extended it to the point of considering it a blessing that Douglass was born in slavery, creating the conditions necessary for the great career that followed. "The life of Frederick Douglass," Washington asserts at the beginning of his biography of Douglass, "is the history of American slavery epitomised in a single human experience. He saw it all, lived it all, and overcame it all. What he saw and lived and suffered was not too much to pay, however, for a great career."[31]

However they account for the trajectory of his life and the profound influence he extended throughout that life, Douglass's admirers come back again and again to the fundamental impact of his career as an editor and especially as an orator. Whatever else might be said of him, whatever the stolen glances into his most private chambers might reveal, Douglass's friends and acquaintances almost always return to Douglass's tremendous power over the written and spoken word, his amazing presence before crowds, his ability to improvise, to entertain, to instruct, to inspire—indeed, to change lives through his eloquent appeals to righteous self-awareness and social justice. Even after all these years, when Douglass's *Narrative* can be viewed as a testimony against an institution, slavery, that was finally defeated, his speeches retain their living presence, and he still challenges our most settled narratives of American history. In his most famous speech, for a Fourth of July celebration in 1852, Douglass challenged his readers even to explain their invitation to him to participate in such an occasion. "Fellow-citizens," he begins, "pardon me, allow me to ask, why am I called upon to speak here to-day? What have I, or those I represent, to do with your national independence?" "Do you mean, citizens, to mock me," he soon adds, "by asking me to speak to-day?"[32] Douglass could not allow his readers the easy comfort of arranging for an antislavery speech on Independence Day without confronting them with the irony of the situation, nor could he avoid pressing the point—that the irony extended to the very foundations of American culture: "The existence of slavery in this country brands your republicanism as a sham, your humanity as a base pretense, and your Christianity as a lie."[33] In many ways, Douglass's career involved an ongoing attempt to insist that words have meaning, and that ideals have practical force, or to expose the fact that all meaning has been undermined by a hypocritical culture.

What made Douglass so powerful, though, was that he believed in the possibility of meaning, and he was a true believer in the principles of those significant words—republicanism, humanity, Christianity. Douglass's approach in many of his speeches focused on the dual presence of hope and hopelessness, both of which depended on a careful reading of one's world. For Douglass, hope could be found by way of a carefully historicized understanding of the present moment, and hopelessness pressed itself in the turbulent currents of that present moment. In his 1876 "Oration in Memory of Abraham Lincoln," for example, presented at the unveiling of the Freedmen's Monument to Abraham Lincoln, Douglass is quite pointed in his management of these competing readings of that commemorative event. He notes, for example, the great progress represented by the moment and exclaims, "In view, then, of the past, the present, and the future, with the very long and dark history of our bondage behind us, and with liberty, progress, and enlightenment before us, I again congratulate you upon this auspicious day and hour."[34] But Douglass also recontextualizes the moment in his identification of Lincoln as "preeminently the white man's President, entirely devoted to the welfare of white men," emphasizing that "in his interests, in his associations, in his habits of thought, and in his prejudices, [Lincoln] was a white man." Identifying the white audience as "the children of Abraham Lincoln" and the black audience as "at best only his step-children, children by adoption, children by forces of circumstances and necessity,"[35] Douglass places the event, the monument, and the man being honored that day within a fractured reading of U.S. history and of a president who represents both progress and the ongoing problems of U.S. cultural, political, and racial life.

Readers will encounter both bright hopes and dark undercurrents in the documents that follow. And in approaching Douglass through the biographical sketches, memoirs, letters, editorials, and other articles about him, readers will encounter the complexity of a life lived on a very public stage, the story of an extraordinary black man in an insistently white world. One might say with considerable justice that the portrait of Douglass that emerges in these pages comes closer to the realities of his life than could any domesticated biographical narrative, for Douglass's life was played out in the pages of newspapers and books, in editorial exchanges and short, sharp notices in newspapers both friendly and antagonistic to his interests. To the extent that our identities depend on others capable of recognizing and validating our own sense of character, purpose, and worth, Douglass's life was complex indeed, and his story ultimately became a narrative woven through the many conflicting strands of the American social and ideological fabric. One wonders how on earth Douglass managed to recognize himself in the jumbled reflections of his life and character provided by those around him. In the attempt of the many writers represented in this volume to identify and claim an understanding of Douglass, we get a sense of the life Douglass lived, both in their ability to get it right and in their inevitable ability to get it wrong. In Douglass's life, and in his complex relations with a number of people over time, we see the history of the country he served so well—both the history we know how to relate and the story we still need to learn to tell. After three autobiographies and numerous biographies, Douglass's life still calls for a just and full telling—one that accounts for the web of relations represented by the following readings and one that calls for the reader's own involvement in this very public life.

The texts printed in this volume have been drawn from a wide variety of sources. I have silently corrected typographical errors and have sometimes changed nineteenth-century spellings. Material that I have deleted from the original text is indicated by bracketed ellipses, and the sets of three asterisks (* * *) that mark breaks in the original texts have been retained. Quotation marks and their placement have been standardized to follow American style. Some documents include the original footnotes. Complete bibliographic information on the source is provided in an unnumbered footnote following each text.

Readers interested in this volume should be interested as well in one published shortly after Douglass's death, *In Memoriam: Frederick Douglass* (Philadelphia: John C. Yorston, 1897). Although the editor of that collection is not listed on the title page, it is generally credited to Douglass's widow, Helen Pitts Douglass. Presented as "a record of the spontaneous expression of grief and surprise evoked by the unexpected death of Frederick Douglass," the volume is devoted to "the world's impulse to honor him who so honored humanity."[36] And, indeed, the world is well represented. The volume is divided into sections on "Obsequies at Washington, D.C.," "Obsequies at Rochester, N. Y.," "Tender Words from Loving Hearts," "Preambles and Resolutions," "Poems and Sonnets," "Memorial Services—Addresses and Sermons," "Tributes of the Press," "Reminiscences," and a closing biographical sketch. Contributions represent well Douglass's global reputation, with letters from places ranging from Toledo, Ohio; Haiti; London; and Paris, among numerous other towns, cities, and countries. Among the many organizations whose resolutions are presented are the Anti-Lynching Committee, London; the Frederick Douglass Literary Association of Baltimore, Maryland; the Frederick Douglass Lyceum of Memphis, Tennessee; Wilberforce University; and the Women's National Council. In all, the book is a wealth of admiring commentary on Douglass by the many worldwide whose lives he touched. With the exception of a couple of poems, I have avoided drawing from that volume for this collection, but I recommend it to all readers interested in what others had to say about Frederick Douglass.

While working on this book, I have had the benefit of outstanding research assistants. I am grateful to Sohinee Roy, Luminita M. Dragulescu, Jim Greene, and Cara Snider for helping me gather material, and I am especially grateful to Douglas Terry for his discoveries, for helping me get this book back on track after a difficult period of distractions, and for his tremendous help in conceptualizing and organizing the book. Due to various personal challenges, this book was frequently delayed. I'm grateful to everyone at the University of Iowa Press, and especially to Catherine Cocks and Joel Myerson, for their patience, their faith in me, and their support for this project, and to Cynthia Lindlof, the most attentive, thoughtful, and professional copyeditor I've encountered in all my years of publishing. Finally, I'm grateful to Denise Ernest for her support and encouragement as I completed this book. She makes everything both possible and meaningful.

NOTES TO THE INTRODUCTION

1. Deborah E. McDowell, "In the First Place: Making Frederick Douglass and the Afro-American Narrative Tradition," in *African American Autobiography: A Collection of Critical Essays*, ed. William L. Andrews (Englewood Cliffs, NJ: Prentice Hall, 1993), 38–39.

2. Robert B. Stepto, *From behind the Veil: A Study of Afro-American Narrative*, 2nd ed. (Urbana: University of Illinois Press, 1991), 18.

3. Ibid., 18–19.

4. William L. Andrews, *To Tell a Free Story: The First Century of Afro-American Autobiography, 1760–1865* (Urbana: University of Illinois Press, 1986), 217.

5. Leon F. Litwack, "The Emancipation of the Negro Abolitionist," in *The Abolitionists*, ed. Richard O. Curry (Hinsdale, IL: The Dryden Press, 1973), 115.

6. Jane H. Pease and William H. Pease, *They Who Would Be Free: Blacks' Search for Freedom, 1830–1861* (New York: Atheneum, 1974), 97.

7. Ibid., 97–98. Parker's letter was published as *John Brown's Expedition Reviewed in a Letter from Theodore Parker, at Rome, to Francis Jackson, Boston* (Boston, 1860); the Peases take the quotation from page 14 of that pamphlet.

8. Ibid.

9. Pease and Pease, *They Who Would Be Free*, 387.

10. *The Letters of William Lloyd Garrison, Volume IV: From Disunionism to the Brink of War, 1850–1860*, ed. Louis Ruchames (Cambridge, MA: The Belknap Press of Harvard University Press, 1975), 693–694.

11. William L. Andrews, "Frederick Douglass, Preacher," *American Literature* 54, no. 4 (December 1982): 593.

12. Frederick Douglass, *My Bondage and My Freedom*, in *Frederick Douglass: Autobiographies*, ed. Henry Louis Gates Jr. (New York: Library of America, 1994), 300.

13. Qtd. in Andrews, "Frederick Douglass, Preacher," 596.

14. Douglass, *My Bondage and My Freedom*, 362.

15. Ibid., 68.

16. Douglass, "Shalt Thou Steal? An Address Delivered in New York, New York, on

8 May 1849," in *The Frederick Douglass Papers, Series One: Speeches, Debates and Interviews*, ed. John W. Blassingame (New Haven, CT: Yale University Press, 1982), 2:175.

17. Frederick Douglass, "Farewell to the British People: An Address Delivered in London, England, on 20 March 1847," in Blassingame, *Frederick Douglass Papers*, 2:29.

18. *Minutes of the National Convention of Colored Citizens: Held at Buffalo, on the 15th, 16th, 17th, 18th and 19th of August, 1843. For the Purpose of Considering Their Moral and Political Condition as American Citizens*, in *Minutes of the Proceedings of the National Negro Conventions, 1830–1864*, ed. Howard Holman Bell (New York: Arno Press and The New York Times, 1969), 15.

19. Frederick Douglass, "Love of God, Love of Man, Love of Country: An Address Delivered in Syracuse, New York, on 24 September 1847," in Blassingame, *Frederick Douglass Papers*, 2:101.

20. Frederick Douglass, "Too Much Religion, Too Little Humanity: An Address Delivered in New York, New York, on 9 May 1849," in Blassingame, *Frederick Douglass Papers*, 2:189.

21. Ibid., 188.

22. Frederick Douglass, "A Reform Absolutely Complete: An Address Delivered in New York, New York, on 9 April 1870," in *The Frederick Douglass Papers, Series One: Speeches, Debates, and Interviews*, ed. John W. Blassingame and John R. McKivigan (New Haven, CT: Yale University Press, 1991), 4:264.

23. "By the Editor," *Christian Recorder*, August 3, 1872, 4.

24. Douglass, "Love of God," 99.

25. Ibid., 99–100.

26. Frederick Douglass, "The Material and Moral Requirements of Antislavery Work: Addresses Delivered in Norristown, Pennsylvania, on 5, 6, August 1847," in Blassingame, *Frederick Douglass Papers*, 2:88.

27. Debates over the scriptural grounds for slavery were quite heated in the nineteenth century and were presented in such books as George Bourne's *A Condensed Anti-Slavery Bible Argument; By a Citizen of Virginia* (1845) and Thornton Stringfellow's *Scriptural and Statistical Views in Favor of Slavery* (1856).

28. Frederick Douglass, "The Liberator, Anti-Slavery Standard, Pennsylvania Freeman, Antislavery Bugle . . . ," *Liberator*, December 16, 1853, 1.

29. Maria Diedrich, *Love across Color Lines: Ottilie Assing & Frederick Douglass* (New York: Hill & Wang, 1999), 183.

30. Ibid., 150.

31. Booker T. Washington, *Frederick Douglass* (London: Hodder & Stoughton, 1906), 15.

32. Frederick Douglass, "What to the Slave Is the Fourth of July?," in *The Oxford Frederick Douglass Reader*, ed. William L. Andrews (New York: Oxford University Press, 1996), 115, 116.

33. Ibid., 126.

34. Frederick Douglass, "Oration in Memory of Abraham Lincoln, Delivered at the

Unveiling of the Freedmen's Monument in Memory of Abraham Lincoln, in Lincoln Park, Washington, D.C., April 14, 1876," in *The Life and Writings of Frederick Douglass*, vol. 4, *Reconstruction and After*, ed. Philip S. Foner (New York: International Publishers, 1955), 310.

35. Ibid., 312.

36. Helen Pitts Douglass, ed., *In Memoriam: Frederick Douglass* (Philadelphia: John C. Yorston, 1897), 3.

1. Frederick Douglass.

2. Sheet music cover for "The Fugitive's Song" by the famed Hutchinson Family Singers (1845).

3. A famous image of Henry Box Brown's arrival in Philadelphia, after having himself shipped from Richmond, Virginia. Although Douglass is included in the reception party, he was not at the event itself. His inclusion here is a sign of his fame and a lesson in the creation of both his legend and Brown's (1850).

4. Frederick Douglass included among Winfield Scott's supporters (1852).

5. Stereographic card of John Brown and Frederick Douglass, manufactured in 1891, indicating how closely the two men were associated long after Brown's failed raid on Harpers Ferry.

6. Illustration featuring Frederick Douglass and various prominent American leaders after passage of the Fifteenth Amendment in 1870.

7. African Americans paying their respects to U.S. Marshal Frederick Douglass (1877).

8. A chromolithograph featuring U.S. Senator Blanche Kelso Bruce, Frederick Douglass, and U.S. Senator Hiram Rhoades Revels. The three men are surrounded by John R. Lynch, Abraham Lincoln, James A. Garfield, Ulysses S. Grant, Joseph H. Rainey, Charles E. Nash, John Brown, and Robert Smalls and by scenes of African American life (1881).

9. Douglass featured at the center of African American leaders from the late eighteenth century to post-Reconstruction America (1883).

10. Cedar Hill, the Douglass family house in the Anacostia section of Washington, D.C.

11. Frederick Douglass seated beside grandson Joseph Douglass, playing violin (ca. 1890s).

12. Portrait of Douglass.

13. A lithograph including a portrait of Douglass as one of thirteen scenes pertaining to African American history (1897).

Chronology

1818	FEBRUARY. Frederick Douglass born in Talbot County, Maryland, to an enslaved black woman, Harriet Bailey, and a white father; named Frederick Augustus Washington Bailey by his mother; owned at birth by Aaron Anthony; separated from his mother and lived with his maternal grandmother, Betty Bailey
1826	Sent to Wye House plantation, under overseer Aaron Anthony, at about age six Following Anthony's death, inherited by Thomas Auld, Anthony's son-in-law, who sends him to live with his brother in Baltimore, Hugh Auld, where at about the age of twelve, Frederick starts to learn the alphabet from Auld's wife, Sophia; when Hugh Auld stops the lessons, inadvertently teaching Frederick the importance of literacy by treating it as a threat, Frederick continues his lessons by persuading neighborhood children to teach him
1828	Harriet Bailey dies when Frederick is about ten
1834	Hired out to Edward Covey, who has a reputation as a "slave breaker," in an effort to break his spirit; eventually resists Covey, a physical confrontation that he later identifies as a turning point in his life
1835	While hired out to William Freeland, tries to escape from slavery in league with other slaves, but the plot is discovered and the group placed in jail
1836–1838	Works as a caulker in Baltimore shipyards; meets Anna Murray, a free black woman who works as a laundress and housekeeper and helps him plan his escape
1838	3 SEPTEMBER. Escapes from slavery, using forged papers to pose

as a sailor; travels by railroad, eventually making it to New York City

15 SEPTEMBER. Marries Anna Murray and moves to New Bedford, Massachusetts, where he adopts the name Frederick Douglass

1839 24 JUNE. Daughter Rosetta (1839–1906) born; by this time Douglass subscribes to, and reads voraciously, William Lloyd Garrison's abolitionist newspaper the *Liberator*

1840 9 OCTOBER. Son Lewis Henry (1840–1908) born

1841 10–12 AUGUST. Attends and makes impromptu speech at anti-slavery event in Nantucket; Garrison and other white abolitionists impressed and persuade Douglass to become a traveling lecturer for American Anti-Slavery Society

1842 3 MARCH. Son Frederick Douglass Jr. (1842–1892) born

1843 15–19 AUGUST. National Convention of Colored Citizens held in Buffalo, New York, at the same time as the meeting of the Liberty Party, which differs from the Garrisonian abolitionists on the commitment to political approaches to the abolition of slavery; attends both conventions, playing an especially prominent role in the National Convention of Colored Citizens

1844 21 OCTOBER. Son Charles Remond (1844–1920) born

1845 Publishes *The Narrative of the Life of Frederick Douglass, an American Slave. Written by Himself*; the *Narrative* makes him especially visible, so makes a lecture tour in England, Scotland, and Ireland to avoid recapture

1846 British supporters raise money and purchase Douglass's freedom from Hugh Auld

1847 Returns to the United States and relocates family to Rochester, New York, where he establishes the *North Star*; aided by printer John Dick, co-editor Martin R. Delany, and black abolitionist and social reformer William C. Nell; finances the paper for many years from his savings, supportive contributions, and lecturing; by 1851, tells a friend the paper is finally self-sustaining

1847	6–9 OCTOBER. National Convention of Colored People meets in Troy, New York, with Douglass again playing a prominent role
1848	19–20 JULY. Attends the first women's rights convention at Seneca Falls, New York 6 SEPTEMBER. Presides as president of the Colored National Convention in Cleveland, Ohio
1849	Julia Griffiths, a white woman whom Douglass met during his British tour, moves to Rochester to help Douglass with the paper and to tutor his children 22 MARCH. Daughter Annie Douglass (1849–1860) born
1851	Ends publication of the *North Star* and merges with white abolitionist Gerrit Smith's *Liberty Party Paper* to form *Frederick Douglass' Paper*
1852	5 JULY. Delivers what will become his most famous speech, "What to the Slave Is the Fourth of July?," at Corinthian Hall in Rochester
1853	Publishes his one work of fiction, *The Heroic Slave*, which appears both in *Autographs for Freedom*, edited by Julia Griffiths, and in *Frederick Douglass' Paper* 6–8 JULY. Brings the Colored National Convention to Rochester, New York
1855	Publishes second autobiography, *My Bondage and My Freedom*; Julia Griffiths returns to England
1856	German journalist Ottilie Assing travels to Rochester to interview Douglass, a meeting that began a long and intimate friendship; when Assing was not visiting the Douglass home over the next twenty-six years, they corresponded regularly
1857	Rochester public schools desegregate after years of protestations by Douglass and others
1858	John Brown visits Douglass in Rochester while developing plans for encouraging a slave revolt
1859	Travels to Canada and then sails to England, worried that he would be viewed as an accomplice in John Brown's raid on Harpers Ferry, Virginia

1860	Returns to the United States when informed of the death of daughter Annie
1863	Congress authorizes black enlistment in the Union army, and Douglass asked to help in the recruitment for the Massachusetts 64th Regiment; visits the White House to urge Lincoln to adopt equal pay for black soldiers
1864	Visits the White House again at the president's request to confer with Lincoln
1869	Denounces racial prejudice at the Equal Rights Association annual convention and argues that voting rights for black men should not be postponed for the cause of women's suffrage
1870	Becomes owner and editor of the *New National Era*, a weekly newspaper in Washington, D.C.
1871	Appointed assistant secretary to the Commission of Inquiry into the possible annexation of Santo Domingo
1872	Nominated to be vice president by Equal Rights Party on a ticket headed by Victoria Woodhull; Douglass did not seek the nomination, is not associated with the party, and does not meet Woodhull until many years later
	Loses home in Rochester, along with many of his papers, in a suspicious fire; although urged to rebuild in Rochester, Douglass moves family to Washington, D.C., increasingly the center of his work
1874	Named president of the Freedman's Savings and Trust Company
1876	14 APRIL. Delivers "Oration in Memory of Abraham Lincoln" at the unveiling of the Freedmen's Monument in Lincoln Park, Washington, D.C.
1877	Appointed U.S. marshal of the District of Columbia and serves from 1877 to 1881
1878	Purchases Cedar Hill, a nine-acre estate in the Anacostia section of Washington, D.C.
1881	Appointed recorder of deeds for the District of Columbia and

	serves from 1881 to 1886; publishes third autobiography, *Life and Times of Frederick Douglass*
1882	4 AUGUST. His wife, Anna Murray Douglass, dies
1884	24 JANUARY. Marries his secretary, Helen Pitts, a white woman born in Honeoye, New York, in 1838, against great resistance from family, friends, and the general public 21 August. Ottilie Assing commits suicide in Paris, leaving what remains of her estate to Douglass
1886–1887	Tours England, France, Italy, Egypt, and Greece with Helen
1888	Appointed consul general to Haiti by President Benjamin Harrison
1889	Appointed chargé d'affaires for Santo Domingo as well as minister resident to Haiti
1891	Resigns as minister to Haiti
1892	Publishes an expanded version of *Life and Times of Frederick Douglass*
1895	20 FEBRUARY. Dies from a heart attack at Cedar Hill after attending a women's rights meeting

"Wye House, Talbot County, Maryland, Lloyd" (1914)

JOHN MARTIN HAMMOND

"I was born in Tuckahoe, near Hillsborough, and about twelve miles from Easton, in Talbot county, Maryland. I have no accurate knowledge of my age, never having seen any authentic record containing it." So begins the *Narrative of Frederick Douglass, an American Slave* (1845), Douglass's first autobiography. It is difficult for today's readers, or even most readers in Douglass's own time, to fully appreciate the sad significance of this statement. In effect, Douglass begins his life story by trying to locate himself both geographically and historically. What a contrast, then, is this other statement of the central plantation of Douglass's childhood, from John Martin Hammond's 1914 tour of the region's great houses in *Colonial Mansions of Maryland and Delaware*. The subjects of this sketch are the owners of the Wye House, the Lloyd family, whose estate once extended to forty-two thousand acres, land worked by more than a thousand slaves. Hammond, who wrote about "quaint and historic forts of North America" in one of his other books, is simply interested in history—and he finds a rich history in virtually every aspect of the house and the people he describes. Revealingly, though, he seems uncertain of what to do with the history Douglass brings to this tour of the Lloyds' house.

NO NAME IN Maryland history is evocative of richer historic memories than that of Lloyd. Seven generations of this illustrious family have lived at Wye House in Talbot County, beginning with Edward Lloyd, the First, who established himself there in 1668. Since that time the estate has been handed down from one generation of Edward Lloyd to another.

The first two Edwards returned to England and died there, but in the old family burying ground at Wye, which stands back of the manor-house, there lie four succeeding generations of the name. Edward Lloyd the First and his brother Cornelius settled in Virginia about 1685, in which year each received from Capt. John West grants of land on the Elizabeth River.

Edward Lloyd was a justice and lawyer at Norfolk in 1645, and a member of the House of Burgesses from 1644 until 1649, in which latter year he joined the Puritan Colony in Maryland. On the 20th of April, 1650, the district embracing Providence was erected into a county and given the name of Anne Arundel, and Edward Lloyd was made commander of this county by Governor Stone. On the organization of Talbot County in the year 1660, having large landed estates on the Eastern Shore, he removed to that county and built his residence on the Wye River, calling it Wye House.

In the year 1660 Caecilius Calvert, second Lord Baltimore, commissioned Col. Edward Lloyd—among others—to be Deputy Governor of Maryland in the event of the death of Governor Philip Calvert. Philemon Lloyd dying before his father, the estate passed to his son Edward Lloyd, the Second, grandson of the first master of Wye.

The original Wye House was burned by the British in 1776, and was looted of its fine paintings and rich plate and other treasures. All the old records of the Lloyd family up to that time were then destroyed. After the war several pieces of plate bearing the family arms were returned by the crown.

Of the original manor house only a fragment remains, and that is now used as an outbuilding. The present Wye House was built just before the end of the Revolutionary War by Edward Lloyd, the Fourth, and remains intact to-day just as constructed more than a century and a quarter ago.

The main building is of two lofty stories, containing the hall, drawing-room, parlour, dining-room and chambers, all of noble proportions, and connects by corridors with one-story wings, in which are the library on one side and domestic offices on the other, presenting a pleasing façade of two hundred feet, commanding a superb view of the Wye River and the bay.

Back of the manor-house is an old garden with many winding walks bounded by box-wood hedges. To one side of the garden is a beautiful stretch of lawn bounded on each side by hedges, at the ends of which is an imposing old building, the conservatory—a relic of colonial days. To the left of the structure is an arch of brick flanked on each side by a wall fast crumbling away. No one seems to know how old this wall is, but it was probably built when the original house was constructed. [. . .]

Each Edward Lloyd, seven of whom have been masters of Wye House, in succeeding to the great ancestral estates of Wye, fell heir to offices of public trust and honor, and we find in this distinguished family three governors, councillors, burgesses, members of Assembly, presidential electors, captains and colonels in colonial and revolutionary times.

Edward Lloyd, the Fourth, was a conspicuous patriot through the entire revolutionary period. He was a member of the Provincial Conventions in 1775 and 1776. He was chosen by the convention of 1775 a member of the commission of safety of the Eastern Shore. In 1780, he was a delegate to the lower house of Assembly, and in 1781–1786 and 1791 was elected to the State Senate. In 1783–1784, he was delegate from Maryland to the Continental Congress, and in 1788 was a member of the State Convention to ratify the Federal Constitution.

His son Edward was a member of Congress from 1806 to 1809, in which latter year he became Governor of Maryland. He was also a presidential elector in 1812, and cast his vote for Madison. From 1816 to 1826, in which year he resigned, he served in the United States Senate. His successors have continued to live the life of wealthy country gentlemen, but have ever responded to the call for public service, in the discharge of which they have reflected credit upon their family name, and upon the State of Maryland.

With Wye House is connected the name of that strange historic character, Fred Douglass. This mulatto boy, the illegitimate son of a white man of considerable learning and a coloured woman who was owned by a sailing master in the employ of Governor Lloyd, was born at St. Michael's. Until he was eight years of age this Fred Douglass was much at Wye, and played not only with the little pickaninnies there, but frequently with the governor's son, Daniel.

When about nine years of age, the boy, who had accompanied his master on a trip to Baltimore, ran away and was lost sight of for years, until he turned up in the person of Fred Douglass, a well-educated and traveled man of the world. He was said to have been the first coloured man who was ever dined by Queen Victoria, an honour which was later accorded to Booker T. Washington. He was also entertained at the White House by President Cleveland, although in so doing the President was severely censured. Douglass was at one time Minister to Hayti, and later became Marshal of the District of Columbia.

About 1881, the old man was moved to visit the scenes of his childhood. In company with several custom officers from Baltimore, he one day journeyed to Wye, and in the absence of Col. Edward Lloyd was shown over the estate by the colonel's son Howard. Although he was but a child when he had last visited Wye, he recalled by name many of the points, creeks, bayous, which had even then been forgotten by the boatmen around St. Michaels.

It is said that the venerable old negro, apparently oblivious of his companions, fell to musing in a negro dialect: "Dar," he said, "is war me and Mars Dan useter trap rabbits."

Some years later Mr. Howard Lloyd, riding to Philadelphia, noticed the aged figure of Fred Douglass in the fore part of the car. Before reaching his destination, Mr. Lloyd went forward to speak to him. At first Douglass seemed not to recognize Mr. Lloyd and greeted him with a cold stare.

"I don't believe you recognize me, Marshal."

The marshal paused, looked at him keenly, then jumping to his feet, hat in hand, he exclaimed, "Yes, I do; it is Mr. Howard Lloyd."

Douglass begged to be allowed to hold the watch of the former governor which the great-grandson wore at the time of the meeting. Speaking of this distinguished son of Maryland, Douglass said: "How well I remember him, stately old gentleman, moving about the farm in that quiet, dignified way of his, with his high hat and cane. I remember when the governor imported a bull of special breed and went out one day to inspect the animal. As he moved across the pasture, the bull glared at him with lowered head, but the governor, not scenting trouble, went on. Presently, with a roar, the animal made for the old gentleman. "That," said Douglass, "was the only time I ever saw the governor act in an undignified manner, his hat went one way, his cane another, while the governor made for the fence."

Letters found in possession of John Brown implicated Douglass to a certain extent. Governor Wise of Virginia made a requisition on President Buchanan for the person of "Frederick Douglass, a negro man, supposed now to be in Michigan, charged with murder, robbery and inciting servile insurrection in the State of Virginia." Douglass went to Canada and then to England, and upon his return to America the matter had been lost sight of.

John Martin Hammond, *Colonial Mansions of Maryland and Delaware* (Philadelphia: J. B. Lippincott, 1914), 152–160.

From *Acts of the Anti-Slavery Apostles* (1884)

PARKER PILLSBURY

Parker Pillsbury was a radical white abolitionist who delighted in taking on the powers that be—from the slaveholding powers to his fellow workers in the antislavery movement. He was, by any measure, a force to be reckoned with—and he did not hesitate to apply that force even to his antislavery allies when they disagreed with him. He was particularly harsh with Douglass when the great black abolitionist separated from the Garrisonian abolitionists and embraced political measures in the antislavery struggle. In the mid-1850s, when Douglass was still married to his first wife, the illiterate black woman who aided Douglass in his escape from slavery and then followed him to the North, Pillsbury publicly questioned Douglass's relationship with his publishing partner, Julia Griffiths, a white Englishwoman whom Pillsbury called "Miss Jezebel Douglass." This mention of Douglass in Pillsbury's 1884 memoir, *Acts of the Anti-Slavery Apostles*, captures a calmer and more supportive moment in the two men's relationship that helps one appreciate Douglass's own separation from established churches. Like Douglass, Pillsbury was sharply critical of what he viewed as the complicity of churches in the maintenance of slavery, and his criticism caused him to lose his license to preach from the Congregational Church in 1840. This excerpt from his memoir includes mention of his association with other radical abolitionists—including Thomas P. Beach, Stephen Symonds Foster, and Nathaniel Peabody Rogers—who attacked churches for being "the stronghold of religion" and were denounced as fanatics and, in one memorable instance, "Gab-olitionists."[1] The work of these devoted activists is the subject of this telling of one of the most frequently repeated stories about Douglass.

MANY MORE WERE roughly removed from meetings where they attempted to speak in most decent and proper manner for the enslaved, some of them women of spotless purity of heart and life. The churches lost many of their choicest members and the *Come-outer* connection greatly increased, especially in Massachusetts and New Hampshire. Hayward's "Book of Religions" contains an excellent descriptive account of them, written by William Bassett, whose name has already graced honorably these pages. Many meetings of them were established, and the present Free religious societies, now so widely known, may be truly said to have had their beginnings then and there. Lynn furnished memorable instances. Two months after the Sunday demonstration there by Beach and Foster [. . .] Mr. Rogers was again there and attended the regular "Come-outer" meeting. He wrote: "Though the clergy taunt them for their homely name, they must have trembled yesterday when they saw the people throng to their meeting in such numbers." Among the speakers on that day was Frederick Douglass, then comparatively new on the anti-slavery platform. He spoke on the subject of prayer, and illustrated it by his own experience while a slave. He said he prayed long and earnestly for freedom in words as he had been taught but nothing came of it. At length he addressed his legs: "O legs, give me freedom! O legs, bring me to freedom! And as you see," he said, "they did it. They answered my prayer."

And Douglass might have added, perhaps he did add, *you "Come-outers" are but fugitive slaves escaped from your spiritual and ecclesiastical plantations.*

NOTE

1. Duane Hamilton Hurd, ed., *History of Essex County, Massachusetts: With Biographical Sketches of Many of Its Pioneers and Prominent Men* (Philadelphia: J. W. Lewis, 1888), 1:506.

From Parker Pillsbury, *Acts of the Anti-Slavery Apostles* (Boston: Cupples, Upham, 1884), 322–323.

From *Sketches of Lynn; or, The Changes of Fifty Years* (1880)

David N. Johnson

David N. Johnson was a leading figure in Lynn, Massachusetts, to which Douglass and family moved in 1841 at the start of Douglass's career as an antislavery lecturer. Johnson was a member of the editorial staff of the *Lynn Transcript* and was a founding officer of the city's Young Men's Debating Society. Today, he is known primarily for this valuable work of local history, *Sketches of Lynn*, in which he faithfully records a very racist debate over "the justice and expediency of the immediate abolition of slavery" that took place sometime during the 1850s.[1] In the excerpt that follows—addressing the Silsbee Street Debating Club, which also debated issues related to slavery but with greater sophistication than did the young men's society—Johnson focuses on the man who would become Lynn's most famous former citizen, Frederick Douglass, and a famous early attempt to challenge discrimination on public transportation. We will have occasion to meet Douglass's companion in this episode, the white abolitionist James N. Buffum, when he gives his own account of this episode.

MR. DOUGLASS LIVED in Lynn about this time. He was not then the polished orator that he has since become, but even at that early day he gave promise of the grand part he was to play in the conflict which was to end in the destruction of the system that had so long cursed his race. He was more than six feet in height, and his majestic form, as he rose to speak, straight as an arrow, muscular, yet lithe and graceful, his flashing eye, and more than all, his voice, that rivaled Webster's in its richness, and in the depth and sonorousness of its cadences, made up such an ideal of an orator as the listeners never forgot. And they never forgot his burning words, his pathos, nor the rich play of his humor. He had just escaped from the "house of bondage";

and as he recited his experience as a slave, his sufferings as he grew old enough to realize the bitterness of his lot, his alternate hope and despair as he attempted to lift the vail [*sic*] of the future—his eyes would now flash with defiance, and now grow dim with emotions he could not control; and the roll of his splendid voice, as he hurled his denunciations against the infamous system, would pass to the minor key whose notes trembled on his tongue. Then with inimitable mimicry he would give a droll recital of some ludicrous scene in his experience as a slave, or with bitter sarcasm he would tell a tale of insult offered by some upstart who fancied he held his title to manhood by the whiteness of his skin; and then again, with flashing eye, he would hurl his indignant denunciation at "wickedness in high places," against men who, under the pretended sanction of religion, defended the "infernal institution" whose horrors had filled his days with dread, and his night dreams with terror. An incident, which the writer heard him relate in his peculiar manner, half amusing, and half indignant at the outrage he had suffered, occurred about this time. Its recital will sound strangely some years hence. These were the days when "negro cars" were on our railroads. Mr. Douglass, and his friend, James N. Buffum, having purchased their tickets, entered one of the cars, not taking special pains to get into the negro car. It was on the Eastern Railroad, and they were bound for Newburyport. The conductor came along, and spying Mr. Douglass, asked him what he was in that car for. Mr. Douglass replied in substance that he wanted to go to a certain place, and thought that the most direct way. The conductor ordered Mr. Douglass to leave. Mr. Douglass assured the conductor that he was satisfied with his seat, and excused himself from accepting the invitation. The conductor called to his aid two or three brakemen, who proceeded to make a demonstration that looked as though Mr. Douglass was to be taken from the car without gaining the consent of his will, or the aid of his limbs. It was amusing to hear Mr. Douglass relate this part of the scene. "When they took hold of me," said Mr. Douglass, with a broad grin, "I felt my hands instinctively clutch the arms of the seat where I sat, and I seemed to be very firmly attached to the place." But two or three stout brakemen were too much for young Douglass, though he had the grip of a giant; or rather, they were too strong to deal with the kind of car furniture then in use. Douglass left the car, and left behind him an empty space in one end of it where seats *had been*. This was before nitro-glycerine was known; otherwise, one might have supposed that a small can of that article had exploded in the end of the car. This was near the middle of the nineteenth century.

NOTE

1. David N. Johnson, *Sketches of Lynn; or, The Changes of Fifty Years* (Lynn, MA: Thos. P. Nichols, 1880), 243.

From David N. Johnson, *Sketches of Lynn; or, The Changes of Fifty Years* (Lynn, MA: Thos. P. Nichols, 1880), 230–232.

From *Life and Correspondence of Henry Ingersoll Bowditch* (1902)

VINCENT Y. BOWDITCH

Henry Ingersoll Bowditch was a prominent physician and ardent abolitionist. Born in Salem, Massachusetts, in 1808, Bowditch was converted to the abolitionist cause by two defining events. The first was his attendance at the funeral of British abolitionist William Wilberforce, whose writings had already influenced Bowditch greatly, in England in 1833. The second was his witnessing of a Boston mob attempting to tar and feather abolitionist William Lloyd Garrison in 1835. Bowditch devoted himself not only to the antislavery cause but also to the antiracist cause, and he both participated in and helped found organizations devoted to countering slavery and resisting those who hunted fugitive slaves. Although Bowditch's abolitionist zeal made him unpopular with many, he distinguished himself as a leading physician over the course of his career and eventually would serve as president of the American Medical Association, among numerous other distinguished posts. In the following tale, introduced by his son, Bowditch remembers a time when making a public statement against slavery and racism was itself a radical act.

IT WAS DURING this episode that my father gave an instance of his pluck and determination to espouse the cause of anti-slavery by walking arm in arm with Frederick Douglass, at that time a runaway slave, through the Boston streets. It is hard to realize at this day what such an action meant; and as a proof of the disapproval, to say the least, which my father's course subjected him, the following extract is given from the "Thirty Years' War of Anti-Slavery."

I have only to mention a few facts connected with myself. Only a few days before one of our meetings, a young lady had hoped that I "would never become an Abolitionist," and about the same time Frederick Douglass appeared as a runaway slave. He was at the meeting in Marlboro' Chapel. Of course I was introduced to him, and, as I would have invited a white friend, I asked him home to dine with me in my small abode in Bedford Street. It is useless to deny that I did not like the thought of walking with him in open midday up Washington Street. I *hoped* I would not meet any of my acquaintances. I had, however, hardly turned into the street before I met the young lady who had expressed her wish as before stated. I am glad now to say that I *did not skulk*. I looked at her straight and bowed in "my most gracious manner," as if I were "all right," while I saw by her look of regret that she thought me "all wrong." It was, however, somewhat like a cold sponge bath,—that Washington Street walk by the side of a black man,—rather terrible at the outset, but wonderfully warming and refreshing afterwards! I had literally jumped "in medias res." But I did not hear until years afterwards, and a long time after Douglass had held office in Washington under the Federal Government, and the slavery of his own race had been washed out in blood, what I was doing for him at the moment when as a friend I asked him to walk home with me to dinner. How little do we appreciate acts that seem trivial or something worse to us, but which to others, affected by such acts, are of inexpressible importance! Beautiful to me seems now the act, inasmuch as it helped to raise a poor down-trodden soul into a proper self-appreciation. And how much I thank God that He led me by giving me a love of freedom, and something like a conscience to act as I did then!

From Vincent Y. Bowditch, *Life and Correspondence of Henry Ingersoll Bowditch* (Boston: Houghton, Mifflin, 1902), 1:137–138.

From *Commemoration of the Fiftieth Anniversary of the Organization of the American Anti-Slavery Society in Philadelphia* (1884)

JAMES N. BUFFUM

James N. Buffum was, like David N. Johnson, a citizen of Lynn, Massachusetts, where he also served as an officer of the Old Silsbee Street Debating Club. Born in North Berwick, Maine, in 1807, Buffum later became mayor of Lynn, a member of the Massachusetts House of Representatives, and an influential advocate of the antislavery cause. Earlier, we witnessed the time when Buffum and Douglass faced racial segregation on American trains. In this speech we get Buffum's account of that memorable day, as well as his memories of broader travels with his friend and colleague. Buffum traveled with Douglass to the British Isles in 1845 to protest the Free Church of Scotland's acceptance of money from American slaveholders, and he comments on that trip here as well. In his memory of both events, Buffum recognizes the significance of the economics of slavery, from the purchase of train fare to the purchase of a man. Along the way, we encounter John A. Collins, the white abolitionist and member of the Massachusetts Anti-Slavery Society who was instrumental in persuading Douglass to devote his life to antislavery work.

THE CHAIRMAN.—I have now the pleasure, ladies and gentlemen, of introducing to you one of the earliest and most indefatigable workers in our anti-slavery cause, and who, in a very important time in the history of that cause, represented us ably in England.

Hon. James N. Buffum. Ladies and gentlemen: It is so long since I have spoken on this subject that I don't know whether I can interest you; but if I do succeed it must be in relating some of my reminiscences.

When I entered the cause I did not suppose I should ever be called upon to speak, and I never should have done so, had it not been for the outrageous prejudices against, and treatment of, the colored race. I will try to give you an account of some of my first efforts in that direction. We had to combat great prejudices, and it was almost impossible to find a place where we would be allowed to speak. I remember the first tour I made, when I attempted to take the field with a young man who was on a vacation from one of the western colleges. We went to Albany, and upon arriving there, found that we could not procure a place to hold a meeting in, and that no notices had been given by the press, who would not assist us. I remember that we went and got some large card boards, lettered them, and one of our number had one in front and one behind him, showing our advertisement; and so we went through the streets, notifying the people where we should speak that evening. We had a good meeting.

In 1843 I went to New Bedford to attend an Anti-slavery Convention—I was a young man and full of enthusiasm—and there I found Frederick Douglass, rolling oil casks on the wharves of New Bedford. By persuasion he went to one of our meetings, and he spoke with such power and effect that everybody was moved by it. He had just come out of slavery, a graduate from that great institution, and had his diploma written on his back with cowhide. We got him to come to Nantucket, and he made five speeches with convincing power; and Mr. Garrison and myself thought it would be a good thing if a man who had endured some of the penalties of slavery, could go out and tell his story, and tell what slavery was. And so he was engaged as an agent to come to Essex County, and there begin his work. A few weeks afterward he came to my house with John A. Collins. We had to attend a Convention at Newburyport; and I went over to the railway station and procured three tickets, all alike, all one color, all one destination, all the same price. Then we got into one of those long cars, and there were but five people in the other end, and we took our seats. Pretty soon the conductor came to collect the tickets. Looking at Douglass, he said, "you must get off; we don't have colored people here."

"Why are you going to put him off?" said I.

"Because he is colored, and the rules of this company don't allow us to carry colored people."

"But his fare is paid; here is his ticket."

"He will have to get off," said the conductor.

"Then turn me out, too"; said I. "How black must a man be, or how white, to escape that calamity?"

"He will have to get off," repeated the conductor.

"I have paid for this seat," said Douglass, "and I will keep it."

He went out and got his brakeman, and came back to enforce the orders of his company.

I had just got up from a bed of sickness, and was in no condition to fight; so I came out quietly, but when Collins and Douglass came out, they brought three seats with them.

The conductor came up to me, and said, "You can get in, if you want to."

"No; if you won't let Mr. Douglass ride, I won't ride"; and I went across the road and got a horse that had no prejudices against color; and so we went to Newburyport.

When we got there we found one of the most enthusiastic meetings. All the facts had gone on before us. We had a regular inspiration, and for the first time in my life, I found myself on the platform talking.

Two days after that I went into that same car, with the same conductor, and on the first two seats at my left as I entered, were three of the dirtiest sailors that I ever saw, with the ugliest monkey, standing right up straight, that God ever made. There he was like any other gentleman. I could not speak with the eloquence of a Phillips, but I could see a point. I called to the conductor, who came to me, and I said, "How is this? Two days ago you put my friend Douglass out because he was a link between a man and a monkey; now you have skipped the link and take the monkey himself." Upon this, the sailor who had the animal, immediately said, "Young man, you need not trouble yourself about my monkey; I can pay for him"; and he took a half dollar and offered it to the conductor to pay his monkey's fare. The conductor looked non-plussed for a while, and at last said, "Never mind about that, put it up." And he put it up.

I went up to Faneuil Hall, and there offered a resolution of this kind; Resolved, that we petition our next legislature to compel the corporations they have created, to grant to intelligent and respectable colored people the same rights and privileges that are enjoyed by dogs and monkeys. [. . .]

Afterwards the fugitive slave-law was passed, and Frederick Douglass was not safe; and all his friends advised that he should go across the Atlantic to find freedom under a monarchy. I accompanied him. We went to Dublin where we had an audience four times as large as this, and the Lord

Mayor presided. Not only presided, but invited us to a banquet, and invited all the city government officials, and distinguished citizens to meet us, because we were anti-slavery men. Wherever we went, we were received with the greatest consideration; and I trust we did a good work. At any rate they gave me the evidence of satisfaction before I returned.

I never in my life was so ashamed of my country, as when I was in England. I went into the old Tower one day, and by paying an extra shilling, I was allowed to see the Queen's jewels. I had just come from Ireland where people were starving and I said, "I thank God that I don't live in a country, where one woman wears a million pounds on her head, and another woman is starving because the potato crop has failed." There was a soldier there who had been in the battle of New Orleans, and turning to me, he said, "Young man you may thank God for what you please, but I thank God that I don't live in a country where all men are born free and equal, and there are three million slaves."

I was recently invited to go to England again. If I were not so old, and tied so strongly here, I would go over, and I would tell them that no such taunts could be uttered against us now. Now our flag floats, ever unstained by the institution of slavery.

I remember one night Fred. Douglass had received a paper from this country, which gave him the information that his old master, Thomas Auld, of Baltimore, had given him away to his brother Hugh; and if he ever stepped foot on American soil, he would have him put to work on a cotton plantation. Douglass took that paper with him that evening, and after speaking nearly an hour in his most eloquent strain, he took it up and said to the audience; "The very steamer which brought my letters, has brought also a newspaper in which I find that my old master, Thomas Auld, of Baltimore, has given me away, and he read it to them. Then he turned and uttered one of the most grand and eloquent speeches that I ever heard from his lips. He said, "Ladies and gentlemen think of it; in that country where I was born, and where they declare that all men are born free and equal, and are endowed by their creator with certain inalienable rights, among them those of life, liberty and the pursuit of happiness, there I was a slave. There was no place where I could stand up and call these hands, this head, my own. Wherever the American flag floated, there I was a slave. I had to fly from the screeching of the eagle, and take shelter in the lap of the lion."

I never saw such a demonstration as his words created. It was an enthusiastic ovation. Finally the women of England sent over to Baltimore and bought Frederick Douglass. They would not allow him to come back here a slave; and they raised the money, paid it, and gave the deed of emancipation to Frederick himself.

They talk about politicians being bought; they say Daniel Webster was bought by British gold. I never knew of but one man being bought by British gold—that man was Frederick Douglass.

From *Commemoration of the Fiftieth Anniversary of the Organization of the American Anti-Slavery Society in Philadelphia* (Philadelphia: Thos. S. Dando, 1884), 42–46.

"The Hundred Conventions" (1843)

William A. White

Those who served on the antislavery lecture circuit regularly did so at great risk to their personal well-being, even to their lives. The following letter offers an account of one such attack, one of many Douglass and his longtime friend William A. White experienced when the two men lectured in Indiana and Illinois in 1843. A few years later, Douglass would remember their time together in a letter to White, noting, "I shall never forget how like two very brothers we were ready to dare, do, and even die for each other. Tragic awfully so—yet I laugh always when I think how comic I must have looked when running before the mob, darkening the air with the mud from my feet. How I looked running you can best describe but how you looked bleeding—I shall always remember."[1] White, originally from a wealthy family in Massachusetts and brother-in-law of the poet James Russell Lowell, was a devoted lecturer, writer, and editor for both the abolitionist and the temperance causes. The other prominent abolitionist mentioned in this account is George Bradburn, a Massachusetts politician and Unitarian minister known for his work against slavery and for women's rights.

NEWCASTLE, (IND.) SEPT. 22d, 1843

Dear Friend:

Instead of writing to you of the great gathering of anti-slavery friends at Oakland, as I promised, I must write of a pro-slavery mob which opposed us at Pendleton, and which it is most painful to think of, for it presented us men, not acting as reasonable creatures, but rather like devils in human form; men actuated by the passions of brutes, and using the intellects of men to carry out those passions.

We arrived at Dr. Fussell's in Pendleton, on the evening of the 14th, and there learned that a mob had threatened to come down from Columbus, a miserable, rum-drinking place, about six miles distant, and break up the meeting. The people in Pendleton are not anti-slavery, but are willing to hear the question discussed. In the morning we held our meeting in the

Baptist church. Frederick spoke, and there was no interruption, though I observed a great number of men, such as do not usually attend our meetings. As we started for our meeting in the afternoon, we learned that we could not have the church, as the trustees feared the building would be injured. When we arrived on the spot, we found a mob of thirty or more people collected, very much excited, and learned that Dr. Cook, a citizen of the town, had attempted, by addressing them, to allay the excitement. Many of the mob were much intoxicated, and their threats most violent. As the church had given us over to them, they felt encouraged to go all lengths. We went in among them, and talked in a conversational way for some time, when Bradburn mounted the steps, and commenced speaking without interruption; but we were soon driven home by a shower, and our first day's meeting was over.

In the evening there was a meeting of the citizens of the place, in which resolutions disapproving the course of the mob, and expressing a determination to resist it, were offered, and after a few words from Bradburn and myself, unanimously passed. A good feeling pervaded the meeting, and we hoped we should have no more trouble.

The next morning being pleasant, we held our meeting in the woods, where seats and stands had been arranged. At the opening of the meeting there were only eleven of the mobocrats present, and we trusted they had seen the resolutions passed the evening before, which were posted in various parts of the town, and would not trouble us; but the fact was, though the citizens had passed the resolves, they were not decided, and it was known that one or two leading men in the town secretly winked at the doings of the mob. We opened the meeting with a song, after which I made a few remarks, and was followed by Bradburn. While he was speaking, the mob continued to collect, but were quiet. At a given signal, they all withdrew, and left us for a time. The audience now numbered one hundred men, and thirty women. In a few moments we heard a shout, and saw the mob coming through the woods, thirty or more in number, two and two, armed with stones and eggs, and led on by a fellow in a coon skin cap, tail and all, as a representation of the great Whig party, and another barefooted man, with nothing but a dirty shirt and pantaloons on, and the former half off his shoulders, as a representative of the democracy of the country. The audience immediately on their appearance rose, and were about to retreat. I requested them to be seated, which some of them did. All the women sat down; but some of the men withdrew; and it is but justice to the women to say, that throughout the whole they showed themselves the more courageous party, as they ever have done. The cry now was, "surround them"; and the mob went up behind the audience, and in front of the stand, and the coonskin man ordered us to be off. This command was followed by a volley of eggs and stones, after which there was a lull for a moment, as the mob seemed at a loss what to do, as their arguments had produced no impression. A parley now took place, and Dr. Cook attempted to address the mob; but they would not hear him, and continued to approach the stand. A man named James Jackson asked us why we did not go to the South and preach. Bradburn replied to him, and Jackson was making an answer, when I invited him to take the stand, which he did, and made a most ridiculous spectacle, interlarding his speech with copious oaths, and ending off by saying "he could not talk, but he could fight—that he had too much good blood in his veins to let us go on; &c." I replied, and at this time, if the citizens of Pendleton had taken a decided stand, all would have been well. One of the mob named Rik, while Jackson was speaking, came up to the stand, and saying that "he saw that nothing was going to be done without he did it," seized hold of the table, overturned it, and began to pull the stand to pieces. The mob joined in, and commenced pushing the audience back and knocking them down. Micajah White, a warm friend, was knocked down, with another friend named Graham. Frederick Douglass who, at the time, was safe among the friends, not seeing me, thought I was knocked down, and seizing a club, rushed into the crowd. His weapon was immediately snatched from him, and he finding he had attracted their anger against himself, fled for his life, and ten or more of the mob followed, crying, "Kill the nigger, kill the damn nigger." I hope never to look upon so fearful a sight, as poor Frederick flying before these hell-hounds, panting for his blood. It was a fearfully true picture of the flight of the fugitive slave, and it was fitting it should take place on the soil of this pro-slavery State. The leader of the mob soon overtook him, and knocked him down and struck him once with a club, and was raising it the second time to level a blow which must have been fatal had it fallen, but I, by dint of hard running, came up in time to throw myself upon him, and stop him in his murderous purpose. One of the wretches hurled a stone which struck me in the back of the head, and but for my hat would have done me a severe injury. I turned to go to Frederick, and three more struck me in front, but doing no decided injury. By this time, the crowd came up, and farther violence was stopped. Frederick was taken up, and though at first he seemed to have been severely injured, he soon recovered, and was able to lecture the next day. Dr. Vaughan, a warm friend, was also hurt. Bradburn was not hurt. The mob themselves I do not much blame; they were but tools in the hands of designing men. When you learn that a member of the Methodist church, and another of the Baptist were among the leaders of the mob, you will see where some of the responsibility rests. I was also told that a Mr. McAllister, of Columbus, a member elect of the Legislature, secretly encouraged the proceedings. When the so-called wise and good of the land countenance such things, what can we expect of an ignorant drunken mob? The wretches threatened to march into town and pull down Dr. Fussell's house in the evening, and the citizens armed themselves, and, owing to this circumstance, the mob did not make their appearance. Dr. Fussell behaved nobly, and the western abolitionists have to endure now, all that was suffered by abolitionists with us three years since. This mob has opened the eyes of many here, for, as one man said, they see which side the devil is on.

Yours, most truly,
W. A. White

NOTE

1. Frederick Douglass, letter from Edinburgh, Scotland, July 30, 1846, to William A. White, in *Life and Writings of Frederick Douglass*, ed. Philip Foner (New York: International Publishers, 1950), 1:181.

William A. White, "The Hundred Conventions," *Liberator*, October 13, 1843, 163.

[Two Reports by an Antislavery Editor] (1841 and 1843)

NATHANIEL P. ROGERS

Nathaniel Peabody Rogers edited the Concord, New Hampshire, antislavery newspaper *Herald of Freedom* from 1838 to 1846, and in the following two articles for his paper Rogers testified to the power—as a speaker, as a presence—that so quickly brought Douglass to prominence as an abolitionist lecturer. The first of these articles, published in the December 3, 1841, issue of *Herald of Freedom*, introduces Douglass to Rogers's readers; the second, published in the paper's February 16, 1844, issue, testifies to the emotional power Douglass both exuded and inspired, as Rogers quite nearly merges his voice with Douglass's in his report. In both articles, Rogers's own uncompromising views are clear, including his dismissal of American churches for their acceptance of the system of slavery.

[Rhode Island Meeting (1841)]

FRIDAY EVENING was chiefly occupied by colored speakers. The fugitive Douglass was up when we entered. This is an extraordinary man. He was cut out for a hero. In a rising for Liberty, he would have been a Toussaint or a Hamilton. He has the "heart to conceive, the head to contrive, and the hand to execute." A commanding person—over six feet, we should say, in height, and of most manly proportions. His head would strike a phrenologist amid a sea of them in Exeter Hall, and his voice would ring like a trumpet in the field. Let the South congratulate herself that he is a *fugitive*. It would not have been safe for her if he had remained about the plantations a year or two longer. DOUGLASS is his *fugitive* name. He did not wear it in slavery. We don't know why he assumed it, or who bestowed it on him—but there seems *fitness* in it, to his commanding figure and heroic port. As a speaker he has few equals. It is not declamation—but oratory, power of debate. He watches the tide of discussion with the eye of the veteran, and dashes into it at once with all the tact of the forum or the bar. He has wit, argument, sarcasm, pathos—all that first-rate men show in their master efforts. His voice is highly melodious and rich, and his enunciation quite elegant, and yet he has been but two or three years out of the house of bondage. We noticed that he had strikingly improved, since we heard him at Dover in September. We say thus much of him, for he is esteemed by our multitude as of an inferior race. We should like to see him before any New England legislature or bar, and let him feel the freedom of the anti-slavery meeting, and see what would become of his inferiority. Yet he is a *thing*, in American estimate. He is the chattel of some pale-faced tyrant. How his owner would cower and shiver to hear him thunder in an anti-slavery hall! How he would shrink away, with his infernal whip, from his flaming eye when kindled with anti-slavery emotion! And the brotherhood of thieves, the *posse comitatus* of divines, we with a hecatomb or two of the proudest and flintiest of them, were obliged to hear him thunder for human liberty, and lay the enslavement of his people at their doors. They would tremble like Belshazzar. Poor Wayland! we wish he could have been *pegged* a seat in the Franklin Hall, the evening the colored friends spoke. His "limitations" would have abandoned him like the "baseless fabric of a vision."

Nathaniel Peabody Rogers, "Rhode Island Meeting," in *Collection from the Miscellaneous Writings of Nathaniel Peabody Rogers*, 2nd ed. (Boston: Benj. B. Mussey, 1849), 203–204.

"Southern Slavery and Northern Religion: Two Addresses" (1844)

Frederick Douglass lectured here Sunday evening, to a crowded Court House. He was here during all Sunday, and spoke at our Sunday meetings, and it was known generally to the people, and there was great curiosity to see him, and hear his eloquence. But no meeting house was offered to him,—or to the people, rather, who wished to hear him—and would have been profoundly interested in the grandeur of his speech. He had to speak, and the audience had to hear, in an inconvenient, uncomfortable room. The sects know here, that Anti-slavery will never again ask them for a meeting house. We will furnish them orators of the first cast, and they are in famishing want of good speaking—but they must come to the cold and noisy Court Room and dirty Town Hall, to hear, so long as they shut up their clean and comfortable synagogues against us. We have asked for them long enough. It would be dishonorable begging, to ask again. If the meeting house is *capable* of being opened to the truth, they had better offer them to us. I believe it is not capable of it—and therefore that they will never open them to anti-slavery. I would here suggest that there ought to be a Lyceum Hall erected in this place, where TRUTH could be spoken. What a commentary on the character of the numerous Temples here. I tell the people the Truth *can never be admitted into an Idol Temple.*

Douglass spoke excellently Sunday afternoon, and to a pretty numerous audience—many of them not accustomed to attend our meetings.—He was advertised as a "fugitive *from* slavery." He said he was not a fugitive *from* slavery—but a fugitive *slave.* He was a fugitive, he said, not *from* slavery—but *in* slavery. To get from it—he must go beyond the limits of the American Union. He asked them why it was that he—such as they saw him before them, must wander about in their midst, a *fugitive* and a *slave.* He *demanded* the reason. It is because of your Religion, he sternly replied, which sanctifies the system under which I suffer, and dooms me to it, and the millions of my brethren now in bondage. Your religion justifies our tyrants, and you are yourselves our enslavers. I see my enslavers here in Concord, and before my eyes—if any are here who countenance the church and the religion of your country. Other influences helped sustain the system of slavery, he said, but this is its sanctioner and main support.

In the evening Douglass made a masterly and most impressive speech. The house was crowded, and with the best of our people—no clergy—and but few of the bigots, who are past hearing. He began by a calm, deliberate and very simple narrative of his life. He did not detail personal sufferings—though he said he might—if inclined to. His fate had been mild compared to that of slaves generally. He, to be sure, had to go naked, pretty much during the earlier years of childhood, and feed at a trough like a pig, under the care of his old grandmother, who, past her labor, was turned out, charged to dig her own subsistence, and that of a few little ones, out of a patch of ground allotted her. These little ones were separated from their mothers, that they might early be without ties of kindred. He did not remember his mother, I think he said, and never knew who was his father. He never knew in his first six years anything about a bed—any more than the pigs did. He remembered stealing an old salt bag, into which he used to creep, and sleep, on the earth floor of the negro hut, at his old grandmother's. She, by the way, had reared twelve children of her own, for the market—all sold and gone from her—and she now blind and alone, if she is alive, and none left with her to bring her a cup of cold water. His own back he said was scarred with the whip—but still he had been a favored slave. He was sent to a slave-breaker, when some 16 or 17 years old—his master not being able to manage him. An attempt at breaking him once brought on a struggle between him and the Jockey. The result of it was such that the Jockey did not care to repeat it, while his care for his reputation, as a successful breaker, kept him from getting help to manage a slave boy—and Frederick escaped farther whipping from him afterwards.—After narrating his early life briefly—his *schooling*—the beginning of the wife of his master's relative to teach him letters, and the stern forbidding of it, by her husband—which Frederick overheard—how he caught a little teaching here and there from the children in the streets—a fact, he said, which accounted to him for his extraordinary attachment to children—after getting through this, in a somewhat suppressed and hesitating way—interesting all the while for its facts, but dullish in manner—and giving I suspect, no token to the audience of what was coming—though I discerned, at times, symptoms of a brewing storm—he closed his slave narrative, and gradually let out the outraged humanity that was laboring in him, in indignant and terrible speech. It was not what you could describe as oratory or eloquence. It was sterner—darker—deeper than these. It was the volcanic outbreak of human nature long pent up in slavery and at last bursting its imprisonment. It was the storm of insurrection—and I could not but think, as he stalked to and fro on the platform roused up like the Numidian Lion—how that terrible voice of his would ring through the pine glades of the South, in the day of her visitation—calling the insurgents to battle and striking terror to the hearts of the dismayed and despairing mastery. He reminded me of Toussaint among the plantations of Haiti,—There was great oratory in his speech—but more of dignity and earnestness than what we call eloquence. He was not up as a speaker—performing. He was an insurgent slave taking hold on the right of speech, and charging on his tyrants the bondage of his race. One of our Editors ventured to cross his path by a rash remark. He better have run upon a Lion. It was fearful, but magnificent, to see how magnanimously and lion-like the royal fellow tore him to pieces, and left his untouched fragments scattered around him.

Nathaniel P. Rogers

Nathaniel P. Rogers, "Southern Slavery and Northern Religion: Two Addresses," *Herald of Freedom* (February 16, 1844), reprinted in *The Frederick Douglass Papers Series One: Speeches, Debates and Interviews*, ed. John W. Blassingame (New Haven, CT: Yale University Press, 1979), 1:23–27.

"Farewell Soiree to Mr. Frederick Douglass" (1847)

[Anonymous]

At the beginning of his abolitionist career, Douglass was still legally enslaved and a fugitive from the law. Especially when he wrote and published his *Narrative of the Life of Frederick Douglass, an American Slave* in 1845, Douglass could not be sure of his safety. Moreover, he was one of the most powerful speakers the American antislavery movement had yet produced. Accordingly, it was decided that Douglass should go abroad, where the international antislavery movement was strong and he could enjoy relative safety. Douglass did not return to the United States until his freedom had been purchased through money raised by Ellen Richardson, a British teacher active in the antislavery movement. Before Douglass's return, his British friends and supporters gathered to send him off. The chairman of this farewell gathering was the formidable British abolitionist George Thompson, who gives one of the two speeches in the following excerpt from an extensive account of the event. The other speaker featured here is Douglass himself, who uses the occasion to associate himself with the work of Daniel O'Connell, the Irish political activist, and to quietly contrast British and American statesmen—the eloquent Lord Brougham, who rose from the position of a lawyer in Scotland to the position of Lord Chancellor of Great Britain, and the slaveholding John C. Calhoun (who was, incidentally, of Scots-Irish descent).

A FAREWELL SOIREE was given last evening to Mr. Frederick Douglass, at the London Tavern, Bishopsgate-street, previous to his departure for America, in testimony of his public virtues and private worth. This grateful tribute of free Englishmen to one who had been for many years an American slave, was given principally by the advocates for the abolition of slavery, and attended by upwards of 400 persons of great respectability. Very many elegantly dressed ladies graced the scene with their presence, and, in addition to an excellent band stationed in the gallery, Mr. Henry Russell was engaged, and sung the "Slave Ships," and several others of his exquisite

American songs. After the company had regaled themselves in an adjoining apartment, with admittance of excellent tea, coffee, and confectionery, they adjourned to the place of meeting, and a few minutes past seven o'clock, the Chair was taken by George Thompson, Esq. On the right of the Chairman sat the respected guest, Mr. Frederick Douglass, and in the vicinity of the Chair, on the platform, the Rev. Mr. Comming, the Rev. Dr. Price, W. Howitt, Esq., the Rev. Dr. Cox, W. H. Ashurst, Esq., F. Bennoch, Esq., Rev. J. Tod Brown, Rev. D. Thomas, Dr. Conquest, Dr. Oxley, Dr. Estlin, Deputy Stevens, E. Miall, Esq., Joseph Griffiths, Esq., Rungo Bapogee, Vakeel of the Rajah of Sattara, Mr. Hare, Esq., and D. W. Wire, Esq.

The Chairman, on taking the chair, said that it was not his intention to detain the meeting, the more so because he was to be followed by Mr. Frederick Douglass, and others, previous to his departure for his native country, where he would confer great benefit in the cause of freedom, not less by his private virtues than by the exercise of those talents which he had at his command. They were met that night to testify to him their affection for his person, their entire approbation of his labors, and admiration for his attachment to the great cause with which he stood identified. They were there also for another purpose, namely: to cherish and encourage him in his future labors, because they desired to recognize him as entitled to their esteem, regard and brotherhood. That meeting was called less for the purpose of doing honor to an individual, than of manifesting their warm and unalterable attachment to the cause which he represented. Mr. Douglass visited this country, not only accredited by abolitionists of all parties, but as one of the most efficient laborers in the cause, and one too who had endeared himself to all who had any knowledge of his personal virtues. He has since traveled its length and breadth, and made himself acquainted with every corner of the land. Highly gifted as he was, he had attracted wherever he went large audiences, and awakened thousands to a sense of their duty, in effecting the personal enfranchisement of thousands of his fellow beings. His mission was then ended; he was about to leave on the 4th of April, and it was thought right that his friends should congregate that evening to do him that honor which his virtues commanded. (Cheers.) One word as to the general question of slavery. Let them not forget that amid their triumph at home over slavery, little had been done in other parts of the world. Africa was still robbed of her children, and as great sufferings inflicted as when the eloquent voices of Wilberforce and Clarkson were raised in their behalf. Let them not forget either that throughout the empire of Brazil, in the U. States, in the colonies of Spain, France, and Holland, the system was as rife as ever, and although the example of England had had its usual good effect, little more in reality had been done. They were able to influence the United States and all Christian people throughout the world, but most of all, in America. They were descended, read the same literature, and had the still greater advantage of commercial intercourse; and could they impress on the minds of that people, that their three millions of slaves were human creatures, on a footing of perfect equality with themselves, they would shrink from a continuance of such a system. By some extraordinary delusion, however, they cannot be convinced of the crimes of which they were guilty against humanity, and they point in triumph to the degraded condition of the slave, which they themselves brought about, as a reason and justification for their conduct. It ought not to be forgotten, that the land where slaves first came from was once a land of eminent statesmen and prelates, and men of letters, and that Africa was celebrated for its learning, piety, and literature, even when Britain was immersed in slavery, and Britons deemed unfit to be sold in the public slave market of Rome. Let them then, that evening, show Frederick Douglass, that though he was proscribed in America—though he was deemed unfit to associate with his fellow-men—in this country he was looked on as a brother, and that he would be enabled to say when he returned to that country, that in England, in Ireland, in Scotland, and in Wales, he was recognized as a man and a brother, and he could therefore well afford to hear the indignities to which he would be subjected. (Cheers.) They were not there that night self-complacently to deride America. There was no man there who wished to see her greatness diminish. Long may she live to circulate their language, their literature, their virtues—but not their vices. Long may her greatness continue to extend; but it was their duty to protest against a system which enslaved their fellow-creatures, and to cry aloud against it as long as it existed. He would not longer trespass on their attention, except to inform them that several sentiments would be proposed for their approbation by gentlemen then on the platform, as well as by Mr. Douglass, who would that night give them a parting word. [. . .]

Mr. Douglass then presented himself, and was received with the greatest enthusiasm. When silence was restored, he said he never appeared before an audience like that, without feeling his incompetency to do justice to the cause he was then to advocate, or to meet those expectations which were generally created for him by those kind friends who preceded him. While he felt grateful for the generosity of his friends he avowed he little deserved their eulogiums. He was a plain, humble man—he had been a slave, and never had a day's schooling in his life; for all the information he possessed was stolen during his slavery.—(Cheers.) That he was deeply and earnestly engaged in advocating the cause of his brethren was most true; and their expressions that evening would be treasured in his breast—would be borne by him to that land of liberty and light, as well as slavery; and be used by him for the emancipation of those of his caste and color. (Cheers.) When he arrived in America, he could boldly stand up for his rights; but here, where every denunciation of slavery was admitted to be correct, where the system was denounced, he had very little to do, for they were all for him. (Cheers.) He listened to the respectful language used towards America and Americans, and he confessed, that although he was going back to that country, though he had many friends there, and expected to die there, he had no respect for her politicians or statesmen. (Cheers.) Society in America was one great falsehood in all its steps. (Hear.) Seventy years ago, they made declaration of independence in favor of the rights of man; yet, the very men who signed it were trafficking in their fellow-men. [. . .]

O'Connell once said, in speaking of Ireland, that her history might be tracked like a wounded man in a crowd. So it was with America; blood in the morning, blood in the mid-day, blood at night, and that not only in a country of boasted liberty, but of Christianity, and a country, too, which vaunted of cooperating with England in the great work of evangelizing the world. They had their missionary societies, but it often happened that the ministers who attended meetings of those societies in New York, Philadelphia, and sometimes at Boston, had their pockets stained with the blood of the slave. Then, again, was Mr. John C. Calhoun, the sturdy democrat, the head of the democracy in America, a slave owner, and in order to render himself a man of consequence in the Senate, actually boasted of being an owner of slaves. The Church in America was the friend of slavery, for its ministers preached in its favor, with Bible in hand, to prove its lawfulness; and when it was driven by the abolitionists into the streets among the mob, and from thence to the Church, it found a refuge there, for it was its greatest stronghold.

The eloquent gentleman, after entering into a detailed statement of the cruelties practiced in the Southern States of America on the unfortunate slaves, proceeded:—He was then in England for 19 months: he had gone through every part of it, and was received in a manner which he should never forget. It would not be right or proper for him, out of deference to any one, to fail to allude to the greatest omission which he believed was ever committed by British Christians, he meant the conduct of the Evangelical Alliance which lately met at Exeter Hall. They were hoodwinked, they were cajoled, in a manner which no after circumstances, he feared, could retrieve. They were raised on a pinnacle, they were set on a hill where the Evangelical could look over them; and three millions of slaves earnestly implored them with entreaties to have pity, slaves, too, who had no voice or representation among them—but it was in vain. (Cheers.) They passed them by on the other side; they had, he believed, repented of the course they took, but from the very feeling of having been betrayed by their American brethren, they would, no doubt, redouble their efforts in future for the abolition of slavery. (Cheers.) With respect to those who purchased his freedom, he was deeply grateful, but he was not responsible for the act, and if there was any violation of principle, he should content himself by living in England for the remainder of life. There was, however, none; it was a question of expediency, and done without any application from him, but he could not help expressing his gratitude to those who did so.

He recommended, at that important moment, the formation of an Anti-Slavery League, for the purpose of improving the moral sentiment in England, and of adding still more to the hatred of the people against slavery; and with respect to America, while the damning blot remained on her escutcheon, let her not proclaim her hypocritical pretensions to the advancement of human liberty.

As that was probably the last time he should ever address a London audience, he had, he was glad to say, been treated with the utmost kindness wherever he went; and, certainly, for the last nineteen months, he, for the only time, learned what real liberty was under a monarchy, as contradistinguished from that of a republic. (Cheers.) Before he left Boston, he was kicked from an omnibus. He would not be allowed to go to a theater, a lyceum, or any place of amusement or instruction. He was driven from every place—he was buffeted by every white man, no matter how black his breast was; but the moment he landed in Liverpool, all was different. He looked around for an insult, for a sign of disapprobation. He visited England, Ireland, and Scotland. He traveled in highways and byways, and in railways, and not one word or act was uttered or occurred, which he could interpret as an insult, or an intention to insult. He visited the House of Lords and Commons, and heard, where he could only hear, the eloquence of Lord Brougham; and most unfeignedly could he assure them, that in whatever manner he should be treated in America, he was, at least, at home in England. (Cheers.) He had had every inducement to remain here; he was offered houses and lands, and money, to bring his family over, and settle down in England, but he determined to go back for the sake of his brethren—to speak for them—to write for them—to lift up his voice for them—in order to insure their emancipation. (Cheers.) He knew he should be met with contumely in America; but he cared not. He should tell his brethren what sympathy they had among Englishmen, and thus encourage their hearts to bear with patience the toil to which they were subjected. With these remarks he should bid them all a long and affectionate farewell. (Great cheering.)

The thanks of the meeting were then passed to the Chairman, after which the meeting separated.

"Farewell Soiree to Mr. Frederick Douglass," *Liberator*, April 30, 1847, 17–18.

[Incident aboard the *Cambria*, En Route to England] (1848)

[ANONYMOUS]

Although Douglass hoped for a more enlightened world in Great Britain than he had known in the United States, his journey toward that new life was not encouraging. He and his traveling companion, James N. Buffum, had been denied a cabin on the *Cambria* and had to settle for passage in steerage. Among those who were not discriminated against were other travelers from the United States, men who made their prejudices, and their resentment of Douglass's presence, clear. When the ship's captain invited Douglass to present a speech, Douglass lashed out against slavery and against the ships that had brought human cargo to the States. A powerful speech, it was not received well by two passengers who tried to shout Douglass down. The captain intervened. Upon Douglass's return to the States, the incident was still remembered, and the captain was still determined that Douglass should enjoy the respect he deserved on his voyage. The following notice from the *United States Magazine and Democratic Review* is a reaction against that "brutal display of hostility to American prejudices."

THE CUNARD STEAMER LINE from Boston to Liverpool, are coming hereafter to New York, as the proprietors are alarmed at the rivalry so suddenly evidenced by the appearance of the American line of steamers from New-York, via Southampton to Bremen. So far, these transatlantic steamers have been wholly supported by American patronage, which, if once withdrawn, will throw them probably on their beam ends. And this is a result likely to occur from present symptoms. If the American line prove itself to be equal in safety and speed—and who can doubt that American skill is not equal to British any day, on sea or land—it is beyond all question certain, that every true hearted American will cheerfully lend every encouragement to his own country's enterprise. There is another reason stronger still why we should give a rebuke to this English Cunard line, which, in the day of its ascendancy, dared to venture upon a brutal display of hostility to American prejudices that should be remembered now.

Only last year, that black vagabond, Douglass, who spent his time in England propagating his filthy lies against the United States, which were greedily swallowed by English hypocrites and fools, returned to this country in the Cambria, under the especial protection of Capt. Judkins, who first insisted that this offensive negro should sit at table with American gentlemen, and, failing in this, he magnanimously gave up to his odorous protegé his own bed and state room. The year before that, Capt. Judkins, whose black propensities are strong in the ascendant, authorized this selfsame negro to hold forth on his deck against the cruelty and infamy of lying America, that talked of liberty in one breath, and refused to live cheek-by-jowl with their nigger brethren in the next. On remonstrances being temperately made by some American gentlemen, this insolent cub of the sea, Capt. Judkins, threatened to *put them in irons*! Ought we not to get him up a public dinner, and a cold bath to boot, on his advent in New York? This suggestion, we learn, is under meditation.

United States Magazine and Democratic Review, n.s., 22 (January 1848): 90.

“Reception of Frederick Douglass at the Belknap-Street Church, Boston” (1847)

[Anonymous]

Douglass's return to the United States was much celebrated, and one can see the development of his reputation and legend in the stories of his reception. Many of the most prominent black abolitionists were in attendance at this meeting, as well as the two most prominent white abolitionists, William Lloyd Garrison and Wendell Phillips. Among the African American abolitionists noted in this report, those who spoke or otherwise played a prominent role include John T. Hilton, one of the founders of the Massachusetts General Colored Association; Josiah Henson, the former slave who became famous for allegedly inspiring Harriet Beecher Stowe in her portrayal of the fictional Uncle Tom; Isaac H. Snowden, who would soon be known as one of three African American students admitted to Harvard Medical School in 1850, only to be pressured to leave after an uprising by the white students and faculty; Henry Bibb, former slave and author of one of the best-known narratives of slavery of the time, who, like Douglass, had founded a newspaper (*The Voice of the Fugitive*, published in Canada); William G. Allen, the formidable African American scholar and educator who would, in 1850, be appointed belles lettres professor at New York Central College in McGrawville; and William C. Nell, a close ally of both Garrison and Douglass who would later publish an important history of African Americans in the Revolutionary War. In his remarks, Douglass pays tribute as well to George Thompson, whom we encountered earlier, and Henry C. Wright, an ardent white abolitionist and feminist. Douglass refers also to another white ally in the antislavery cause, the Reverend Samuel H. Cox, with whom he had had a very public dispute. Reverend Cox was in attendance in 1846 at the World Temperance Convention, held at Covent Garden Theatre in London, and had objected to Douglass's remarks at the event. Because Douglass used the occasion to criticize the American delegates for their association with the system of slavery, Reverend

Cox thought he had been deliberately disruptive, thus damaging the cause of temperance, a cause to which Douglass, like Cox, was a devoted advocate.

In the following account of this reception, especially interesting is the emphasis on formality, including the appointment of officers for the occasion. Such details were important to African American communities then engaged in establishing organizations and associations by which they might address the needs of their communities, needs ignored by the standing governments, councils, and professional organizations of the dominant culture. In the development of such efforts, this was an important event—the return of an internationally recognized leader. In the same issue of the *Liberator* in which this report was published is another piece, "Reception of Frederick Douglass by the Colored People," reporting on a similar reception, also with officers appointed for the occasion, at Zion's Church in New York.

AT AN EARLY HOUR on Monday evening, May 3d, 1847, the house was filled to overflowing with a highly respectable audience. After a voluntary on the organ, by Mr. Bowen, the meeting was called to order by John T. Hilton. The following gentlemen were appointed officers, viz:

William C. Nell, *President*; Robert Morris, Jr., Jonas W. Clark, *Vice Presidents*; Edward B. Lawton, George Allen, *Secretaries*.

The guest of the evening, Frederick Douglass, was then conducted to the pulpit, accompanied by William Lloyd Garrison, and Wendell Phillips, Esq., whereon being seated he was greeted by repeated demonstrations of applause.

The throne of grace was then fervently addressed by Rev. Mr. Henson, of Canada, at the conclusions of which, the chairman introduced Mr. Douglass to the meeting, preceded by the following remarks:—

LADIES AND GENTLEMEN:

We have assembled this evening, to extend the hand of welcome to our distinguished friend, and humanity's eloquent advocate, Frederick Douglass, who, after an absence of twenty months in the old world, where he has won for himself, and the cause so near his heart, laurels of victory, returns to us renewed in spirit, and eager for the conflict with American pro-slavery and prejudice.

We are happy to reciprocate, on this occasion, the sentiments advanced by the Chairman of the farewell meeting, tendered him at London—"That we testify to him our affection for his person, our entire approbation of his labors, and admiration for his attachment to the great cause, with which he stands identified."

It affords us the most heartfelt satisfaction, to acknowledge the respect and attention exhibited by all classes in England, Scotland, and Ireland, to our friend, while traversing the length and breadth of the land in fulfilment of his mission.

In England, whose soil will not bear the impress of a slave, sacred as the birthplace of Wilberforce and Clarkson, honored by the united labors of a constellation of true men and women pledged ever to do battle for the enslaved of every land, there Douglass was made Welcome and "stood *redeemed*, regenerated and disenthralled by the irresistible genius of UNIVERSAL EMANCIPATION." In Scotland, too, renowned in her struggles for liberty by the heroic deeds of Wallace and Bruce, and his own great prototype Douglass, a land illustrious in poetic associations of Burns the ploughman poet, and Walter Scott of Abbotsford—there from the elite of Edinburgh and Glasgow, as also the peasantry of Loch Katrine,

> O'er hill and dale,
> By the bonnie highland heather.

in contrast with the awards of Republican America, Frederick Douglass was honored, as the language of Scotia's own bard proclaimed,

> A man for a' that.

And glorious liberty-loving Ireland,—"First flower of the earth, first gem of the sea,"—though persecuted and famishing, yet responded harmoniously to the teachings of Daniel O'Connell, and to Webb, Allen, Haughton, and of a host of true hearts, themselves the chief, and who greatly facilitated his labors of love among the people.

We should indeed be ungrateful as Abolitionists, did we fail to record our tribute of thanks to all those friends, who have thus aided by their time, talent, money, and influence, as accelerating the car of Emancipation. May the time speedily arrive, when the British Lion and American Eagle, encircled with the appropriate banner conspicuously adorned with the blended

Thistle and Shamrock, unite in one jubilee of thanksgiving, that the last night of American Slavery is past, and that all upon her soil, of whatever color or clime, are indeed free and independent.

Our friend has had every inducement to remain abroad. Houses, lands and money were proffered himself and family, but true to the Amor Patriæ which burns so vividly on the altar of every American heart, he preferred the "hills and valleys green" of his own native land, for with "all its faults, he loves it still," and as he expressed himself, "determined to come back for the sake of his brethren—to speak for them—to write for them—to lift up his voice for them—in order to ensure their emancipation."

Permit me, without further trespass upon your patience, in your behalf to greet Frederick Douglass with a cordial welcome home, and to invoke for him your diligent attention to the words of instruction with which he may be disposed to favor the meeting.

Mr. Douglass, on rising, received the hand of the chairman, which was loudly approbated by the whole audience.

Mr. Douglass confessed being much embarrassed at finding himself thus warmly greeted by his Boston friends, for which testimonial he had no words to express his gratitude. He had returned from his labors across the water, where every mark of esteem was tendered him, and where he had addressed numerous large assemblies in behalf of humanity. But duty to those at home had induced him to resume his post by the side of the faithful and true; to labor with them for the redemption of the slave. Mr. Douglass presented in detail many incidents of his tour—from the exhibition of American pro-slavery on board the Cambria, outward bound, (which was, however, much ameliorated by the noble conduct of Capt Judkins,) contrasted with the treatment awarded him by all classes on the soil of Old England; during his remarks, presenting a graphic delineation of the Free Church of agitation, the Evangelical Alliance, his controversy with Dr. Cox at the great Temperance Meeting in Covent Garden Theatre, which, being characterized by the orator's blended power of wit and satire, drew forth repeated shouts of laughter and applause. A grateful tribute was also awarded those devoted friends of the slave, George Thompson and Henry C. Wright—the mention of whose names was a signal for renewed applause.

Mr. Douglass, after an allusion to his late ransom, acknowledged in an elegant flow of language the eminent services of the British, Scotch and Irish friends, concluding by an earnest exhortation to all present, in imitation of those devoted and gifted champions, William Lloyd Garrison and Wendell Phillips, to an uncompromising warfare with American Slavery.

Isaac H. Snowden submitted the following resolutions, which were subsequently adopted and ordered to he published.

Resolved, That we have listened with unallayed delight to the eloquent address of our guest, Frederick Douglass, and would tender him our congratulations on his safe return home; with the hope that his life may long be spared, enabling him to urge, with characteristic ability, upon the people of America, the opening of the prison doors to them that are bound.

Resolved, That we regard his late mission abroad, in union with Wm. Lloyd Garrison, George Thompson, James N. Buffum and Henry C. Wright, as of the utmost importance to the cause of human brotherhood; and the manner in which it has been fulfilled, as reflecting upon them the highest credit—commanding the admiration and warmest gratitude of every lover of truth, justice, and humanity.

Resolved, That the exclusion of Frederick Douglass from the cabin of the Cambria homeward-bound furnishes another proof of the omnipotence and omnipresence of American colorphobia.

Resolved, That whatever opinions may be held, relative to the purchase of Frederick Douglass, our thanks are nevertheless due those English friends, who felt such anxiety for his safety as to submit to be robbed by soul-drivers and man-stealers.

Mr. Garrison, who, on being introduced by the Chairman, was heartily cheered, bore his testimony to the zeal and ability manifested by Mr. Douglass while in Europe—remarking that there he was entirely exempt from the annoyance of that ally of slavery—prejudice against color. It is unknown everywhere but in America. He rejected indignantly the absurd dogma, that such prejudice was natural; for if so, all nations would exhibit it. He condemned such a feeling as brutal, anti-republican and anti-Christian.

Wendell Phillips, Esq., whose presence was unanimously applauded, kindly acknowledged his appreciation of the favor extended him by the meeting, and would improve the opportunity to endorse the remarks to which they had listened—concurring in the tribute to Mr. Douglass, and concluded by advocating the adoption of the resolutions.

Henry Bibb, the eloquent fugitive, came forward at call of the meeting, and offered a brief exposition of his feelings—rejoicing in the success of his brother Douglass, and hoping that he might long continue to wield his influence against the system of American slavery. He was succeeded by William G. Allen, of Troy, N. Y., editor of the National Watchman, who, in a few fervent remarks, illustrated the condition of the nominally free colored American—his disabilities in the various States of the Union—also the prevalence and force of that vulgar prejudice which had been so truthfully delineated—expressing himself happy in thus participating in the welcome of Frederick Douglass.

At half past eleven o'clock, the crowded assembly adjourned, after uniting in three welcome shouts for Frederick Douglass, which did indeed make the welkin ring—every heart responding to the satisfaction imparted by the joyous occasion.

WILLIAM C. NELL, *President*
ROBERT MORRIS, Jr. }
JONAS W. CLARK } *VICE DO.*
EDWARD B. LAWTON }
GEORGE ALLEN } *SECRETARIES*

"Reception of Frederick Douglass at the Belknap-Street Church, Boston," *Liberator*, May 21, 1847, 2–3.

"Frederick Douglass" (1869)

SAMUEL J. MAY

Samuel Joseph May was born to an upper-class Boston family. One gets more than a glimpse of his sister, Abby May Alcott, in the pages of the popular novels of her daughter, Louisa May Alcott. May himself was similarly possessed with a generous spirit, and his career as a leading Unitarian minister included devoted efforts at social reform, including antislavery as well as educational reform and women's rights. An important figure in the antislavery movement, he looked back on this work after the Civil War and offered this portrait of Douglass's early career. In addition to the now-familiar stories of Douglass's association with John A. Collins and James N. Buffum, May mentions the Hutchinson Family, a famous singing group who regularly devoted their talents to social causes. The sheet music for one of their songs, "The Fugitive's Song," featured an image of Douglass on the cover.

I NEED GIVE but one more example of a colored man of my acquaintance who has exhibited great intellectual ability as well as moral worth. And he is one extensively known and admired throughout our country, Great Britain, and Ireland. Of course I mean Frederick Douglass. His well-written, intensely interesting autobiography, entitled "My Bondage and My Freedom," has probably been read so generally that I need not attempt any sketch of his life. Suffice it to say he was born a slave in Maryland. He experienced all of the indignities, and suffered most of the hardships and cruelties, that passionate slaveholders could inflict upon their bondmen. When about twenty-one years of age he resolved that he would endure them no longer, and in 1838 he found his way from Baltimore to New Bedford, the best place, on the whole, to which he could have gone. There, with his young wife, he commenced the life of a freeman. The severest toil now seemed light. He worked with a will, because the avails of his labor were to be his own. Being, as most colored persons are, religiously inclined, he soon became a member of a Methodist church, and ere-long was appointed a class-leader and a local preacher.

While in slavery Mr. Douglass had contrived, in various ingenious ways, to learn to read and write. So soon, therefore, as he came to live in Massachusetts, he diligently improved his enlarged opportunities to acquire knowledge. Ere long he became a subscriber for *The Liberator*, and week after week made himself master of its contents, in which he never found a silly or a worthless line. Of course its doctrines and its purpose were altogether such as his own bitter experience justified. And the exalted spirit of religious faith and hope, at all times inspiring the writings and speeches of Mr. Garrison, awakened in the bosom of Mr. Douglass the assurance that he was "the man,—the Moses raised up by God to deliver his Israel in America from a worse than Egyptian bondage."

In the summer of 1841 there was a large antislavery convention held in Nantucket. Mr. Douglass attended it. In the midst of the meeting, to his great confusion, he was called upon and urged to address the convention. A number were present from New Bedford who had heard his exhortations in the Methodist church, and they would not allow his plea of inability to speak. After much hesitation he rose, and, notwithstanding his embarrassment, he gave evidence of such intellectual power—wisdom as well as wit—that all present were astonished. Mr. Garrison followed him in one of his sublimest speeches. "Here was a living witness of the justice of the severest condemnation he had ever uttered of slavery. Here was one 'every inch a man,' ay, a man of no common power, who yet had been held at the South as a piece of property, a chattel, and had been treated as if he were a domesticated brute," &c.

At the close of the meeting, Mr. John A. Collins, then the general agent of the Massachusetts Antislavery Society, urgently invited Mr. Douglass to become a lecturing agent. He begged to be excused. He was sure that he was not competent to such an undertaking. But Mr. Garrison and others, who had heard him that day, joined Mr. Collins in pressing him to accept the appointment. He yielded to the pressure. And, in less than three years from the day of his escape from slavery, he was introduced to the people of New England as a suitable person to lecture them upon the subject that was of more moment than any other to which the attention of our Republic has ever been called.

Mr. Douglass henceforth improved rapidly. He applied himself diligently to reading and study. The number and range of his topics in lecturing increased and widened continually. He soon became one of the favorite anti-slavery speakers. The notoriety which he thus acquired could not be confined to New England or the Northern States. A murmur of inquiry came up from Maryland who this man could be. A pamphlet which he felt called upon to publish in 1845, in answer to the current assertions that he was an imposter, that he had never been a slave, made it no longer possible to conceal his personality. The danger of his being captured and taken back to Maryland was so great that it was thought advisable he should go to England. Accordingly, he went thither that year in company with James N. Buffum, one of the truest of antislavery men, and with the Hutchinson family, the sweetest of singers.

Although not permitted to go as a cabin passenger, many of the cabin passengers sought to make his acquaintance and visited him in the steerage, and invited him to visit them on the saloon-deck. At length they requested him to give them an antislavery lecture. This he consented and was about to do, when some passengers who were slaveholders chose to consider it an insult to them, and were proceeding to punish him for his insolence; they threatened even to throw him overboard, and would have done so had not the captain of the steamer interposed his absolute authority: called his men, and ordered them to put those disturbers of the peace *in irons* if they did not instantly desist. Of course they at once obeyed, and shrank back in the consciousness that they were under the dominion of a power that had broken the staff of such oppressors as themselves.

This incident of the voyage was reported in the newspapers immediately on the arrival of the vessel at Liverpool, and introduced Mr. Douglass at once to the British public. He was treated with great attention by the Abolitionists of the United Kingdom; was invited to lecture everywhere, and rendered the most valuable services to the cause of his oppressed countrymen. So deeply did he interest the philanthropists of that country that they paid seven hundred and fifty dollars to procure from his master a formal, legal certificate of manumission, so that, on his return to these United States, he would be no longer liable to be sent back into slavery. They also presented him with the sum of twenty-five hundred dollars for his own benefit, to be appropriated, if he should see fit, to the establishment of a weekly paper edited by himself, which was then his favorite project.

Soon after his return in 1847 he did establish such a paper at Rochester and conducted it with ability for several years. He has since become one of the popular lecturers of our country, and every season has as many invitations as he cares to accept. He is extensively known and much respected. Many there are who wish to see him a member of Congress; and we confidently predict that, if he shall ever be sent to Washington as a Representative or a Senator, he will soon become a prominent man in either House.

Samuel J. May, *Some Recollections of Our Antislavery Conflict* (Boston: Fields, Osgood, 1869), 292–296.

"Reminiscences of Frederick Douglass" (1895)

Jane Marsh Parker

How well do your neighbors know you? The following piece is written by one of Douglass's neighbors in Rochester, New York, and someone who knew him very well, as this piece suggests. Douglass's young neighbor Jane Marsh Parker, only eight when her family moved to Rochester, was in a position to witness many of Douglass's famous visitors. Beyond Douglass's infamous relationship with John Brown, Parker mentions the lawyer and politician Robert G. Ingersoll, who would later become known as a powerful orator and "The Great Agnostic," and Swedish writer and feminist Fredrika Bremer. Parker's preacher father moved the family to Rochester to edit publications on the Millerite movement, named for William Miller, who believed (and convinced many others) that the end of the world was imminent—specifically, sometime in 1843 or 1844 (the date changed as Miller recalculated his prophecy). When the world failed to end, the Millerites were broadly ridiculed, an experience that stayed with Parker throughout her life, who abandoned religion for a time but later became a devoted member of the Episcopal Church. Kept out of school in anticipation of the world's end, Parker eventually completed her education and went on to become a very active writer, as well as a devoted mother and one of Rochester's leading women. The friendship suggested by the following remembrance was real. When Douglass was appointed U.S. minister to Haiti, he invited Parker to join a small group accompanying him to the island, where Parker stayed for three months while researching various topics for later publications.

How well I remember this flutter our suburban and aspiring neighborhood was thrown into when, some time in 1847, soon after Frederick Douglass came to Rochester to live, it was known that he had bought a house on our street—and a very good house, too—and was about to move his family into the same! He had bought of an Abolitionist, and the property-owners on either side of him were Abolitionists, one of whom was my father. Naturally, there was open protest from the rest; but soon after the arrival of the new neighbors, all opposition to their presence disappeared. Frederick Douglass was a gentleman, and a good neighbor. Mrs. Douglass chose seclusion, and the children were models of behavior.

That house on Alexander Street, a two-story brick, of about nine rooms, on a large lot about one hundred feet in width, was a handsome property for an ex-slave to buy, a runaway of only ten years before, whose manumission papers bore date December 5, 1846. It must have been the first house he ever owned. One of the first things he did after settling in it, and making a private study of a hall bedroom on the upper floor, was to write a letter to his old master, Thomas Auld, in which he said: "So far as my domestic affairs are considered, I can boast of as comfortable a dwelling as your own." It may be doubted if many slave-kept homes were as comfortable and well ordered, for Mrs. Douglass was a model housekeeper, her thrifty care of her family and her watchful supervision of expenditure making the financial venture of her husband in undertaking the publication of the "North Star" far less hazardous than many believed. She was laying the foundation of his prosperity, insuring his future independence. Anna Murray Douglass was a free woman when she helped her lover to escape from Maryland, following him at no small peril to New York, where they were married, she going out to service until he found steady employment on the docks of New Bedford. She was a pure-blooded negro, of the best type, with severe notions of the proprieties and duties of life. Her training had evidently been in Southern families of high standing; for, like her husband, she had what her new neighbors called "very aristocratic ideas." She read character with marvelous accuracy, and was a wholesome check on her husband's proneness to being imposed upon. Her greatest discontent was when his admirers persisted in dragging her into notice—when she had to receive visitors merely to gratify curiosity. Little if any service was hired in that admirably kept home. A sister of Mrs. Douglass assisted her in fulness and systematic industry. Did not Rosetta make a shirt for her father, every stitch, before she was ten years old? Mrs. Douglass disapproved, decidedly, of the idle, pleasure-taking ways of the other little girls in the neighborhood, and she did not hesitate to correct their lapses in good manners. This is to show the footing the family soon had in the neighborhood.

Every one of note who came to the city was pretty sure to call upon Frederick Douglass; we had only to watch the front door to see many famous men and women; which, with his connection to the Underground Railroad (known only to his anti-slavery neighbors), added much to a locality which before had been rather dull. Frederika Bremer was one of his many famous visitors in those days; and what a thrill it gave me to turn over the pages of the full set of her writings which she had left upon the Douglass parlor table, her autograph on the fly-leaf of each volume!

"For Frederick's sake," Mrs. Douglass, that first summer of their living on Alexander Street, consented, rather reluctantly, to have a teacher in the house for herself as well as the children—an English woman, of whom she faithfully tried for a while to learn to read and write; but when it came to neglecting housewifely duties for copy-book and speller, the experiment ended; and Mrs. Douglass was glad to be released, referring to the episode afterwards as an amusing experience to Frederick as well as herself, and one that settled the matter of her ever becoming an educated woman. Small circles of young ladies used to meet at the house in those times to make fancy articles for the anti-slavery fairs, and once, when one of them had finished a book-mark with *Fredrick* Douglass upon it in cross-stitch, Mrs. Douglass was the first to see the mistake, showing that there was one name in the world that she could read and spell, even if she did make her signature with her X.

But the excitement caused in the neighborhood by the settlement of the Douglass family among us was as nothing to what came to pass when two English sisters arrived, spinsters of means and culture, and it was announced that they were to be members of the Douglass household for some time, and co-workers with Frederick Douglass in the anti-slavery cause, assisting in the office of the "North Star." Enthusiasts for the abolition of American slavery, these two English ladies had consecrated their means and service to the cause. The appearance upon the main street of Frederick Douglass with one of these ladies on either arm seriously threatened the order of the town for a while, and threats were openly made of what would be done if such aggressive demonstration of race-mixture were persisted in. Frederick Douglass kept his head high as ever, the ladies filling the role of possible martyrs unflinchingly. After a while the threatenings of storm died away; one of the ladies married a leading Abolitionist, and the older remained for several years the associate editor of the "North Star," giving to Frederick Douglass that assistance in his work which he could ill have done without. "Think what editing a paper was to me before Miss Griffiths came! I had not learned how to spell; my knowledge of the simplest rules of grammar was most defective. I wrote slowly and under embarrassment—

lamentably ignorant of much that every school-boy is supposed to know." He rewrote his autobiography under her supervision, and she did much for his education in many ways, returning to England after a few years, when she was married to a clergyman of the Established Church.

That little den-like upstairs study of Frederick Douglass with its small table and a few books—how well I remember it! and how we used to keep there a list of the words he found it hard to spell. He did learn to spell, however, and in a very short time. Had he drawn up the Constitution of John Brown's Asylum Republic (the original copy as written by John Brown was one of the treasures of Cedar Hill), there would not have been those slips in orthography.

Frederick Douglass was highly esteemed by his neighbors, and most popular with the children. When the boys stole his apples he made them ashamed, and they became his loyal admirers forever after. If he knew that a group of children were gathered before his window on a warm summer night when he was singing to his violin, he was sure to give them what he knew they were waiting for—"Nelly was a Lady" or "Old Kentucky Home"—coming to the door and bowing his acknowledgment of their hearty applause. Nobody could sing "Oh, carry me back to ole Virginny" as he could. He had a rich baritone voice and a correct ear, and it was something to hear him sing in the latter years of his life from "The Seraph," the very same old singing-book which he had slipped into his bundle when he skipped out of Maryland for freedom. There was another book in his library that had had much to do with his destiny—"The Columbian Orator," the identical book he had bought with his carefully hoarded pennies when a slave boy, that he might learn something to speak at the Sabbath-school exhibitions of the free negroes, which he attended by stealth, and where he was beginning to shine as an orator. That "Columbian Orator" contained a dialogue between a master and a slave (a Turkish master), and he, as a boy, delighted to repeat the long, big-worded soliloquy of the slave—". . . All nature's smiles are frowns to him who wears the chains of slavery."

Later on Mr. Douglass bought a house with much larger grounds on the woody hillside south of the city—a neighborless place, its only roadway at that time the private road leading to his door. It was there that John Brown visited him, full of his project of raiding the border slave States and of establishing a refuge for fugitives in the mountains, and there that he laid his plans, often demonstrating, to the delight of the Douglass children, each detail with a set of blocks, making long tramps alone over the hills when he had a hard problem to solve. Mr. Douglass was absent from home much in those days, a great part of his time being spent in Washington and in lecturing and attendance upon conventions.

Frederick Douglass had his education in four great schools, graduating from one to the other in natural sequence and with honors—Methodism, Garrisonianism, Journalism, Political Campaignism. Had not the great mass of the slaves been religious, had they not been held in check by their strong emotional religious feeling, surely slavery would have been terribly different from what it was. And so, had not Frederick Douglass been a Methodist, had the deepest springs of his nature been unlocked by some other force, might they not have found an outlet sweeping him to disaster rather than salvation? It was in the Methodist prayer-meetings that he found that he could speak so that every one would listen to him, and that few, if any, could speak as he could. He was innately religious—it was his temperament; his underlying characteristic was a reverent faith in the Unseen. Irreverence always shocked him. Religious cant—or, as he would call it, *ir*religious cant—was his aversion. He subscribed to no creed, having tolerance for all. He knew the Bible better than most men; he read it more; his readiness in quoting texts never failed him; that was one secret of his old-time telling assaults upon a slave-defending Christianity. He has been heard to say in his later years, "I have no uneasiness about the hereafter. I am in the trade-winds of God. My bark was launched by him, and he is taking it into port." Again, "Perhaps I should have made a good Roman Catholic. I have a kinship with that Church, I think sometimes; but one must be born with it, nurtured in it, or always an alien." Once, when urged by an over-zealous Churchman to join the Episcopal Mission at the foot of Cedar Hill, he mused some time in silence. "I can't forget," he said, softly, "that your Church would not baptize slave babies. The Episcopal Church was consistent there, as it is in everything, but it left me out." He was the warm friend of Robert G. Ingersoll, their acquaintance beginning, if my memory is right, long before Ingersoll was known to the world, and when he opened his door one night to Frederick Douglass, who otherwise would have walked the street, the hotels refusing him admission. "I was a stranger—more than that, a negro—and he took me in."

"One of the hardest things I had to learn when I was fairly under way as a public speaker was to stop telling so many funny stories. I could keep my audience in a roar of laughter—and they liked to laugh, and showed disappointment when I was not amusing—but I was convinced that I was in danger of becoming something of a clown, and that I must guard against it." His keen sense of the ludicrous saved him from many a mistake; his quick wit in repartee could effectually silence his antagonists. Under it all was the deep minor key of his prevailing melancholy—that depth of feeling he seldom suffered to master his outward cheerfulness.

As "a graduate from slavery, with his diploma written on his back," the Garrisonian platform gained much in enrolling him under its banner; and he found upon it, perhaps, the single door for advancement beyond the mental calling by which he had barely earned his bread. As a Methodist exhorter he had learned to speak so fluently and well that it was no wonder that many who heard him in the anti-slavery meetings had doubts if he had ever been a slave, and said so openly.

Public speaking and the drill of conventions fitted him for journalism as nothing else could have done. Again his horizon was widened, and he was brought into fuller touch with men of the world and public affairs. Only ten years out of slavery, and seated in an editorial chair! Who, then, was so qualified in his peculiar way for "stumping the North" in Presidential campaigns? From Fremont to Harrison, great was his service to the Republican party.

It has been said that the career of Douglass would have had its fitting and glorious ending on the scaffold with John Brown. He never thought so. His heart was never fully given to John Brown's scheme; he had discouraged it; had thought it visionary and impracticable; and yet his complication with it nearly cost him his life. He was always open in saying that he did not boast of having much martyr-stuff in him—that is, when he could just as well live for his cause as die for it. The intensity of his emotional nature, when aroused, had given him a habit, in denunciation, of shutting his jaws tightly together at the close of his sentences. Once, when speaking before a large audience, he actually crushed his upper front teeth, but so perfect was his self-control that he betrayed nothing in his delivery or facial expression, but finished his address before leaving the platform.

He never became a student, even when the victory of his cause had been won, and he had the leisure for study. Composition was never easy for him, unless his soul was stirred in its depths; nor was public speaking, unless his tongue was on fire. His literary lectures upon subjects foreign to his personal experience were largely disappointing. "The Honorable Frederick Douglass" was never the orator that "Fred Douglass" had been in the old pre-emancipation days. He sometimes said in his old age that he had outlived his cause. "Never did I dream, in my most hopeful moods, when I was pleading for my brothers in bonds, that I would ever see the end of American slavery."

He liked a good novel—of the stirring kind. Dumas was one of his favorites, and of "The Three Musketeers" he never tired. Nothing pleased him more, upon his arrival in Port-au-Prince, than to be told by the Parisian Haytians that he bore a strong resemblance to Victor Hugo.

Jane Marsh Parker, "Reminiscences of Frederick Douglass," *Outlook* 51, no. 14 (April 6, 1895): 552–553.

"A Leaf from My Scrap Book: Samuel R. Ward and Frederick Douglass" (1849)

William J. Wilson

Throughout U.S. history, whenever any African American male has become prominent, he has been placed in competition with another—sometimes to represent (usually inaccurately and always reductively) different ideological or social positions. Booker T. Washington and W. E. B. Du Bois, Martin Luther King Jr., and Malcolm X. Americans, both black and white, seem to favor black leaders in pairs. Given his prominence in the nineteenth century, it is perhaps inevitable that Douglass was frequently compared to other leaders, sometimes to his advantage and sometimes not. The following, written by an African American writer who often wrote under the pseudonym "Ethiop," William J. Wilson, compares Douglass with Samuel Ringgold Ward, one of the most important black abolitionists of his time. Like Douglass, Ward was born in slavery, and following his escape he became a Congregational minister and editor of the *Provincial Freeman*, the newspaper he founded in Canada in 1853. Wilson, known for his wit, his satirical edge, and his willingness to take on difficult subjects, was in many ways the perfect person to compare these two great orators. Obviously an admirer of Douglass when this piece was written in 1849, Wilson seems to give the edge to Ward, though Wilson's admiration of Douglass would continue to develop. He was a contributor to Douglass's paper, and he later included Douglass among a pantheon of revolutionary leaders in an 1859 piece written for the *Anglo-African Magazine*.

Perhaps a fitter occasion never presented itself, nor was more properly availed of, for the exhibition of talent, than when Frederick Douglass and Samuel R. Ward debated the "question" whether the Constitution was or not a pro-slavery document.

With the "question" at issue we have, at present, nothing to do; and with the arguments so far only as they exhibit the men.

Both eminent for talent of an order (though differing somewhat in cast) far above the common level of great men.

If any inequalities existed, they served rather to heighten than diminish the interest of the occasion, giving rise to one of the severest contests of mind with mind that has yet come to my notice.

Douglass, sincere in the opinions he has espoused, defends them with a fervor and eloquence that finds scarcely a competitor.

In his very look—his gesture—in his whole manner, there is so much of genuine, earnest eloquence, that they leave no time for reflection. Now you are reminded of one rushing down some fearful steep, bidding you follow; now on some delightful stream, still beckoning you onward.

In either case, no matter what your prepossessions or oppositions, you for the moment, at least, forget the justness or unjustness of his cause and obey the summons, and loath, if at all, you return to your former post.

Not always, however, is he successful in retaining you. Giddy as you may be with the descent you have made, delighted as you are with the pleasure afforded, with the elysium to which he has wafted you, you return too often dissatisfied with his and your own impetuosity and want of firmness. You feel that you had had only a dream, a pastime, not a reality.

This great power of momentary captivation consists in his eloquence of manner—his just appreciation of words.

In listening to him, your whole soul is fired—every nerve strung—every passion inflated—every faculty you possess ready to perform at a moment's bidding. You stop not to ask why or wherefore.

'Tis a unison of mighty yet harmonious sounds that play upon your imagination; and you give yourself up, for a time, to their irresistible charm.

At last, the *cataract* which roared around you is hushed, the *tornado* is passed, and you find yourself sitting upon a bank (at whose base roll but tranquil waters), quietly meditating that why, amid such a display of power, no greater effect had really been produced.

After all, it must be admitted, there is a power in Mr. Douglass rarely to be found in any other man.

With copiousness of language, and finish of diction, when even ideas fail, words come to his aid—arranging themselves, as it were, so completely, that they not only captivate, but often deceive us for ideas; and hence the vacuum that would necessarily occur in the address of an ordinary *speaker* is filled up, presenting the same beautiful harmony as do the lights and shades of a picture.

From Mr. Douglass, in this, perhaps, as much as in any other respect, does Mr. *Ward* differ. Ideas form the basis of all Mr. Ward utters. Words are only used to express those ideas.

If words and ideas are not inseparable, then, as mortar is to the stones that compose the building, so are his words to his ideas.

In this, I judge, lays Mr. Ward's greatest strength. Concise without abruptness—without extraordinary stress, always clear and forcible; if sparing of ornament, never inelegant. In all, there appears a consciousness of strength, developed by close study and deep reflection, and only put forth because the occasion demanded,—a power not only to examine but to enable you to see the fairness of that examination and the justness of its conclusions.

You feel Douglass to be right, without always seeing it; perhaps it is not too much to say, when Ward is right you see it.

His appeals are directed rather to the understanding than the imagination; but so forcibly do they take possession of it, that the heart unhesitatingly yields.

If, as we have said, Mr. Douglass seems as one whirling down some steep descent whose very impetuosity impels;—ere you are aware of it, it is the quiet serenity of Mr. Ward, as he points up the rugged ascent, and invites you to follow, that inspires your confidence and ensures your safety. Step by step do you with him climb the rugged steep; and, as you gain each succeeding eminence, he points you to new scenes and new delights;—now grand—sublime; now picturesque and beautiful;—always real. Most speakers fail to draw a perfect figure. This point I think Mr. Ward has gained. His figures, when done, stand out with prominence, possessing both strength and elegance.

Douglass' imagery is fine—vivid—often gaudily painted. Ward's pictures —bold, strong, glowing.

Douglass speaks right on; you acknowledge him to have been on the ground—nay, to have gone over the field; *Ward* seeks for and finds the corners; sticks the stakes, and leaves them standing; we know where to find them.

Mr. Douglass deals in generals; Mr. Ward reduces everything to a point.

Douglass is the *lecturer*; Ward the *debater*. Douglass powerful in invective; Ward in argument. What advantage Douglass gains in mimicry Ward recovers in wit.

Douglass has sarcasm, Ward point.

Here, again, an essential difference may be pointed out:—

Douglass says much, at times, you regret he uttered. This, however, is the real man, and on reflection you like him the better for it. What Ward says you feel to be but a necessity, growing out of the case,—that it ought to have been said—that you would have said precisely the same yourself, without adding or diminishing a single sentence.

Douglass, in manner, is at all times pleasing; Ward seldom less so; often raises to the truly majestic, and never descends below propriety. If you regret when Douglass ceases to speak, you are anxious Ward should continue.

Dignity is an essential quality in an orator—I mean true dignity.

Douglass has this in an eminent degree; Ward no less so, coupled with it great self-possession. He is never disconcerted—all he desires he says.

In one of his replies to Mr. Douglass I was struck with admiration, and even delight, at the calm, dignified manner in which he expressed himself, and his ultimate triumph under what seemed to me very peculiar circumstances.

Douglass' was a splendid effort—a beautiful effusion. One of those outpourings from the deeps of his heart of which he can so admirably give existence to.

He had brought down thunders of well-merited applause; and sure I am, that a whisper, a breath from almost any other opponent than Mr. Ward, would have produced a tumult of hisses.

Not so, however, now. The quiet, majestic air, the suppressed richness of a deep-toned, but well-cultivated voice, as the speaker paid a few well-timed compliments to his opponents, disturbed not, as it had produced, the dead stillness around.

Next followed some fine sallies of wit, which broke in on the calm.

He then proceeded to make and accomplished one of the most finished speeches to which I have ever listened, and sat down amidst a perfect storm of cheers.

It was a noble burst of eloquence,—the gatherings up of the choicest possible culled thoughts, and poured forth, mingling with a unison of brilliant flashes and masterly strokes, following each other in quick succession; and though felt—deeply felt, no more to be described than the vivid lightning's zig-zag, as produced from the deep-charged thunder-cloud.

If Douglass is not always successful in his attempts to heave up his ponderous missiles at his opponents, from the point of his descent, he always shows determination and spirit.

He is often too far down the *pass*, however, (herculean though he be,) for his intent.

Ward, from the eminence he has gained, giant-like, hurls them back with the force and skill of a practiced marksman, almost invariably to the detriment of his already fallen victim.

In Douglass you have a man, in whose soul the iron of oppression has far entered, and you feel it.

He tells the story of his wrongs, so that they stand out in all their naked ugliness.

In Ward, you have one with strong native powers,—I know of none stronger; superadded a careful and extensive cultivation; an understanding so matured, that fully enables him to successfully grapple with men or errors, and portray truth in a manner equaled by few.

After all, it must be admitted, both are men of extraordinary powers of mind.

Both well qualified for the task they have undertaken.

I have, rather than anything else, drawn these outline portraits for our *young men*, who can fill them up at leisure.

The subjects are both fine models, and may be studied with profit by all,—especially those who are destined to stand in the front rank.

Note.—It has been some years since the above sketch was drawn; and though my impressions, especially of Mr. Douglass, have undergone some slight change since,—seeing in him enlarged, strengthened, and more matured thought, still I think, on the whole, the careful observer will attest substantially to its correctness.

William J. Wilson, "A Leaf from My Scrap Book: Samuel R. Ward and Frederick Douglass," in *Autographs for Freedom*, ed. Julia Griffiths (Auburn, NY: Alden, Beardsley, 1854), 165–173.

"Outline of a Man" (1853)

R. R. Raymond

A white minister of a Baptist church in Syracuse, New York, R. R. Raymond was an active supporter of the antislavery movement. In 1850, he supported the black reverend Jermain W. Loguen's call to resist the Fugitive Slave Law at a Syracuse meeting called to discuss the law, and he was one of thirteen men appointed to a Vigilance Committee by A. H. Hovey, mayor of Syracuse, to resist any attempts to recapture fugitive slaves. The piece that follows is Reverend Raymond's contribution to *Autographs for Freedom*, a collection edited by Douglass's friend Julia Griffiths to raise money and sympathy for the cause. Raymond presents Douglass as an almost mythical figure, rising to fulfill the requirements for Raymond's imagined black abolitionist hero. Indeed, Raymond presents not only his past imaginings of a man, who turns out to be Douglass; he also presents an imagined past for Douglass, based on the outlines of Douglass's story. Along the way, Raymond quotes extensively from Douglass's autobiographies, presented in footnotes (excluded here). Raymond's sketch of Douglass appeared in the same volume as Douglass's only work of fiction, the novella *The Heroic Slave*.

IN SOME OF THOSE castle-building day-dreams, in which, like all youth of an imaginative turn, I was wont, in my early days, to indulge, a favorite image of my creation was an *Africo-American for the time*,—a colored man, who had known by experience the bitterness of slavery, and now by some process free, so endowed with natural powers, and a certain degree of attainments, all the more rare and effective for being acquired under great disadvantages,—as to be a sort of Moses to his oppressed and degraded tribe. He was to be gifted with a noble person, of course, and refinement of manners, and some elegance of thought and expression; by what unprecedented miracle such a paragon was to be graduated through the educational appliances of American slavery, imagination did not trouble herself to inquire. She was painting fancy-pieces, not portraits.

Having thus irresponsibly struck out upon the canvas her central figure, she would not be slow to complete the picture with many a rose-colored vision of brilliant successes and magic triumphs won by her hero, in his great enterprise of the redemption of his people. A burning sense of their wrongs fired his eloquence with an undying, passionate earnestness, and as he alternately reproached the injustice, and appealed to the generosity of his oppressors, all opposition gave way before him; the masses, as one man, demanded the emancipation of his long-denigrated deeply injured race; and millions of regenerated men rose up, upon their broken chains and called him blessed.

Years rolled away, and these poetic fancies faded "into the light of common day." The cold, stern, pitiless reality remained. The dark incubus of slavery yet rested down upon more than three millions of the victims of democratic despotism. But the triumphant champion of the devoted race had melted away, with the morning mists of my boyish conjuring.

One morning in the summer of 1844, walking up Main-street in the city of Hartford, I was attracted by the movements of a group of some twenty-five or thirty men and women, in a small recess, or court, by the side of the old Centre Church. They appeared to be organized into an assembly, and a tall mulatto was addressing them. I drew near to listen. The speaker was recounting the oft-enacted history of a flight from slavery. With his eye upon the cold, but true north star, and his ear ever and anon bent to the ground, listening for the "blood-hound's savage bay," sure-footed and panting, the fugitive was before me! My attention had been arrested; I was profoundly interested. The audience was the American Anti-slavery Society, then just excluded from some of the public halls of the city, and fain to content themselves, after an apostolic sort, with the *next best* accommodations. The orator was FREDERICK DOUGLASS, the most remarkable man of this country, and of this age; and—may I not dare to add—the almost complete fulfilment of my early dream!

Since that day, through assiduous application, and a varied experience, he has continued to develop in the same wonderful ratio of improvement, which even then distinguished him as a prodigy in self-education. Unusually favored in personal appearance and address, full of generous impulse and delicate sensibility, exuberant in playful wit, or biting sarcasm, or stern denunciation, ever commanding in his moral attitude, earnest and impressive in manner, with a voice eminently sonorous and flexible, and gesture full of dramatic vivacity, I have many times seen large audiences swayed at his will; at one moment convulsed with laughter, and at the next, bathed in tears; now lured with admiration of the orator, and now with indignation at the oppressor, against whom he hurled his invective. But in my boyhood's quasi-prophetic fancy of such a man and his inimitable success, I had not counted upon one antagonist, whose reality and potency, the observation of every day now forces painfully upon me. I mean the strange and unnatural *prejudice against mere color* which is so all-prevalent in the American breast, as almost to nullify the influence of *such* a man, so pleading; while his dignity, his urbanity, his imperturbable serenity and good nature, his genuine purity and worth all fail, at times, to secure him from the grossest indignities, at the hands of the coarse and brutal. Nobody who knows him will be inclined to question our estimate of his character, but it still comports with the intelligence and refinement and piety of a large proportion of American society to label him "nigger," and the name itself invites to safe contumely, and irresponsible violence.

I have spoken of Frederick Douglass as an interesting man—a wonderful man. Look at him as he stands to-day before this nation; and then contemplate his history.

Begin with him when, a little slave-child, he lay down on his rude pallet, and that slave-mother, from a plantation twelve miles away, availed herself of the privilege granted grudgingly, of traveling the whole distance, after the day's work, (on peril of the lash, unless back again by sunrise to her task,) that she might lie there by his side, and sing him with her low sweet song to sleep. "I do not recollect," says he, "of ever seeing my mother by the light of day. She was with me in the night. She would lie down with me, and get me to sleep, but long before I awaked, she was gone." How touching the love of that dark-browed bondwoman for her boy! How precious must the memory of that dim but sweet remembrance be to him, who though once a vassal, bound and scourged, and still a Helot, proscribed and wronged, may not be robbed of this dear token that he, too, *had once a mother*! Her low sad lullaby yet warps his life's dark woof—for she watches over his pathway now with spirit-eyes, and still keeps singing on in his heart, and nursing his courage and his patience.

Follow him through all the tempestuous experience of his bondage. His lashings, his longings, his perseverance in possessing himself of the key of knowledge, which, after all, only unlocked to him the fatal secret that he was a slave, a thing to be bought and sold like oxen. Imagine the tumult of his soul, as standing by the broad Chesapeake, he watched the receding vessels, "while they flew on their white wings before the breeze, and apostrophized them as animated by the living spirit of freedom"; or when reading in a stray copy of the old "Columbian Orator," (verily, all our school-books must be expurgated of the incendiary "perilous stuff" in which they abound,) the "Dialogue between a Master and his Slave," and Sheridan's great speech on Catholic Emancipation. See to what heroic resistance his proud heart had swollen, when he turned outright upon his tormentor—pious Mr. Corey [*sic*], the "nigger-breaker"—and inflicted condign retribution on his heartless ribs; "after which," says he, significantly, "I was never whipped again; *I had several fights* but was never whipped." Attend him in his exodus from our republican Egypt. Witness his struggles with poverty; his vain attempts to find employment at his trade, as a colored man, in the *free* North. Behold him at last emerging from his obscurity at the Anti-slavery Convention in Nantucket. Somebody, who is aware of his extraordinary natural intelligence, invites him to speak. Tremblingly he consents. "As soon as he had taken his seat," said Mr. Garrison, after describing the tremendous effect of his remarks upon the audience, "filled with hope and admiration, I rose and declared that Patrick Henry, of revolutionary fame, never made a speech more eloquent in the cause of liberty, than the one we had just listened to from the hunted fugitive."

That was just *eleven years ago*,—and what is Frederick Douglass now? I would fain avoid the language of exaggeration. It is ever a cruel kindness which over-praises, exciting expectations, which cannot but be disappointed. But when, in view of the fact that the subject of this sketch was but thirteen years ago A SLAVE, in all the darkness and disability of Southern bondage, I affirm that his present character, attainments, and position constitute a phenomenon hitherto perhaps unprecedented in the history of intellectual and moral achievement, none who know and are competent to weigh the facts, will account the terms extravagant. It is not to be expected but that his mental condition should betray his early disadvantages. His information, though amazing, under the circumstances, will not of course bear comparison, in fulness and accuracy, with that of men who have been accumulating their resources from childhood. In his writings, the deficiency of early discipline is most manifest, rendering them diffuse and unequal, though always interesting, and often exceedingly effective. He is properly an *orator*. His addresses, like those of Whitfield, and many other popular speakers, lose a large proportion of their effect in reading. They require the living voice, and the magnetic presence of the orator. But even in this respect, Douglass is not uniform in his performance, but is quite dependent on his *surroundings*, and the inspiration of the moment. But when, all these consenting, he becomes thoroughly possessed of his theme, and his tall form—six feet high and straight as an arrow,—his bearing dignified and graceful,—self-possessed, yet modest,—his countenance flexible, and wonderful in power of expression, and his voice, with its rich and varied modulation, are all summoned to the work of enchantment, many a rapt assembly, insignificant in neither numbers nor intelligence, can testify to the witchery of his eloquence.

And, after all, the *moral* features of this interesting character constitute its principal charm. The integrity and manliness of Frederick Douglass, potent and acknowledged where he is at all known, have much to do with his influence as a popular orator. It has been customary, with a certain class of Shibboleth-pronouncers to class him with infidels, but this is only the appropriate and characteristic retort of a certain sort of "highly respectable" Christianity to his uncompromising denunciations of its hollow and selfish character. *I* think Frederick Douglass is a Christian; he is a gentleman, I *know*. There are few white men of my acquaintance, who could have borne so much adulation, without losing the balance of their self-appreciation. Nobody ever knew Frederick Douglass to over-rate himself, or to thrust himself anywhere where he did not belong, or upon anybody who might by any possibility object to his companionship,—unless, in the latter case, when he deemed necessary the assertion of a simple right. Whence he got his retiring and graceful modesty, and his nice sense of the minute proprieties,—unless it be somehow in his *blood*—is a mystery to me. Can it be possible that such refinements are *scourged* into men "down South"? An illustration of this may be seen in his response to those gentlemen of Rochester, who, by way of gratifying a grudge against the Anti-slavery faction of their party, nominated Douglass for Congress in derision.

GENTLEMEN:—I have learned with some surprise, that in the Whig Convention held in this city on Saturday last, you signified, by your votes, a desire to make me your representative in the Legislature of this State. Never having, at any time that I recollect, thought, spoken, or acted, in any way, to commit myself to either the principles or the policy of the Whig party; but on the contrary, having always held, and publicly expressed opinions diametrically opposed to those held by that part of the Whig party which you are supposed to represent, your voting for me, I am bound in courtesy to suppose, is founded in a misapprehension of my political sentiments.

Lest you should, at any other time, commit a similar blunder, I beg to state, once for all, that I do not believe that the slavery question is settled, and settled forever. I do not believe that slave-catching is either a christian duty, or an innocent amusement. I do not believe that he who breaks the arm of the kidnapper, or wrests the trembling captive from his grasp is "a traitor." I do not believe that Daniel Webster is the saviour of the Union, nor that the Union stands in need of such a saviour. I do not believe that human enactments are to be obeyed when they are point-blank against the law of the living God. And believing most fully, as I do, the reverse of all this, you will easily believe me to be a person wholly unfit to receive the suffrages of gentlemen holding the opinion and favoring the policy of that wing of the Whig party denominated "the Silver Grays."

With all the respect which your derision permits me to entertain for you,

I am, gentlemen,

Your faithful fellow-citizen,

FREDERICK DOUGLASS

The perpetrators of the wanton and gratuitous insult which elicited this beautiful rebuke, would be sadly outraged, were we to insist on withholding the title of "Gentlemen" from those who could, on any pretense, trample on the feelings of such as they esteem their inferiors. If they half begin to comprehend the meaning of the term, much more to feel its power, their cheeks must have crimsoned with shame, when they saw their own unprovoked assault, contrasted with the calm and self-respectful serenity of this reply.

Another instance of this dignity under circumstances of peculiar trial, may be found in his own account—in the columns of "Frederick Douglass' paper"—of a rencontre with a hotel clerk in Cleveland. It is as follows:

At the ringing of the morning bell for breakfast, I made my way to the table, supposing myself included in the call; but I was scarcely seated, when there stepped up to me a young man, apparently much agitated, saying: "Sir, you must leave this table." "And why," said I, "must I leave this table?" "I want no controversy with you. You must leave this table." I replied, "that I had regularly enrolled myself as a boarder in that house; I expected to pay the same charges imposed upon others; and I came to the table in obedience to the call of the bell; and if I left the table I must know the reason." "We will serve you in your room. It is against our rules." "You should have informed me of *your rules* earlier. Where are your rules? Let me see them." "I don't want any altercation with you. You must leave this table." "But have I not deported myself as a gentleman? What have I done? Is there any gentleman who objects to my being seated here?" (There was silence round the table.) "Come, sir, come, sir, you must leave this table at once." "Well, sir, I cannot leave it unless you will give me a better reason than you have done for my removal." "Well, I'll give you a reason if you'll leave the table and go to another room." "That, sir, I will not do. You have invidiously selected me out of all this company, to be dragged from this table, and have thereby reflected upon me as a man and a gentleman; and the reason for this treatment shall be as public as the insult you have offered." At these remarks, my carrot-headed assailant left me, *as he said*, to get help to remove me from the table. Meanwhile I called upon one of the servants (who appeared to wait upon me with alacrity) to help me to a cup of coffee, and assisting myself to some of the good things before me, I quietly and thankfully partook of my morning meal without further annoyance.

Whatever may have been the duty of Mr. Douglass, (and none who know him can for a moment doubt what his inclination would have been,) in case the proscriptive "rules of the house" had been previously made known to him, the justice, as well as the gentlemanly self-possession of his bearing, in relation to this public outrage, must, I think, be sufficiently obvious.

R. R. Raymond, "Outline of a Man," in *Autographs for Freedom*, ed. Julia Griffiths (Boston: John P. Jewett, 1853), 148–160.

[The Great Controversy] (1847–1891)

[Various Authors]

Praise can be expressed briefly, but criticism takes more time. One of the most trying periods of Douglass's post-emancipation career began in 1853, when Douglass seemed to be at odds with virtually every black and white abolitionist with whom he had once been great friends. The following gathering of newspaper articles and letters is lengthy, but it would be unjust to all concerned, and certainly unjust to history, to pass by this period too quickly. What I am calling "the great controversy" probably had its roots in Douglass's deep independence and his resentment at being restrained, controlled, or otherwise treated condescendingly. In his 1855 autobiography, *My Bondage and My Freedom*—considered by some to be his declaration of independence from his Garrison-sponsored 1845 autobiography, *Narrative of the Life of Frederick Douglass*—Douglass complained of being constrained by white abolitionists on the antislavery lecture circuit, noting, "I was generally introduced as a '*chattel*'—a '*thing*'—a piece of southern '*property*'—the chairman assuring the audience that *it* could speak." Increasingly, Douglass reports, "It did not entirely satisfy me to *narrate* wrongs; I felt like *denouncing* them." The advice he was given, though, was not simply to tell his story but to perform his assigned role. As one adviser put it, "Better have a *little* of the plantation manner of speech than not; 'tis not best that you seem too learned."[1] When he returned from his travels in Great Britain in 1847, Douglass was determined to think and act in accordance with his own intellectual and moral compass. Garrison first started to feel Douglass's distance in 1847, when Douglass seemed insufficiently unsettled by Garrison's illness at the time and, more significantly, when Douglass announced his decision to start his own paper, the *North Star*. As editor of the primary abolitionist paper, the *Liberator*, Garrison naturally resented this competition from his protégé. But the divisions became especially pronounced when Douglass turned away from Garrison's approach to the cause, with a focus on nonresistance and moral suasion, and agreed with those who looked to political action to end slavery. Having once accepted Garrison's view that the U.S. Constitution was a proslavery document, Douglass changed his mind and advocated political resistance to the forces sustaining slavery. So incensed and bewildered was he by Douglass's seemingly dramatic change of heart and mind that Garrison went so far as to speculate that Douglass was under the spell of Julia Griffiths, the white British woman who had come to Rochester to help Douglass with his newspaper. Garrison was not alone in portraying Griffiths as a seductive home wrecker who was turning Douglass's head and corrupting his character. In response, Douglass's wife, Anna, sent a letter to the *Liberator* denying that Griffiths was a disruptive presence—but Susan B. Anthony, who had access to Anna's private views, believed that Anna was indeed threatened by Griffiths and that the letter had been staged by Griffiths and Douglass. As we saw earlier, however, Douglass's neighbor Jane Marsh Parker had a much different way of characterizing the importance of this relationship, highlighting Griffiths's help as Douglass developed his skills as a writer and editor.

Such intimate accusations—of political, marital, and generally moral infidelity—abounded during this dispute played out in the antislavery press. Of course, Douglass was never shy or ambiguous in positioning himself in relation to others, and his criticism of Garrisonian abolitionism, and of the American Anti-Slavery Society, was equally sharp, quickly drawing the wrath of those, both white and black, who remained loyal to Garrison and his cause.

What follows is just a sampling of this very public controversy as it played out in the press. Although there were many people involved, it will help to identify a few primary actors in this unfortunate drama. Primary among them is William Lloyd Garrison, whose preeminence in the movement was unquestioned and whose popularity within the black community was both broad and deep. Wendell Phillips, a white abolitionist who was known as one of the most powerful orators of his day, was also allied with Garrison and was much admired by William C. Nell and many other African Americans. George Thompson, a renowned British abolitionist, was noted for his fearless activism and greatly admired in the United States. Gerrit Smith was a wealthy white social reformer, occasional presidential candidate, and ardent abolitionist who was influential in persuading Douglass to renounce an exclusive reliance on moral suasion and turn to political activism. Theodore Parker was a minister whose congregation included William Lloyd Garrison, but Parker did not hold himself to the Garrisonian model of abolitionism. Parker was a leader in efforts to resist, by force if necessary, the provision of the Compromise of 1850 that allowed for fugitive slaves to be captured in the North and returned to the South. Other prominent white abolitionists also found their way into this controversy, either by being mentioned and implicated by others or by stepping in to defend themselves and others. Among those mentioned in the following documents, including some we heard from before, are Parker Pillsbury, Henry C. Wright, Stephen S. and Abbey Kelley Foster, Lewis Tappan, Edmund Quincy, and George W. Putnam.

A few black abolitionists also play an important role in these public exchanges. Primary among them is William C. Nell, an extraordinary black abolitionist and community leader who worked with Garrison on the *Liberator* and who was so much in agreement with Garrison that the U.S. Constitution was a proslavery document that he would not vow to uphold it, a decision that kept him from being certified as a lawyer. Two other black abolitionists, Charles Remond and Robert Purvis, both active in the movement and admired by Douglass, also bear the weight of Douglass's public criticism.

In the background of these exchanges is a who's who of American politics, journalism, and literature, including the formidable statesman Daniel Webster (still recently denounced by most abolitionists for his role in the Compromise of 1850, which included a renewed Fugitive Slave Law); Senator Thomas Corwin, who had been encouraged by abolitionists to run for president in 1848; Senator Charles Sumner, perhaps the most respected antislavery legislator in the country; Horace Mann, best known for his work in education reform; Unitarian minister and philosopher William Henry Channing; the journalist and publisher Jane Swisshelm, known for her advocacy of the antislavery and women's rights causes; and the woman who, from the first installment of *Uncle Tom's Cabin* in the *National Era* on June 5, 1851, had risen to unprecedented prominence as an antislavery writer, Harriet Beecher Stowe.

Such are the primary actors in the tragedy that follows, though, as is often the case with tragedies, there was enough ill will and harsh words to reach virtually everyone involved in the antislavery movement. For perspective (perspective favorable to Douglass), this long interlude concludes with excerpts from Frederic May Holland's 1892 biography of Douglass.

NOTE

1. Frederick Douglass. *My Bondage and My Freedom*, in *Frederick Douglass: Autobiographies*, ed. Henry Louis Gates Jr. (New York: Library of America, 1994), 366–367.

Excerpt from Letter from William Lloyd Garrison to Helen E. Garrison

Cleveland, Oct. 20, 1847
[in a postscript]

Is it not strange that Douglass has not written a single line to me, or to any one, in this place, inquiring after my health, since he left me on a bed of illness? It will also greatly surprise our friends in Boston to hear, that, in regard to his project for establishing a paper here, to be called "The North Star," he never opened to me his lips on the subject, nor asked my advice in any particular whatever. Such conduct grieves me to the heart. His conduct [. . .][1] paper has been impulsive, inconsiderate, and highly inconsistent with his decision in Boston. What will his English friends say of such a strange somerset? I am sorry that friend [Edmund] Quincy did not express himself more strongly against this project in the Liberator. It is a delicate matter, I know, but it must be met with firmness. I am sorry to add, that our friend Saml. Brooke is at the bottom of all this, and has influenced Douglass to take this extraordinary step, as he thinks the Bugle might as well be discontinued, or merged in Douglass's paper! Strange want of forecast and judgment!—But, no more now.

NOTE

1. The letter is torn. [Original footnote to Excerpt from Letter from William Lloyd Garrison to Helen E. Garrison]

From *The Letters of William Lloyd Garrison*, vol. 3, *No Union with Slaveholders, 1841–1849*, ed. Walter M. Merrill (Cambridge, MA: The Belknap Press of Harvard University Press, 1973), 532–533.

From "Frederick Douglass in Boston"

Mr. Douglass was next introduced to the meeting, and discoursed in his characteristic manner upon the horrors of American slavery. At the conclusion of his address, the claims of his paper were again brought forward. The object of his paper, its nature, and *peculiar* claims upon them were lucidly presented.

Mr. William C. Nell, the man whom all know, but to love him, arose at this crisis, and remarked that a very unpleasant duty devolved upon him.

He felt called upon to say a word in reference to Frederick Douglass and his paper; and what he said would be said in a spirit of kindness. He thought Frederick Douglass had been unkind, ungenerous, and ungrateful to his old and tried friends, particularly to Mr. Garrison. He said this was his opinion—an opinion formed by reading the very paper the claims of which have been represented before us. If he was wrong he was willing to be corrected, and he hoped Frederick Douglass would now feel called upon to defend his position, and explain if he could, to the satisfaction of Mr. Garrison's friends, the obnoxious article upon which he has based his opinions.

Frederick Douglass called for the articles. Mr. Nell remarked that as he has not come thither with the desire or expectation of provoking a discussion he had not brought the articles to the meeting.

Frederick Douglass informed him that opportunity should be presented for the investigation of the whole matter.

He then deliberately reviewed his whole course in reference to him. After some desultory remarks from others, the claims of the paper were again presented and several subscribers obtained. The meeting then adjourned. [. . .]

Frederick Douglass stated that he considered it a duty devolving upon Mr. W. C. Nell, either to retract, or endeavor, to substantiate the accusations he had brought against him.

Mr. Nell, promptly responded, but remarking was not conscious of having brought any accusations against Frederick Douglass. He had merely stated his opinions with reference to certain matters. He considered that he had a right to his opinion and a right to express it. He then read an article from "*Frederick Douglass Paper*" and alluded to others which in his judgement justified the opinion he had formed of Frederick Douglass. That latter gentleman explained the meaning of the articles which appeared to some obnoxious.

Robert Morris, Esq., then arose and made what we conceive to be a most ungenerous and ungentlemanly attack upon Mr. Nell; descending to personalities of the grossest character. His remarks were upon a subject of an extraneous nature, and his attack wholly gratuitous. We must learn to be more united. In Union, there is strength. The converse of this proposition is also true. —In disunion, there is weakness.

We cannot all think alike, because of a diversity of our mental constitution. Show me a race of people, made alike in every respect, mentally, morally, physically, and I will show you a people who think alike, we will continue to act differently.

W.J.W.

Boston, Aug. 6th, 1853

From "Frederick Douglass in Boston," *Frederick Douglass' Paper* 6, no. 31 (August 12, 1853): 3.

"Spirit of Frederick Douglass's Paper"

The following editorial articles, taken from recent numbers of "*Frederick Douglass's Paper*," indicate what manner of spirit the editor is of, touching his old anti-slavery associates, both white and colored.

No. IV

Mr. Douglass has recently visited Boston, and this is his account of one of his meetings in the Belknap street meeting-house:—

BOSTON, Mass., Aug. 9th, 1853.

Well, I have had a busy week in Boston; and it will hardly be believed, by the anti-slavery reader, that much of my work has been to defend the late Colored National Convention from the ill-natured and treacherous misrepresentations of its private and public enemies. I had thought, till I came to Boston, that the colored people were about unanimous in commending the character and action of that Convention; and was much surprised that both *Remond* and *Purvis*, had been here, and had handed the Convention, and its most important doings, over to condemnation. The "*National Council*" came in for an especial measure of these gentlemen's galls. Surprised at this feeling towards the Council, I was not, however, surprised that the writer hereof was handled roughly by these gentlemen. He expects nothing else from them, neither now or hereafter. They have not ceased to seek his anti-slavery destructions since they sought to blast him in Rochester. It is about time that they knew their malice is despised, and their assaults defied. The object of their vengeance is a *free man*, and, by the help of God, he will remain so. Neither sudden prosperity nor blood-stained riches can bow his spirit before malicious and sycophantic foes. The grief which he felt at the treachery of his old friends a year ago, has given way to a feeling *far* more enduring than grief. But enough is said on this point. It is indeed extraordinary that *Remond*, *Nell*, and *Purvis*—three colored men—should be found among the most untiring enemies of the existence of the only paper devoted to the interests of the colored people, and published by one of their number; and this fact shows to which side they belong. I hold them as *my* bitterest enemies, and the *practical* enemies of the colored people.

Let it not be inferred, from what I have now said, that the colored people of Boston sympathize in the assaults made upon me by Messrs. *Remond, Nell*, and *Purvis*. Such is far from being the case. Whatever may have been the case before, the colored people of Boston are unwilling that a single hair of my head should be given to gratify the malice of the disaffected three. Their very opposition has riveted the affections of old friends, and brought to my side new ones. At the close of one of my meetings, when one of my friends had very kindly recommended my paper to the support of the colored citizens of Boston, William C. Nell rose, to put them on their guard against subscribing for a paper, the editor of which he charged with ingratitude and unkindness towards William Lloyd Garrison!! He said just at that point, "he had a duty to perform." [Contemptible tool.] He said, further, it was a "disagreeable duty" (the words of Webster, in his great kidnapping speech, in front of the Revere House). Nell's duty was about as disagreeable, and a little more disgraceful than Webster's. He would, doubtless, be very happy to see my paper destroyed—and destroyed it may be; but while it lives, it will be a free and independent sheet, pursuing its course, without fear of, or favor to its enemies. The paper can be killed, but it cannot be enslaved. If, after struggling nearly six years to establish a paper which should, to some extent, defend the rights of the colored people of the United States, the enterprise should fail, by the treacherous opposition referred to, the responsibility will not be mine. If any think this resentment too vehement, let them remember (in the language of Hon. Horace Mann) how easy it is to bear insults offered to others. I deal not with honorable men, but with traitors, from whom I neither ask nor expect quarters.—Bravely as Mr. Nell stood forth, at the first, to stamp me with base ingratitude—the meanest of all human vices—he was glad before he discharged "*his duty*," to disclaim the attitude of an accuser before that audience. After a very few rounds, he cunningly said, "I am the injured party here—I am the man on trial." And so indeed he was.—But he was his own accuser, and the author of his own injury. He had made charges against another gentleman in the audience, and had two accounts to settle at once, and a most pitiful work he made of it. Without strength to sustain his allegations either against myself, or Robert Morris, Esq., he was equally destitute of the magnanimity to withdraw those charges, but merely whined over his good intentions in making them. While he doggedly insisted upon the goodness of his motives, which, by the way, we do not remember to have heard called in question. But I leave Mr. Nell, hoping that his experience in this business will leave him a wiser and a better man. I had intended, when I commenced this letter, to have paid my respects to Mr. Wendell Phillips, but time will not now permit. He shall be attended to in good season. It shall not be said that I shrink from answering any of the questions which he put to me at the Framingham celebration. [. . .]

Having thus grossly outraged the spirit, language and course of Mr. Nell, the latter asked to be heard in his own defense, and got for his pains the following despicable rejoinder:—

William C. Nell is informed that he, having in Boston done what he could to prevent the circulation of *Frederick Douglass's Paper*, the editor of the paper does not feel called upon to give his columns to the circulation of his speeches or letters. When a man seeks to cut out his neighbor's tongue, he must not be surprised to find that tongue refusing to testify in his favor; besides, Mr. Nell will recollect that the Secretary of the meeting (whose partiality to Mr. Nell cannot be doubted) has already given, in our columns, the official report of what transpired at the meeting, thus rendering anything from him, in the way of a report of his sayings on the occasion, quite unnecessary.

"Spirit of Frederick Douglass's Paper," *Liberator*, August 26, 1853, 1.

"Frederick Douglass and His Paper"

Esteemed Friend Garrison:

Frederick Douglass, at Framingham, August 2d, remarked, "that he held his columns free to any one who should think injustice had been done to any party." Having myself been the victim of his injustice, in his paper of August 12th, I solicited a hearing therein, which has been denied me—August 19th—thus:—"The editor does not feel called upon to give his columns to the circulation of his [my] speeches or letters." Will you promote the cause of truth and free discussion by inserting in THE LIBERATOR the following rejected communication?

W.C.N.

Boston, August 19th, 1853.

Boston, August 13, 1853.

MR. DOUGLASS:

In your paper of Aug. 12th, you have grossly misrepresented my sayings and doings at the meeting recently held in Boston. I, therefore, ask you to publish the following communication.

In the first place, I must express to you the surprise manifested here in view of the language of your editorial; for, at the meeting, you acquitted me of any dishonorable or personal motive in the presentation I felt called upon to make relative to your course, and, moreover, promised you would do all in your power to promote harmony and allay controversy; but the first development to your readers is applying to me the epithet, "contemptible tool."

You put words into my mouth which I never used. I did not say, "I am the injured party here; I am on trial." What I did say was, "I am the persecuted party"—persecuted, I meant, by yourself and Mr. Morris. I made no allusion to being "on trial," there being no occasion for it. I have no fears of any trial before a Boston audience.

As to your holding me up as a practical enemy of the colored people, my pen smiles at the idea. When are you going to commence the task of proving your assertion?

I heed not your innuendoes nor your comments; I can wait the decision of an impartial community. But your readers should know what I said and did on that occasion, hence I submit my remarks, as offered.

REMARKS OF THE FIRST EVENING.

MR. CHAIRMAN,—Concurring, as I am happy to do, in the general train of remark which we have just heard from Mr. Douglass, I the more deeply regret his omission of another topic, which others besides myself anticipated his making some allusion to. But as neither himself nor any other person has done so, the duty seems to devolve upon me.

It is, of course, known to most of those present, that the time has been when Mr. Douglass sustained very friendly relations toward Mr. Garrison and the Pioneer Society. It is also well known that now that relation is changed, and within a few months past, his spirit seems more than ever alienated, and in his paper he has made use of language which to many, and certainly to me—when considering his former identity of interests with them—seems unkind, ungenerous and ungrateful. I say this more in sorrow than in anger; but as I have long and intimately known Mr. Douglass—been associated with him in the publication of his paper—familiar with him and the old Society in their day of harmony and cooperation—and, moreover, as I have, to persons present and elsewhere, in speaking of his paper, cheerfully commended, though not afraid to blame—it occurs to me that I am no less his friend than before, because I ask him to explain his new position. There are those here who desire it, and the words that he may offer may correct us if in error, and render his paper the more acceptable.

I have not risen to defend Mr. Garrison and his coadjutors; for, thank God! from me, and in this place, they need no defense. I have not risen to offend Mr. Douglass and his friends; to any thing of that kind, I am opposed by my whole moral, mental and physical constitution. But here, in the city where Mr. Garrison and the Pioneer Society are known and loved, it is fitting that an opportunity should be tendered for explanation.

SECOND EVENING.

MR. CHAIRMAN,—I disclaim any wish or desire to curtail the list of subscribers for Mr. Douglass's paper. I would not blot from the moral firmament one anti-slavery star. The colored people of Boston, like those of other places, are very delinquent in supporting anti-slavery papers, for even the pioneer sheet, THE LIBERATOR, has not from them a tithe of the patronage to which it is preeminently entitled. Let them all remain, to shed light on the slave's path to freedom. It is only because I would have Frederick Douglass's Paper emit a more friendly light, that I stand before you this evening.

Among the articles in Mr. Douglass's paper which I submit in justification of my statement, is that published by him May 27th, headed "Infidelity," followed with some of Mr. Garrison's comments, in THE LIBERATOR of June 10th.

This censure of the old Society, in consequences of the oft-exploded charges of infidelity against some of its agents, brings to my mind that most eloquent passage in the anti-slavery lecture of Mr. Douglass, a few years since:—"Commend me to that infidelity which takes off chains, rather than to the Christianity which puts them on."

Mr. Douglass, on one occasion, dealt very unhandsomely with George Thompson; but as I have reason to believe he regretted the course he took and the language he used on that occasion, I will waive the reading of his remarks, and the comments of Mr. Thompson's friends in England. But it seems appropriate that I should present, in this connection, what I then expressed in letters to my friends, and what I always feel when he utters an unkind word toward any of his old friends:—

> My abiding feeling is one of sincere regret that George Thompson should have been attacked by a colored man, at least such an one historically as Frederick Douglass. He should have pondered *long* and *well*, before allowing his pen to indite or tongue to utter any thing disparagingly of George Thompson.
>
> If there had been a crime committed, and a necessity for its exposure, the matter would present a wholly different aspect; as it is, I think an indecent haste was exhibited in the performance of a very ungrateful act.

In Mr. D's paper of July 22, he calls upon Geo W. Putnam of Lynn, who has recently become disaffected towards the Mass. Anti-Slavery Society in a manner invoking a renewal of his warfare against them.

But I care not to enlarge, or go into details. My object is not controversy, but simply a presentation of facts, for all parties interested.

Mr. Douglass remarked that two or three more such speeches as were delivered here by Mr. Foss would heal the wound, (which, after all, was not a very deep one,) between him and his old friends. Happy indeed would I be, Mr. Chairman, if my words on this occasion would be accepted in that light. Let us compare notes by the way-side—let Mr. D. cease his direct and indirect hostility toward his old friends, speak well of or laud to the skies any individuals or parties he may feel disposed to, discuss and argue with them, show his to be a more excellent way than theirs—all this is well and proper; but in doing this, let him not defect from and drag others down; for he and they, though honestly differing as to ways and means, can both work in a general way for the downfall of our common enemy, slavery.

WILLIAM C. NELL.

REMARKS. The grossly personal and wholly unjustifiable assaults of Mr. DOUGLASS upon Mr. NELL, Mr. PURVIS, and Mr. REMOND, demand some notice from us, which we are again obliged to defer.—ED. LIB.

"Frederick Douglass and His Paper," *Liberator*, September 2, 1853, 138.

"The Liberator, Anti-Slavery Standard, Pennsylvania Freeman, Antislavery Bugle—William Lloyd Garrison and Frederick Douglass; or, A Review of Anti-Slavery Relations," by Frederick Douglass

I am now entering upon a work personal to myself, and shall, therefore, dispense with the *we*, and speak in the pronoun singular. This work, dear reader, is one which, for reasons easily rendered appreciable, I have long postponed, and, indeed, have sought much to avoid. For several of the late years of my anti-slavery experiences, incidents have been occurring, and coming to my knowledge with more or less frequency, painfully foreboding a fierce and bitter warfare upon me, under the generalship of Wm. Lloyd Garrison, with a view to destroy my anti-slavery usefulness, and, possibly, to drive me from the field of public anti-slavery effort. All this, of course, will be disclaimed: it has already been disclaimed; but the purpose of men is often better learned from their deeds than from their words. *Word-wise*, these Garrisonians are my best friends: *deed-wise, I have no more vigilant enemies*. This long apprehended attack has already commenced, and has pretty well developed, its peculiar character. Yes! the spectacle of *a rich and powerful organization*, largely provided with the appliances of moral warfare, is now seen marshaling its forces, its presses, and its speakers, for the moral extermination of one humble, solitary individual. Start not at this as an unwarrantable assertion, and do not regard it, either, as an exhibition of egotism on my part. *Facts are facts*, and facts shall bear me out in this assertion. It shall presently be made fully to appear, that "the American Anti-Slavery Society," claiming to be, *par excellence*, the Anti-Slavery Association of this country, and, withal, soliciting and obtaining funds in this country, and in Great Britain, upon the strength of this arrogant title, yet exerting its energies and expending its funds for the purpose, small or great, of *silencing and putting to open shame a fugitive slave*, simply (as I contend and mean to prove) because that fugitive slave has dared to differ from that Society, or from the leading individuals in it, as to the manner in which he shall exercise his powers for the promotion of the anti-slavery cause, and the elevation of the Free People of Color in the United States. The hatchet of fratricidal war is uplifted: nay, it is now flung at the head of its appointed victim, with the combined force of three strong arms, and with the deadly aim of three good marksmen.

I must, however, own, dear reader, that it has cost me much to place myself in my present attitude of defense. It has been a question with me, and that not an idle question, whether I ought not for the sake of the peace and the harmony of our great national, anti-slavery family, to allow myself to be dispatched thus summarily without uttering a shriek, or giving the alarm of foul play to the bystanders. Whether or not the cause of the poor, bleeding, and perishing bondman, whose professed friends all my assailants are, might be more advantageously served by my consenting to leave the field, giving up my mission in the world, abandoning my paper, flinging down my pen, shunning the platform, ceasing to speak any more in the name of the slave, and in the name of his holy cause, and consenting, for the rest of my life, long or short, silently to stand and receive all the reproach, bitter contempt, and supercilious scorn *which Garrisonians understand well how to pour out* upon all such as they are pleased to denominate deserters from their fold: whether I had not better get me back to the shades of the ships in New Bedford, where, in my earliest days of freedom, with free hands, I earned my daily bread in peace, *far* out of sight of the great world's eye, indifferent to its seductive applause, unmindful of its frowns, only too glad to get leave to toil; whether I had not better yield to the demand now apparently made, concede at once that no man, black or white, "bond or free, Barbarian or Scythian," in any part, or of any part of this habitable globe, has any business, or can have any business to work in what is called the cause of the slave's emancipation, unless, first of all, he is able to show a most perfect agreement between his views, and those of Mr. Garrison. * * *

The war has been going on these four months, and more in public—and I know not how long it has been raging in private. Since the 1st of August, 1853, the Anniversary of *West India Emancipation*, until now, I have been *pursued, misrepresented, traduced and vilified*, with a bitterness ever increasing, and a steadiness and violence, only *characteristic of malice*, deep, broad, lasting and in its worst form. * * *

I shall be silent no longer. The impunity allowed to my adversaries by my silence, like all other submission to wrong, has failed to soften the hearts of the wrong doers. My seeming retreat has occasioned an additional advance on their part. They have waxed more arrogant as I have waxed humble. Their assaults now are unbearable. Every apology for honorable silence has been wrenched from me—and that too, by *him*, whom, whatever his runners and whisperers may have said to the contrary, I have loved, honored, revered, and faithfully cooperated with until very recently. He has seen fit to invade my household, despise the sacredness of my home, break through the just limits of public controversy, and has sought to blast me in the name of my family. That he has not succeeded in his purpose, is from no want of desire on his part. His motive in the matter is clear to all who read his article. * * *

While my adversaries can find no words too coarse nor too bitter to apply to me, with a power of front which is truly amazing, and *an affectation of piety and long-facedness, laughable to those who know them*, they have coolly turned upon me with a lecture about my unchristian spirit. *This old non-resistance game* has been played, I think, about long enough; when *every species of abuse* may be indulged in, and the worst passions stirred under the pretext of its being "*moral indignation*." * * *

Of late, the *Refuge of Oppression* has become about the best part of Mr. Garrison's paper. *No! it won't do.* No affectation of bravery, such as is evidenced by stringing together a mass of personal abuse for Mr. Garrison's *Refuge of Oppression: which refutes itself, and about which nobody cares a single straw*, is sufficient to show that Mr. Garrison is altogether ready, at all times, to face the music. This old game has been played very often; and I have not been unobservant of the bland smile of complacency with which the *Liberator* has, occasionally, congratulated itself upon its moral intrepidity, candor and fairness. * * *

The *Standard* says, "He (Mr. Douglass) claims the right, in the face of Christ's positive precepts, to kill his enemies."

Now, really, if I claimed or exercised any such right as this, *among the first places where there would be danger to human life, would be "the Standard office"*: for I know of no place where I have a more malignant enemy than Mr. Johnson is giving proof of being. If I thought he cared two straws about Christ's precepts, one way or the other, I might, possibly, discuss the question of *peace* with him; but no man who deals in the vituperative bitterness which he has dealt in towards me, can convince me of the meekness and benevolence of his Christianity. * * *

But it is said the fact that Mr. Garrison and the *National Anti-Slavery Standard* applaud and honor GERRIT SMITH, fellowship THEODORE PARKER, and other men who differ from them about the Constitution, sufficiently refutes the falsehood that the change in my views had any thing to do in producing the hostile movements now made against me by the Garrisonians! Well! this looks plausible, but the sophistry is easily exposed. The case would be quite similar, if they had any likeness to each other. A man might as well argue that because the AUSTRIAN MINISTER expresses his high consideration for the AMERICAN REPUBLIC, therefore, Austria would not hang KOSZTA for promoting Republican views in Hungary. GERRIT SMITH is an *independent nation.* Alas! poor me! I am but a rebel—while those against whom I have rebelled would *treat* with Mr. SMITH, they would hang me. [. . .]

I verily believe that the ear of Mr. Garrison has been most grossly abused by his sycophantic fawners, in respect to the estimate set upon his character by me. It is the misfortune of men occupying the highly influential positions which he does; often to be surrounded by person[s] whose only means of rising into notice is the dealing in extravagant praise of such distinguished ones, and pretending to guard their persons and character against malign influences from abroad. In this way they succeed in having themselves baptized as "*the tried*," "*the true*," "*the reliable*," and so forth. On no other supposition can I reconcile the course pursued by Mr. Garrison toward a friend. But reconciled howsoever it may be, the work is for others, not for me. It is a little remarkable how *reluctantly* Mr. Garrison and his friends have fallen *pele mele* upon me. All their assaults are made with sentiments of the profoundest regret. They have had to overcome mountains of reluctance in getting at me; and 'tis amazing, considering the *ruggedness* of these mountains, that they ever succeeded in crossing their alpine heights.

> One thing should always be remembered in regard to the anti-slavery cause. It is not based upon complexion, but upon justice; its principles are world-wide, though the victims whom it seeks to deliver are groaning in the Southern prison-house; concerns man as man, not merely as an African, or one of African descent.

Theoretically and abstractly, it is easy to admit the truth of this first postulate laid down by Mr. Garrison, as the necessary preliminary to his strictures upon me. Practically, however, and in point of fact, it fails to express the *whole* truth. If Mr. Garrison means here to assert, merely, that the principles of justice and liberty are universal: having neither respect to country, color or condition, I agree with him; but if he means what it seems he really does mean, that white men are as deeply concerned in the success of the Anti-Slavery cause in this country, as are *Africans*, or persons of African descent, he contradicts the plainest truths, and flies directly in the face of facts, with no other apparent motive than to disparage the very people of whose claims to liberty he is the acknowledged defender and advocate.

As if to leave no doubt of this disparagement, Mr. Garrison says:

> Unswerving fidelity to it, (the cause,) in this country, requires high moral attainments, the crucifixion of all personal considerations, a paramount regard for principle, absolute faith in the right. It does not follow, therefore, that because a man is or has been a slave, or because he is identified with a class meted out and trodden under foot, he will be the truest to the cause of human freedom. Already, that cause, both religiously and politically, has transcended the ability of the sufferers from American slavery and prejudice, as a class, to keep pace with it, or to perceive what are its demands, or to understand the philosophy of its operations.

This is about the same idea, rather more plainly brought out in the *Freeman*, by RUSH PLUMLEY, in his high-sounding talk about "moral rulers of mankind," and "Divine right," &c., &c. *If* it *be* true (as Mr. Garrison alleges) that the anti-slavery "cause, both religiously and politically, has transcended the ability of the sufferers from American Slavery and prejudice, as a class, to keep pace with it, or to perceive what are its demands, or to understand the philosophy of its operations," it is equally true that it has transcended the ability of white men as well; and it is, therefore, difficult to perceive any good motive in Mr. Garrison for thus branding the *colored* people—the sufferers from slavery and prejudice—thus invidiously with a want of apprehension and moral capacity. There is just one other judgment to be pronounced on the colored people "as a class," by Mr. Garrison, and the reward of "five thousand dollars" will no longer be offered for his head. It is this: "Liberty, both politically and religiously, has transcended the ability of the sufferers from American Slavery and prejudice, as a class, to keep pace with it, or to perceive its demands, or to understand the philosophy of its operations," with the simple addition, and therefore not fit for freedom, and the wall of partition which separates Mr. Garrison from the rest of his fellow-citizens would instantly fall. In reading this passage from Mr. Garrison, one is led to enquire WHAT there is, either in the "pace," "demands," or "philosophy" of the anti-slavery cause, which is so profound and mysterious that the colored people of the country cannot understand it. I had thought this anti-slavery cause something after the model of Christianity, so plain that the way-faring man, though a fool, might "understand the philosophy of its operations." The colored people ought to feel profoundly grateful for this magnificent compliment (which does not emanate from a Colonizationist) to their high, moral worth, and breadth of comprehension, so generously bestowed by William Lloyd Garrison! Who will doubt, hereafter, the natural inferiority of the *negro*, when the great champion of the negroes' rights thus broadly concedes all that is claimed respecting the negroes' inferiority by the bitterest despisers of the negro race! Of course, after this, we shall hear no more talk, on the part of abolitionists, about "placing themselves in the position of the slave, and seeing his wrongs from his stand-point!" It strikes me that the class who may be presumed to understand this cause, are the actual "sufferers from American Slavery and prejudice."

The iron of slavery and prejudice has entered their souls. What is theory to others is *practice* to them. Every day and hour is crowded with lessons to *them* on the subject, to which the WHITES, as a class, are strangers. I have often traveled on the forward deck of a steamer in the night, while abolitionists have been sleeping soundly in the cabin below. I have been deprived of food, and gone hungry, while abolitionists have dined sumptuously. Abolitionism does not change the color of the skin—so that while *theoretically* and *abstractly*, the cause of anti-slavery is the cause of universal man, it is *practically* and *peculiarly* in this country the cause of the colored man—and any attempt either on the part of Mr. Garrison, or on the part of Rush Plumley, to lift this holy cause into a sublimity, beyond the comprehension of the colored men as a class, deserves to be branded by every colored man with the reprobation due to so stupendous an insult. Had the same sentiment fallen from the lips of Hon. HORACE MANN concerning the colored people as a class, he would, ere this, have been publicly denounced, by speech and by resolution, in mass meetings of the colored people of Massachusetts. Verily! 'tis not good to "have respect to persons" in judgment!

> Another thing should be clearly understood. The difficulty with Mr. Douglass, on the part of his old friends, is not that he has changed his opinions concerning the Constitution, but that he has become alienated in spirit, and no longer treats them with fairness or courtesy.

This is more assertion, so far as it relates to the change of my views concerning the Constitution, &c. As to having become alienated in spirit,

Mr. Garrison should have stated what the history of the affair proves, that the alienation was mutual, and existed as much on their part as on mine.

I know, if *he* does not, that as soon as I changed my views on the Constitution of the United States, leading Garrisonians, who had taken my paper, the *North Star*, flung it back upon me like falling leaves in autumn; and after that announcement, I was never again invited to the platform of the American Anti-Slavery Society!! Now, I affirm that considering how uniformly I had been before welcomed among the Garrisonians, it does seem that (Mr. Garrison to the contrary, notwithstanding,) the change in my views concerning the Constitution, had something to do, and has still something to do with the difficulty between me and my "old friends."

But more on this point by-and-by. Mr. Garrison attempts to make me convict myself of falsehood—because, while I declared that the *Liberator* had opened what it evidently meant should be a very galling and destructive fire upon *Frederick Douglass's Paper*, I afterward said that his promised "strictures" remained to be made. I considered Mr. Garrison's array of extracts from my paper, significantly numbered, artistically arranged, and skillfully introduced, as the opening, and so it really proved to be the opening, of a fire upon *Frederick Douglass's Paper*; and if this be a falsehood, may mortal man never tell a greater!

> The atrocious crime of Mr. Nell was, in modestly asking Mr. Douglass to explain his position to his old friends and coadjutors! The treatment he has received at the hands of Mr. Douglass would be disgraceful to a barbarian.

The "atrocious crime of Mr. Nell" was just no such thing. Mr. Nell, who goes *grumbling* about in private, that he ought to have been successor in the anti-slavery office in Boston, to Henry W. Williams, and complaining that he, a colored man, was pushed out of employment to make way for Mr. Wallcut, whiningly arraigned me before the colored people of Boston, as having been "unkind, ungenerous, and ungrateful" to his Boston anti-slavery friends. I thought him a pitiful tool, and said so. His behavior on that occasion was that of a hanger-on.

> The refusal of Mr. D. to allow Mr. Nell to be heard through his columns, after having grossly misrepresented and assailed him, was an act of unmitigated injustice.

The refusal here alluded to, I hold to have been eminently just. Mr. Nell had, already, been reported in my columns by the Secretary of the meeting, (a personal friend of his,) every justice had been done him. It was, therefore, no injustice to exclude a speech of his prepared after the meeting in question, and which was essentially different from that made on the occasion.

Mr. Garrison concludes his first notice of me with the following bitter judgment:

> He is an altered man in his temper and spirit; the success of his paper he makes paramount to principle; and the curse of worldly ambition is evidently the secret of his alienation.

Whether "the curse of worldly ambition" is on me or not, it is very evident "*the curse*" *of* WILLIAM LLOYD GARRISON is upon me.

There is no proof that, in any case, I have made "*the success*" of my "*paper*" "*paramount to principle*." The charge of "worldly ambition" is quite innocent from the pen of Mr. Garrison, since, I believe there is not a man in the United States oftener accused of "*ambition*" and egotism than he by whom the charge is brought! No! Mr. Garrison, you have not hit the secret of my "*alienation*"—if alienated I may be properly called. Had I been ambitious of praise, ambitious of position, I never would have incurred the displeasure of GARRISONIANS. I should have sought their support, and flattered their pride, acknowledged their claims, prophesied smooth things, withheld distasteful criticism, shaped my course by their wishes, and basked in the sunshine of their smiles.

Upon Mr. Garrison's CHICAGO article, it would be easy to say much, but I am admonished, by the enormous length to which this article has already grown, to use brevity. This article, as Mr. Garrison says, was written from necessity; and what, dear reader, do you think was the necessity! *This* it was, to *my* apprehension. I had held a series of successful anti-slavery meetings in CHICAGO, ILLINOIS. A friend of Mr. Garrison's attended those meetings. He confessed himself pleased with the faithfulness with which I advocated the claims of the cause of freedom. *Now* to destroy the favorable judgment of my labors, and of my character, this article of Mr. Garrison was rendered "necessary." In regard to this article, as in regard to all the others, I shall only strike out, for the reader, the key-stone of the arch of fallacies, and leave details to those who have leisure to peruse them.

> If, rejecting their interpretation of the Constitution, we nevertheless praise and welcome the individual to whom he refers, why should we not act as cordially toward Mr. D., with whom we have been brought into far more intimate relations than with either of the others, in whose remarkable development we have felt an honorable pride, for whose welfare we have cherished a brotherly regard, and whose individuality and independence we have desired to see preserved inviolate?

I have met this argument before, and I shall now meet it again. The argument is, that as certain "individuals" holding opinions in harmony with Frederick Douglass, are praised and welcomed by Garrisonians; therefore, the opinions of Frederick Douglass are not the cause of his being proscribed by Garrisonians. The point of the case is not reached by this argument. The very soul of it is left out. It is not the OPINIONS, but the CHANGE of opinions, the *change* from *theirs* to those of *others*; and this change openly promulgated in the very Garrisonians' camp! Here is the offence. But, again, the cases put are not equal. Such men as are named, are quite as tall as Garrisonians themselves. They have wealth, honors, position; and Boston is not the place to be wholly indifferent to these. Even Charles Remond, who was scarcely recognized as one of the "tried" and the "true," when poor, has since making himself well off by marriage, rapidly risen in Boston favor.

The fact that Garrisonians are lavish of "praise" towards GERRIT SMITH, may deceive others; but it cannot deceive me. It, at best, is but a modern devotion, and has increased in the multitude of its ceremonies, precisely in proportion to the bitterness which its votaries have assailed me. That "noble man," GERRIT SMITH, and that "*base*" man, Frederick Douglass, go hand in hand with this controversy, and the one is seldom seen without the other. There was a time, and that time is not long gone by, when GERRIT SMITH was seldom mentioned in the "Liberator" and "Anti-Slavery Standard," but for the purpose of making him appear ridiculous, as being at the head of the party of a "Baker's Dozen." It is but a very few months since he was branded as an "APOSTATE," by an agent of the American "Anti-Slavery Society," in the columns of the "*Liberator*," when Mr. Garrison did not even interpose the "noble" between Mr. Smith and the brand. What has happened to make Mr. Smith such a prodigious favorite with Garrisonians of late?

Mr. Garrison, like Mr. Johnson and Mr. Plumley, finds evidence of my unworthiness in the commendations bestowed upon me; especially by Dr. CAMPBELL, of the *British Banner.* Now, without for a moment endorsing the soundness of every judgment pronounced by Dr. Campbell upon Anti-Slavery men and measures in this country, I will say that *there is not a man in all England, who has uniformly borne a fuller or a stronger testimony against American Slavery*, in all its parts and particulars, than has Dr. Campbell of the *British Banner*—Certainly, *there is not a man in England, whose friendship I more highly prize, or of whose commendation I ought to be more proud.* His journal, the *British Banner*, stands at the head of the great dissenting interest of England, and in point of moral courage, true manliness, high independence, steadfast adherence to the right, and to the cause of progress, the *Banner* reigns without a superior in the newspaper world. It is all nonsense to call it an "unscrupulous sheet." It may answer where the paper is not known, but it will excite only contempt among those who read the *Banner.* But why have those journals spoken a kind word for me of late? The answer is to be found in the shockingly unjust attacks made upon me by the Garrisonian Press. Mr. Garrison and his friends may thank themselves for those galling commendations.

I am guilty, also, of having been commended by the *Colonization Herald.* I am greatly indebted to the Garrisonian journals for making me acquainted with the fact, for I have not seen the *Herald* containing it. One of these days, I may show that there is not much difference between the estimate set upon *colored* people, as a class, by Abolitionists and Colonizationists themselves. I have certain facts upon that subject, which may be brought to light at a subsequent stage of this controversy.

I have no fear of being thus confounded with Colonizationists; an effort has been made *thus* to confound me, but it proved altogether a miserable failure. The story that I have been in every instance the "aggressor," that I have "ostracized" myself, that my "constitutional opinions" have nothing to do with the matter, that I give "no evidence" of being "satisfied with" my "present position," that I am "doing violence to" my "own convictions," that I have "lost much of my moral power, that I have spoken 'ungenerously, unfairly, and malignantly' of George Thompson, Wendell Phillips, Parker Pillsbury, Stephen S. Foster, Henry C. Wright, Robert Purvis, C. L. Remond, Wm. C. Nell," can be judged of as well by my readers, in the light of views already presented, as from any extended remarks of mine here. I, therefore, dismiss this part of the subject by simply saying, that about nothing have I been so shabbily treated as about the remarks made by me upon a speech made at Bristol, England, in which I deemed him unjust to the LIBERTY PARTY.

> For several years past, he had one of the worst advisers in his printing office, whose influence over him has not only caused much unhappiness in his own household, but perniciously biased his own judgment.

As to whether my "adviser" is the best or "the worst," is a matter of different opinions. I am, at any rate, profoundly grateful for the eminent services of that "adviser" in opening my eyes to many things connected with my anti-slavery relations, to which I had before been partially blind, as well as for holding up my hands right nobly, in my efforts to establish my paper, and to educate my children. The judgment of Mr. Garrison is not the judgment of those who know this "adviser" best. The charge of "unhappiness in my household," is one which I refuse to answer in this place, or in any public journal, unless required to do so by some proper and competent tribunal, known to the laws of the land.

1. Because it involves considerations wholly foreign to the present controversy.
2. Because the public have not been called upon by my "household" to pass upon its affairs, its happiness or its "unhappiness," or upon "the cause" of either.
3. Because, to deny the charge, would be an ex-parte denial.
4. Because, in matters of this sort, ex-parte denials are worthless.
5. Because, such denials would satisfy nobody who was before dissatisfied.
6. Because the precedent of dragging a man's domestic affairs before the public, with a view to damage him in public estimation, is bad.
7. Because a man's wife and children should be spared the mortification involved in a public discussion of matter so entirely private, and which can come to no issue in such a court.
8. Because the stake I hold in the happiness of my household, is greater than that of any other person.

Since writing the above, a letter from Mrs. Douglass has made its appearance in the "Liberator"; and I copy it here, "simply remarking," that in everything essential, the denial is, and was, intended to be a complete answer to the charge made by the "Liberator."

LETTER FROM MRS. DOUGLASS.

We publish the following letter as requested by Mrs. DOUGLASS—simply remarking that it is evasive in its language, as our charge had reference to the past, and not to the present. It is not possible that Mrs. D. means deliberately to affirm, that there has been no unhappiness created in her family, in regard to the person alluded to, though there may be no cause for any such feeling at the present time.

WILLIAM LLOYD GARRISON:

SIR—It is not true, that the presence of a certain person in the office of Frederick Douglass causes unhappiness in his family. Please insert this in your next paper.

ANNA DOUGLASS.

Rochester, Nov. 21st, 1853.

At this point, I might well drop the farther considerations of these *savage attacks*; and wash my hands entirely of the prosecution of this controversy. But I know my assailants too well, and *the unconquerable hate much they bear me*, to suppose, for a moment, that I shall be permitted hereafter to pursue my Anti-Slavery labors in peace. The end of controversy with them, is the end of the material of which it is composed. They will strike so long as there is any body or thing to strike at; and as I have not the slightest intention of withdrawing myself from the field which they so much dislike to see me occupy, I shall hold myself ready to repel, with whatever force I can properly command, this *double-distilled* conspiracy to crush me.

Frederick Douglass, "The Liberator, Anti-Slavery Standard, Pennsylvania Freeman, Antislavery Bugle . . . ," *Liberator*, December 16, 1853, 1–2.

"The Mask Entirely Removed"

Either he must
Confess himself wondrous malicious
Or be accused of folly.
—CORIOLANUS

In his paper of the 9th instant, FREDERICK DOUGLASS occupies twelve columns in reply to sundry brief articles in the *Pennsylvania*

Freeman, *Anti-Slavery Standard*, *Bugle*, and *Liberator*, respecting his feelings and attitude towards his old friends, and associates in the cause of emancipation. Such portions of it as relate to the other journals referred to, we leave them to dispose of as they may think proper. We quote all that is personal to us, in addition to a considerable portion of Mr. D's exordium; and from this sample, our readers can easily infer what the remainder must be.

The history of the Anti-Slavery struggle has been marked by instances of defection, alienation, apostasy, on the part of some of its most efficient supporters for a given time; but by none more signal, venomous, or extraordinary, than the present. Mr. DOUGLASS now stands self-unmasked, his features flushed with passion, his air scornful and defiant, his language bitter as wormwood, his pen dipped in poison; as thoroughly changed in his spirit as was ever "arch-angel ruined," as artful and unscrupulous a schismatic as has yet appeared in the abolition ranks.

Having long endeavored, by extreme forbearance, to avoid any collision with him; having omitted in many cases to make even a passing reference to what we deemed unworthy to his position; having criticized, with brevity and moderation, some very objectionable articles from his pen, only because we could not be true to our convictions of duty, if we suppressed the expression of our surprise and sorrow; and having no feelings of personal animosity to gratify; we have no intention to stake a protracted rejoinder in the present case but shall submit the whole matter, in a very few words, to the impartial judgment of all who take any interest in the controversy.

It is difficult to believe that the author of the article of "enormous" length and character, now under consideration, is the FREDERICK DOUGLASS once so manly, generous, and faithful. The transformation—or, rather, the revelation—is the most astounding and severely painful event in our experience; and "the end is not yet." He now assumes an attitude which is eliciting the warmest encomiums from the most malignant enemies of the Anti-Slavery movement, and which is undisguisedly hostile to his old companions in arms. No marvel, therefore, that he can speak of the "Garrisonians" with as much flippancy as any of our pro-Slavery condemners; or that he can aver, "*Word-wise*, these Garrisonians are my best friends—deed-wise, I have no more vigilant enemies"; or that he is able to say of the "REFUGE OF OPPRESSION," that, "of late, it has become about the best part of Mr. Garrison's paper, and about which nobody cares a single straw"; or that he can utter the monstrous untruth, that "a fierce and bitter warfare" is waged against him, "under the generalship of William Lloyd Garrison," with a view to destroy *his anti-slavery usefulness*!!

The untruthfulness of Mr. D. is matched only by his adroitness in striving to excite popular sympathy, as though he were a poor innocent lamb, about to be torn in pieces by a pack of famished wolves! Though he is the aggressor, he affects to have made no effort even in self-defense, and whiningly says—"I shall be silent no longer (!) The impunity allowed to my adversaries, by my silence, like all other submission to wrong, has failed to soften the heart of the wrong-doers (!) They have waxed more arrogant as I have waxed humble" (!) "Gerrit Smith is an independent nation. Alas! I am but a rebel. While those against whom I have rebelled would treat with Mr. Smith, they would hang me." Again—"I had reason to know that prejudice against color—yes, prejudice against my race, would be invoked, as it has been invoked, on the side of my adversaries (!)—and in all the likelihoods of the case, the question between me and my old friends would be decided in this case as between white and black—in favor of the former, and against the latter—the white man to rise, as an injured benefactor, and the black man to fall, as a miserable ingrate" (!) Again—"The spectacle of a rich (!) and powerful (!) organization, largely provided with the appliances of moral warfare, is now seen marshaling its forces, its presses, and its speakers, for the moral extermination of one humble, solitary individual (!!!)—for the purpose of silencing, and putting to open shame, *a fugitive slave*, (!) simply because that fugitive slave has dared to differ from that Society, or from the leading individuals in it, as to the manner in which he shall exercise his powers for the promotion of the anti-slavery cause, and the elevation of the free people of color in the United States" (!!) Again—"The hatchet of fratricidal war is uplifted; nay, it is now flung at the head of its appointed victim, with the combined force of three strong arms, and with the deadly aim of three good marksmen" (!!!) And this is his estimate of the American Anti-Slavery Society, its presses, and its speakers! Now as a specimen of low cunning and malignant defamation, we have never seen this surpassed. It is too palpable to need a single word in reply, and we should be lost to all self-respect to treat it as worthy of serious consideration.

Mr. Douglass sneers at the regret expressed by us, and others, at the necessity of noticing his hostile assaults, and scoffingly says—"They have had to overcome mountains of reluctance in getting at me; and it is amazing, considering the ruggedness of these mountains, that they ever succeeded in crossing their Alpine heights!" If this does not indicate either that we have never in his opinion, been his true friends, or that, ever selfish and untrue himself, he is incapable of experiencing the pang of misplaced confidence and disappointed friendship, we know not how to interpret language. In either case, it places him in a most unenviable position.

Jaundiced in vision, and informed with passion, he affects to regard us as the "disparager" (!) of the colored race, and artfully endeavors to excite their jealousy and opposition by utterly perverting the meaning of our language. We said, that "the Anti-Slavery cause, both religiously and politically, has transcended the ability of the sufferers from American slavery and prejudice, as a *class*, to keep pace with it, or to perceive what are its demands, or to understand the philosophy of its operations"—meaning by this, that the cause requires religious and political sacrifices, which, "as a class," they do not yet see, or, seeing, are not yet prepared to make, even though they are the victims to be delivered—and also meaning that what was at first supposed to be local, is now seen to have a world-wide hearing, and must be advocated upon world-wide principles, irrespective of complexional differences. There is nothing really or intentionally invidious in a statement like this: and yet how does Mr. Douglas treat it? "The colored man," he says, "ought to feel profoundly grateful for this magnificent compliment to their high moral worth and breadth of comprehension, so generously bestowed by William Lloyd Garrison! Who will doubt, hereafter, the *natural* inferiority of the negro, when the great champion of the negroes' rights *thus broadly concedes all that is claimed respecting the negro's inferiority by the bitterest despisers of the negro race*"!!! Now, if this were blundering stupidity, it might readily be pardoned; but it is unmitigated baseness, and therefore inexcusable.

Again we said—"It does not follow, that because a man is or has been a slave, or because he is identified with a class meted out and trodden under foot, therefore he will be the truest to the cause of human freedom"—a truism which nothing can make plainer. Yet Mr. Douglass presumes upon the color of his skin to vindicate his superior fidelity to that cause, and to screen himself from criticism and rebuke! This trick cannot succeed. Of the colored people he says—"What is theory to others, is practice to them. Every day and hour is crowded with lessons to them on the subject, to which the whites, as a class, are strangers." Very true—but what then? Does it indicate the same regard for universal justice, for those who are oppressed to desire to gain their freedom, as it does for others, not of their complexion, and not involved in their suffering, to encounter deadly perils and make liberal sacrifices in seeking their liberation? The former may be animated by motives limited to a narrow selfishness; the latter must be actuated by feelings of disinterested benevolence and world-wide philanthropy. Once, Mr. Douglass would have promptly recognized this distinction; now, beneath the blackness of his skin he is attempting to hide the blackness of his treachery.

How low he has fallen is farther indicated by his despicable insinuation—"Even Charles L. Remond, who was scarcely recognized as one of the 'tried' and 'true,' *when poor*, has, *since making himself well off by marriage*, rapidly risen in Boston favor"! Is not this at once the acme of absurdity, the extreme of falsehood, and the lowest depth of moral debasement? When Frederick Douglass was "poor," and in utter obscurity, and not as now every where visible, was he a stranger to "Boston favor," and was nothing done to raise him up to respectability and influence? But this is to hint that he is destitute of grateful emotions—and gratitude is something about which he does not like to be reminded.

So, too, when he speaks of the faithful, intelligent and worthy WILLIAM C. NELL as "a hanger-on" and "a pitiful tool"—and of OLIVER JOHNSON as "not caring two straws about Christ's precepts" in regard to peace, whom he (Douglass) would be the first to assassinate, if he believed it right to kill his enemies, as he has not "a more malignant enemy than Mr. Johnson is giving proof of being"—he reveals a state of mind as frightful as it is deplorable.

Referring to the Rev. Dr. Campbell, of the *British Banner*, he says, "There is not a man in England, whose friendship I more highly prize, or of whose commendation I ought to be more proud"; and his *Banner* he places at the head of all other journals for its "moral courage, true manliness, high independence, steadfast adherence to the right, and to the cause of progress"—the last attributes to be attributed to that venomous, Ishmaelitish and really pro-slavery sheet. There is not a more unfair disputant or a more unscrupulous defamer at the head of the press, than this same dogmatical, quarrelsome, and double-dealing Dr. Campbell. The American Anti-Slavery Society and *The Liberator* have not a more malignant and outrageous assailant abroad than himself; and if he were in this country, we have no more doubt that he would be found on the side of pro-slavery conservation, and a holder of slaves if a resident of the South, than we have of the position of Franklin Pierce. The fact that Mr. Douglass deems it an honor to be complimented by such a man, is another melancholy proof of the loss of his integrity to the Anti-Slavery cause.

A word in regard to our allusion to a bad adviser in Mr. D's printing-office, whom we accused of exerting a pernicious influence upon his mind and judgment, and "causing much unhappiness in his own household." That last allusion was not meant unkindly, nor intended to imply any thing immoral; but, though it is strictly true, and we could bring a score of unimpeachable witnesses in Rochester to prove it, we regret it was made, as it had no relevancy. Our only object in referring to that nameless "adviser" was, to indicate to such inquirers as our Chicago correspondent, that there had been secret causes at work to alienate Mr. Douglass from his old associates, and we felt bound to throw out the intimation as a clue to much that would be otherwise inexplicable to those not familiar with the facts in the case. Mr. D. says—"I am profoundly grateful for the eminent services of that 'adviser,' in *opening my eyes* (!) to many things connected with my anti-slavery relations, to which I had before been partially blind." That tells the whole story, and is all we care to extort. In what condition his vision now is—and whither in slumbering in the lap of a prejudiced, sectarian Delilah, he has not at last enabled the pro-slavery Philistines to ascertain the secret of his strength, cut off his locks, and rejoice over his downfall—we leave our readers and the uncompromising friends of the Anti-Slavery cause to judge.

"The Mask Entirely Removed," *Liberator*, December 16, 1853, 196.

[Letter from Harriet Beecher Stowe to William Lloyd Garrison]

Cabin, December 19, 1853
Mr. Garrison.

Dear Sir,—After seeing you, I enjoyed the pleasure of a personal interview with Mr. Douglass, and I feel bound in justice to say that the impression was far more satisfactory than I had anticipated.

There did not appear to be any deep underlying stratum of bitterness; he did not seem to me malignant or revengeful. I think it was only a temporary excitement and one which he will outgrow.

I was much gratified with the growth and development both of his mind and heart. I am satisfied that his change of sentiment was not a mere political one but a genuine growth of his own conviction. A vigorous reflective mind like his cast among those who nourish these new sentiments is naturally led to modified views.

At all events, he holds no opinion which he cannot defend, with a variety of richness of thought and expression and an aptness of illustration which shows it to be a growth from the soil of his own mind with a living root, and not a twig broken off other men's thoughts and stuck down to subserve a temporary purpose.

His plans for the elevation of his own race are manly, sensible, comprehensive; he has evidently observed closely and thought deeply and will, I trust, act efficiently.

You speak of him as an apostate. I cannot but regard this language as unjustly severe. Why is he any more to be called an apostate for having spoken ill-tempered things of former friends than they for having spoken severely and cruelly as they have of him? Where is this work of excommunication to end? Is there but one true anti-slavery church and all others infidels? Who shall declare which it is? I feel bound to remonstrate with this—for the same reason that I do with slavery—because I think it an injustice. I must say still farther, that if the first allusion to his family concerns was unfortunate this last one is more unjustifiable still. I am utterly surprised at it. As a friend to you and to him, I view it with the deepest concern and regret.

What Douglass *is* really, time will show. I trust that he will make no farther additions to the already unfortunate controversial literature of the cause. *Silence* in this case will be eminently—*golden*.

I must indulge the hope you will see reason at some future time to alter your opinion and that what you now cast aside as worthless shall yet appear to be a treasure. There is abundant room in the anti-slavery field for him to perform a work without crossing the track or impeding the movements of his old friends, and perhaps in some future time, meeting each other from opposite quarters of a victorious field, you may yet shake hands together.

I write this note, because in the conversation I had with you, and also with Miss Weston, I admitted so much that was unfavorable to Mr. Douglass that I felt bound in justice to state the more favorable views which had arisen to my mind.

Very sincerely your friend,

H. B. Stowe

Annie Fields, ed., *Life and Letters of Harriet Beecher Stowe* (Boston: Houghton, Mifflin, 1898), 213–215.

"From the National Anti-Slavery Standard: Frederick Douglass"

Were we the "vigilant enemies" of Frederick Douglass—were our feelings toward him those of "unquenchable hate"—were it our purpose to "exert the energies and expend the funds" of the Association we represent, to fling at his head "the head of an appointed victim," the hatchet of fratricidal war—did we mean to "pursue, misrepresent, traduce and vilify him, with a bitterness ever increasing, and a steadiness and violence only characteristic of malice, deep, broad, lasting, and in its worst form"—in short, (not to put altogether too agonizing and fine a point upon it,) were we, in common with all the rest of the American Anti-Slavery Society, its President and Vice-Presidents, its Secretaries and its Treasurers, its Board of Managers, its Executive Committee, and its lay members, both male and female, the abandoned, wicked, malicious, unscrupulous, arrogant, exterminating, negro-hating, and hypocritical conspirators which Mr. Douglass represents us to be, we should rejoice at the article from his paper to which we give so large a space in the present number of our own. In one sense, indeed, we are gratified—that thereby comes an end, we hope, to a very painful controversy, and that Mr. Douglass here acknowledges in terms, and displays in the intensest bitterness of spirit, the enmity to the Anti-Slavery Cause, as it is represented by the American Society and its friends, that has been alleged against him. But not deeming ourselves so full of all uncharitableness, and so influenced by the basest motives, as he regards us, we cannot but regret such a development of character in one whom, for so many years, we honored and esteemed, and whose power of good for an oppressed people we considered hardly second to that of any other human creature. The article, however, long as it is, we copy, as well as another, for not copying which, he complains of us—as it seems to us, unreasonably, as we gave so much of it as touched upon the point at issue between us—that neither he nor any one else shall ever be able to say that we have denied him a hearing, and because we would rather err on the generous side in this matter than even seem to be, in ever so slight a degree, less than generous or just. Bear with us, reader, for this once, and we trust the necessity will not again arise, that your ear or our lips shall be pained by an allusion to a circumstance which can be productive only of evil to a cause which we both cherish, and which, like everything else human, must be subject always to human infirmity and foolishness, and sometimes sacrificed to human selfishness and vanity.

Not indeed that we have much to say, or any intention of replying, article by article, to Mr. Douglass's indictment, or defense, or whatever title he may be pleased to apply to this extraordinary document. The sprawling sportsman, whose gun, though aimed at duck or plover, kicks back and knocks its owner over, is himself the best evidence that his shot has been otherwise harmless. The recalcitration of this piece also is, as between Mr. Douglass and ourselves, the only direction in which it is likely to do any damage. Doubtless there are people who will hold this article as his sufficient justification, but they are of a class whose prejudices preclude the possibility of any other than a foregone conclusion, and who would have held his total silence as equally triumphant. None who thought him wrong before, will think him right now; and the few who have been waiting for further evidence in the case, waiting to hear with patience and without passion, and disposed for a righteous judgment, wherever it might fall, can hardly fail to read in this "enormous length" of vituperation, the condemnation of the man who is so blinded and confused by the violence of his wrath, as to acknowledge the truth of the charge against him, and be himself at the pains to gather together the evidence that his answer to it is altogether idle. Having shown this, we may be, we think, dismissed from the further consideration of the subject.

"From the National Anti-Slavery Standard: Frederick Douglass," *Liberator*, December 30, 1853, 206.

"From the Pennsylvania Freeman: Frederick Douglass"

In his paper of the 9th inst., Frederick Douglass gathers up and groups together several articles from the *Liberator*, *Anti-Slavery Standard*, *Anti-*

Slavery Bugle, and the *Pennsylvania Freeman*, written at various times during several months past, in reply to attacks of his own upon the American Anti-Slavery Society or its prominent friends, and then devotes twelve columns of his sheet to a rejoinder, which, in bitterness of spirit, in violence of hostility, in adroitness of appeal, and in unfairness and untruthfulness of statement, has rarely, if ever, been surpassed in the assaults of our enemies.—The article may be regarded as an open declaration of war against the American Anti-Slavery Society, and the Societies and presses in sympathy with it. It is a melancholy exhibition of the dominance of evil influences and passions, over a man of splendid talents and rare genius, which will sadden the hearts of the friends of the slave, and over which angels might weep. We believe the time will come when Mr. Douglass himself will regret that he ever yielded to the bad counsels, whether from within or without, which he has followed in this matter.

What private griefs, or fancied wrongs, from the loss of subscribers or other causes, he may have had, we know not; but, without provocation from the Anti-Slavery press, as far as we remember, he repeatedly assailed with unjust imputations, misstatements, and insinuations, the managers and prominent friends of the American Anti-Slavery Society. This naturally called forth a defense from the papers friendly to that Society, each one noticing the facts in its own way, as a matter of interest to its own readers, without a thought of "concert" or "combination," or, so far as we know, the interchange of one word upon the subject.

To beguile the judgment of his readers by exciting their sympathy, Mr. Douglass artfully represents himself, a "humble, solitary individual," as the persecuted, long-suffering, and innocent victim of a savage, powerful, and relentless conspiracy of the American and Pennsylvania Anti-Slavery Societies, and all their presses and speakers, combined for his "moral extermination." He asserts that "a fierce and bitter warfare" has been waged upon him, "under the generalship of Wm. Lloyd Garrison, with a view to destroy his Anti-Slavery usefulness," and "to drive" him "from the field of public Anti-Slavery effort"; "that the hatchet of fratricidal war is uplifted" and is "flung at the head of its appointed victim, (himself,) with the combined force of three strong arms, and with the deadly aim of three good marksmen."

The only motive for this unnatural and murderous conspiracy against one humble "fugitive slave," is that "that fugitive slave has dared to differ from" those societies, "or from leading individuals in them, as to the manner in which he shall exercise his powers for the promotion of the Anti-Slavery cause, and the elevation of the Free People of Color in the United States."

The probability of such assertions is about upon a par with their modesty. Have Mr. Douglass's vanity and self-importance really swollen into such enormous proportions that he can believe these diseased fancies?

No, Mr. Douglass, the crown of the martyr or the chaplet of the hero is not so easily earned, else Falstaff or Munchausen had been canonized or deified long ago. Whatever your merit or achievements, you are not yet a second Horatius, battling alone against a Tuscan army, nor a solitary Leonidas facing the hosts of Persia in a new Thermopylæ. * * *

As Mr. Douglass has made his formal declaration of war upon "the Garrisonians," we shall hereafter know what to expect from him, and shall probably have less occasion to notice him than though his position was doubtful. We expect to find more important and more pleasant labor than controversy with him.

"From the Pennsylvania Freeman: Frederick Douglass," *Liberator*, December 30, 1853, 206.

From *Frederick Douglass: The Colored Orator*

The "North Star" fully justified its name by enabling its editor to guide fugitives to freedom; and it also helped him to free himself from a peculiarly Southern view of the United States Constitution, which deprived the Garrisonians of the influence they deserved, and to rise to that higher view which soon gained the supremacy at the North. Our estimate, not only of his mental caliber, but of his fidelity to his cause, will depend largely on our opinion about this question; and it must therefore be examined thoroughly.

The Abolitionists were either disunionists, or else Free Soilers and Liberty party men, according to their view of the Constitution as pro-slavery or antislavery. Douglass had been attacking it as pro-slavery ever since his first speech in 1841; but on May 7, 1851, when the A. A. S. S. was obliged to meet in Syracuse, because no suitable place could be found in New York City, a resolution was proposed, endorsing the "Liberator" and other papers as antislavery organs. Some one asked why the paper edited by Frederick Douglass was not on the list. Then he declared that he preferred to be left out, for he had more sympathy with those Abolitionists who were willing to vote, than with those who would not. He had then been carrying on his paper for three years and a half. How he thought at that time may be imagined from what he said, a few years later, in a lecture, entitled "The Anti-Slavery Movement," and published in Rochester, 1855. In speaking of "the different anti-slavery sects," he says:

> I shall consider, first, the Garrisonian Anti-Slavery Society. I call this the Garrisonian Society, because Mr. Garrison is, confessedly, its leader. This Society is the oldest of modern anti-slavery societies. It has, strictly speaking, two weekly papers, or organs, employs five or six lecturers, and holds numerous public meetings for the dissemination of its views. Its peculiar and distinctive feature is its doctrine of "No union with slave-holders." This doctrine has, of late, become its bond of union, and the condition of good fellowship among its members. Of this Society I have to say, its logical result is but negatively anti-slavery. Its doctrine of "No union with slave-holders," carried out, dissolves the Union, and leaves the slaves and their masters to fight their own battles, in their own way. This I hold to be an abandonment of the great idea with which that Society started. It started to free the slave. It ends by leaving the slave to free himself. It started with the purpose to imbue the heart of the nation with sentiments favorable to the abolition of slavery, and ends by seeking to free the North from all responsibility for slavery, other than if slavery were in Great Britain, or under some other nationality. This, I say, is the practical abandonment of the idea with which that Society started. It has given up the faith that the slave can be freed short of the overthrow of the Government; and then, as I understand that Society, it leaves the slaves, as it must needs leave them, just where it leaves the slaves of Cuba, or those of Brazil. The nation, as such, is given up as beyond the power of salvation by the foolishness of preaching; and hence, the aim is now to save the North, so that the American Anti-Slavery Society, which was inaugurated to convert the nation, after ten years' struggle, parts with its faith, and aims now to save the North. One of the most eloquent of that Society, and the man who is only second to Mr. Garrison himself, defines the Garrisonian doctrine thus: "All the slave asks of us is to stand out of his way; withdraw our pledge to keep the peace on the plantation; withdraw our pledge to return him; withdraw that representation which the Constitution gives in proportion to the number of slaves; and without any agitation here, without any individual virtue, which the times have eaten out of us, God will vindicate the oppressed by

the laws of justice which he has founded. Trample under foot your own unjust pledges; break to pieces your compact with hell, by which you become the abettor of oppression. Stand alone, and let no cement of the Union bind the slave, and he will right himself."

That is it. "Stand alone." The slave is to "right himself." I dissent entirely from this reasoning. It assumes to be true what is plainly absurd, and that is, that a population of slaves, without arms, without means of concert, and without leisure, is more than a match for double its number, educated, accustomed to rule, and in every respect prepared for warfare, offensive or defensive. This Society, therefore, consents to leave the slave's freedom to a most uncertain and improbable, if not an impossible, contingency. As a mere expression of abhorrence of slavery, the sentiment is a good one; but it expresses no intelligible principle of action, and throws no light on the pathway of duty. Defined, as its authors define it, it leads to false doctrines and mischievous results. It condemns Gerrit Smith for sitting in Congress, and our Saviour for eating with publicans and sinners. Dr. Spring uttered a shocking sentiment when he said, if one prayer of his would emancipate the slaves, he would not offer that prayer. No less shocking is the sentiment of the leader of the disunion forces, when he says, that if one vote of his would emancipate every slave in this country, he would not cast that vote. Here, on a bare theory, and for a theory which, if consistently adhered to, would drive a man out of the world—a theory which can never be made intelligible to common sense—the freedom of the whole slave population would be sacrificed.

But again: "No union with slave-holders." I dislike the morality of this sentiment, in its application to the point at issue. For instance: A. unites with B. in stealing my property, and carrying it away to California, or to Australia; and, while there, Mr. A. becomes convinced that he did wrong in stealing my property, and says to Mr. B., "No union with property-stealers," and abandons him, leaving the property in his hands. Now, I put it to this audience, has Mr. A. in this transaction met with the requirements of stringent morality? He certainly has not. It is not only his duty to separate from the thief, but to restore the stolen property to its owner. And I hold that in the Union, this very thing of restoring to the slave his long-lost rights can better be accomplished than it can possibly be accomplished outside of the Union. This, then, is my answer to the motto, "No Union with slave-holders."

But this is not the worst fault of this Society. Its chief energies are expended in confirming the opinion, that the United States Constitution is, and was, intended to be a slave-holding instrument—thus piling up, between the slave and his freedom, the huge work of the abolition of the Government, as an indispens-

> able condition to emancipation. My point here is, first, the Constitution is, according to its reading, an anti-slavery document; and secondly, to dissolve the Union, as a means to abolish slavery, is about as wise as it would be to burn up this city, in order to get the thieves out of it. But again, we hear the motto, "No union with slave-holders"; and I answer it, as that noble champion of liberty, N. P. Rogers, answered it with a more sensible motto, namely—"No union with slave-holding." I would unite with anybody to do right, and with nobody to do wrong. And as the Union, under the Constitution, requires me to do nothing which is wrong, and gives me many facilities for doing good, I cannot go with the American Anti-Slavery Society in its doctrine of disunion. [. . .]

He says, in a letter not before printed:

> I was a non-voter in 1848, though deeply interested in the Free Soil movement, inaugurated in the Buffalo convention in that year. Before 1852 I became a sound convert to the doctrine of the unconstitutionality of slavery and the duty of voting against slavery.

He adds that he gave "active support to all the candidates nominated thereafter, from Hale to Lincoln." The "North Star" changed its name at the time that its editor changed his views. He says that there were "I know not how many other stars in the newspaper firmament," and in order to avoid confusion, the name of "Frederick Douglass's Paper" was adopted at the beginning of the fourth volume, in December, 1850. In 1852 it contained more news, more poetry, more humor, more about politics, and more about Woman's Rights and other new reforms than had been found in the "North Star." Mr. Ward was prominent among the colored contributors, and among the white ones were J. G. Birney and Gerrit Smith. The friend last named was president of the New York State Anti-Slavery Society, which Douglass helped to revise and served as corresponding secretary. Its platform declares that slavery cannot be made legal, and its first meeting was at Rochester, on March 18, 1852, two days before the publication of "Uncle Tom's Cabin." That city was chosen as the place for the subsequent meetings, which were not numerous.

The Free Soilers gave a cordial welcome to their new ally at the meeting of the Ohio Anti-Slavery Society, on May 5, at Cincinnati, where he was made vice-president; and there Burleigh argued for disunion, while Julian defended the men who made him one of their candidates in this year's campaign. Our Douglass devoted himself mainly to exposing the shortcomings of the Church, and his speech contained the following characteristic passage:

> In this connection I am always forcibly reminded of the incomparable illustration of the principle of brotherly love in the New Testament. When the stranger fell among thieves, and was left alone on the highways to perish, there came along three persons, severally representing the classes in society. First came the priest—evidently all priest and no humanity—who passed by entirely "on the other side," and his successors appear to have remained on the other side to this time. [Laughter.] Then came another, a deacon, probably; he seemed half-man and half-priest, for he took a middle course, and seemed wavering; but, unfortunately, the priest predominated, and he followed "in the footsteps of his illustrious predecessor" on the other side. [Great laughter.] But, my friends, there next came that way a man, nothing but a man; yes, a regular human; [renewed laughter] and he went straight up to the suffering stranger, bound up his wounds, and attended to all his wants. [Laughter.] [The peculiar and inimitable facial contortions setting off this narrative, can only be imagined by those who have listened to Tom Corwin.] I can always distinguish the class of time-serving clergymen, wherever I meet them, in the railroad car or steamboat—that is, when they condescend to occupy the same car and cabin—if they approach one of my color at all, the first question is—not "Do you love your neighbor, your brother man?" But, "do you love God?" [Another unreportable expression of countenance.] But, my friends, let me be understood. It is the faithless and recreant priesthood I would hold up; not the true servants of an impartial God, who created us *all* in his likeness. I will never be driven off the platform of the Christian religion in fighting slavery. [Great applause.] But my heart goes out only to a practical religion. I see in this convention an exhibition of adherence to the vitality of religion. Christianity works thus, not alone with the rich and strong, but it reaches its long, beneficent arm down to seize and bear up the last link of humanity. [Applause.] Such Christianity is embodied in the great anti-slavery movement of the nineteenth century—it is expressed in the resolution before us. I am heartily in favor of it.

It is sad to see that after this eulogy upon the Good Samaritan, he failed to meet him at the convention of the A. A. S. S. one week later in Rochester. There he had to defend his change of views, and hear himself denounced as a deserter by Garrison, Phillips, Remond, Mrs. Abby Kelley Foster, and her husband, Stephen. Among other offenses were his advocating the Homestead Bill and his praising Kossuth. He was so provoked at Remond's thanking God for not being the son of a slave, that he made this allusion to the occupation of his critic's father, "I thank God that I am neither a barber nor the son of a barber." Another colored man compared him to a castaway, who had been picked up by the ship of which Garrison was captain, had tried in vain to get himself into command, and then had stolen a boat and fled. Garrison believed so firmly in disunionism, that it seemed to him impossible that any of his disciples had found a single error in the creed. He thought it his conscientious duty to bring a charge of mercenary motives against the friend, who had founded the "North Star" with money which he might honorably have invested for the benefit of his family; who sank in the enterprise, before 1856, at least twelve thousand dollars of his own earnings, according to the testimony of a competent and trustworthy writer, in the introduction to "My Bondage and my Freedom"; and who had made his house not only a refuge for fugitives, but a free boarding-house for poor colored boys who were invited there to learn the trade of printing. No wonder that an exile from Hungary said to one of my friends with uplifted hands, "If I attend any more of your anti-slavery meetings they will make me a pro-slavery man." Douglass said some years later, in his reply to George Thompson:

> No personal assaults shall ever lead me to forget that some who in America have often made me the subject of personal abuse, are at the same time, in their own way, earnestly working for the abolition of slavery. They are men who thoroughly understand the principle that he who is not for them is against them; but unfortunately they do not seem to understand that he who is not against them is on their side.

He has since remarked, that "Mr. Garrison sent a great many people to perdition who obstinately refused to go." Among them, by the way, were Longfellow, Sumner, and Channing. The columns of "Frederick Douglass's Paper," for 1852 and 1853, are entirely free from any bitterness against his assailants; and in the latter year he said, at the May meeting, held at New York by the Tappans and other non-Garrisonian Abolitionists:

> I honor and respect Lewis Tappan; I love and honor William Lloyd Garrison; and may God have mercy upon me when I refuse to strike a blow against slavery in connection with either gentleman. I will work with either; and if the one discards me because I work with the other, the responsibility is not mine.

The Garrisonians, however, continued to attack him so fiercely that there seemed likely, as the "Syracuse Journal" said, "To be a war between the white and black roses." Mrs. Swisshelm, who was in hearty sympathy with the anti-slavery movement, as well as with that in behalf of her sex, says in her own paper, the "Saturday Visitor": "We do believe that the 'Liberator,' 'Standard' and 'Freeman' might be better employed than in blackballing a black man." She adds, in reference to a charge about neglecting Mrs. Douglass, which drew out an indignant letter of denial from the latter, and is fully refuted by one quoted at the close of the next chapter: "In all our experience of very bitter newspaper warfare, we never saw the equal of this; and for all we can see, the three able papers that have united to crush Mr. Douglass, have failed to bring a particle of proof that he is not as good and true as he is eloquent and energetic." He finally found it due to his family as well as to himself, that he should reply once for all. Twelve columns of his paper are occupied with an answer which meets all the charges, and declares that this is done "not to re-open, but if possible to close up our account with these anti-slavery journals. For ourselves," he adds, "we have not now, as we had not in the beginning, the slightest wish to be embroiled in personal conflict with anti-slavery men of any sort. There is better work for all of us to do than to keep up a warfare against each other." [. . .]

Of the severity with which Garrison blamed his giving up disunionism, Douglass wrote me thus:

> The first remark with which my statement was met by Mr. Garrison was this, "There is roguery somewhere." There was no mistaking the meaning; and, coming from any one else, it would have been resented on the spot. [. . .] I do not think that the grand, old anti-slavery pioneer went to his grave thinking there was any "roguery" in me. If he did, I was not alone in this bad opinion of his. No man who ever quitted the Garrisonian denomination was permitted to leave without a doubt being cast upon his honesty. That was one of the Liberator's weapons of war; and it was a weapon which never rusted for want of using. There are spots on the sun; but it shines for all that; and Garrison with all his harshness of judgment is Garrison still, and one of the best men of mothers born.

From Frederic May Holland, *Frederick Douglass: The Colored Orator* (New York: Funk & Wagnalls, 1892), iii–iv, 190–206, 394.

[Exchange with William Wells Brown] (1855)

FREDERICK DOUGLASS AND WILLIAM WELLS BROWN

A former slave whose prominence in the antislavery movement was rivaled only by Douglass himself, William Wells Brown could be a sharp critic of his black abolitionist colleagues. Born in slavery in 1814, Brown escaped in 1834 and soon became active in both the temperance and antislavery movements. He was a prolific writer who published autobiographies, fiction, drama, travel narratives, and histories, and he was an entertaining and persuasive lecturer. Like Douglass, he traveled to Great Britain, both to lecture and to avoid being captured and returned to slavery—and, like Douglass, his freedom was eventually purchased, allowing for his safe return to the United States. Once home, he apparently shared with friends his suspicion that Douglass had spoken against him to one of his British hosts. When Brown heard that Douglass was aware of his complaint, he wrote Douglass a letter, presenting his case in some detail. Douglass didn't publish the letter but instead published the following short notice of the affair, to which Brown responded with the letter that follows, published not by Douglass but in the *National Anti-Slavery Standard*. And thus ended, for the general public, at least, this squabble between two great men of the cause.

"William Wells Brown"

While our distinguished brother, Brown was abroad, laboring, with admirable industry in the cause of human freedom, and adding to his stock of knowledge of men and things, we esteemed it not less a pleasure than a duty to commend him and his work. We rejoiced that so much of talent and industry could be pointed to, (in vindication of our common people,) as were exemplified in Mr. Brown. We do *not* regret any kind word we then said of him; but we *do* regret that he should feel called upon, to show his faithfulness to the American Anti-Slavery Society, by covering us with reproach and dishonor. If Mr. Brown has aught against us, he need not retail his complaints to cliques, parties, and anti-slavery circles, or allow them to be so retailed for him. Put your charges against us, Mr. Brown, in a suitable shape, and they shall appear, not only in the anti-slavery office at Boston, in the private ear of prejudice, but we promise you to publish them to our readers. As an honest man, we hold it to be your duty to do this, or to cease circulation as facts, what we know can be shown to be the merest fictions. Come, Mr. Brown, let us have the facts.

"William Wells Brown," *Frederick Douglass' Paper* 8, no. 2 (March 2, 1855): 2.

"To Frederick Douglass"

Sir: Had not your many changes and re-changes prepared me to be astonished at nothing that you might say, or do, I would have been somewhat surprised at the attack made upon me by you, in your paper of the 2d of March. You commence by saying, "we do regret that he should feel called upon to show his faithfulness to the American Anti-Slavery Society by covering us with dishonor." Let me say to you, Frederick Douglass, that my difference with you has nothing whatever to do with the American Anti-Slavery Society, and no one knows that better than yourself. And I regard such an insinuation as fit only to come from one whose feelings are entirely lost to all sense of shame. My charge against you is, that, just before I left the United States for England, you wrote a *private* letter to a distinguished Abolitionist in Great Britain, injurious to me, and intended to forestall my movements there. In a note which I forwarded to you, to your address in Rochester, on the 20th of January last, I gave you to understand that I had been made aware of your having acted in that underhanded manner. The following is a part of the note I sent you more than a month ago. "During my sojourn in England, and several months after my arrival there, and while spending a few days with a friend of yours, the post brought me a letter, which had been re-mailed in London, and it proved to be from you, dated at New Bedford. After I had finished reading the letter, your friend seemed anxious to learn its contents. I handed it to her, with the request that she would read it; your friend appeared much astonished at the kindness expressed by you to me, and exclaimed, 'Douglass has done you a great injustice,' and immediately revealed to me the contents of a letter which she had received from you, some months before, and which was written a short time previous to my departure from America. I need not say that the very unfavourable position in which your letter placed me before your friend, secured for me a cold reception at her hands. I need not name the lady; you know to whom I refer, unless you wrote to more than one." Your attack upon me, in your paper of the 2d Inst., in which you ask for "facts," when my note containing the above had been in your possession more than a month, shows too well your wish to make a sneaking fling at me, instead of seeking for "facts," and acting the part of an honorable man. Why did you not give my note a place in your paper, and make such comments as you thought best? No, that would not have suited you. But, anxious to heap insult upon injury, you resort to the mode most congenial to your feelings and sense of justice. Had I not thought it due to the public to state the above "facts," I would have treated your scurrilous paragraph with that silence and contempt that all such articles so justly deserve. However, no future insinuation of yours, no matter how false or unjust, shall provoke from me reply.

William Wells Brown, "To Frederick Douglass," *National Anti-Slavery Standard* 15, no. 42 (March 10, 1855).

Introduction to *My Bondage and My Freedom* (1855)

JAMES MCCUNE SMITH

Although I am not including any of the other introductory material from Douglass's three autobiographies, the one written by Dr. James McCune Smith for Douglass's *My Bondage and My Freedom* is a worthy exception—in part for what it reveals about Douglass, and in part to represent the perspective of another of nineteenth-century America's remarkable intellectuals and leaders. Born in slavery, Smith became the first African American to hold a medical degree, having graduated at the top of his class from the University of Glasgow, Scotland. He received his medical degree in 1837 and completed an internship in Paris. Following his return to the United States, Smith maintained an active medical career, though he was never admitted to the American Medical Association or to local medical associations. Still, his great intellect could not be denied, and he was elected a founding member of the New York Statistics Society in 1852, and he was elected a member of the American Geographic Society in 1854. Smith's interests were many, his understanding deep, and his influence enormous, and Douglass found in him a thoughtful and inspiring friend who shaped his life significantly. In turn, Smith offered an introduction to Douglass's autobiography significantly different from those by William Lloyd Garrison and Wendell Phillips that graced Douglass's 1845 *Narrative*. In addition to a broad intellectual appreciation, Smith places Douglass in an elite pantheon of African Americans, including some we encountered earlier—William Wells Brown and Samuel Ringgold Ward—and others who were regularly mentioned in accounts of black achievements: abolitionist and mathematician Charles L. Reason; businessman William Whipper; and James W. C. Pennington and Jermaine Wesley Loguen, both of whom had been born in slavery but eventually achieved freedom and entered the ministry. Mentioned as well are the great writer Alexandre Dumas, actor Ira Aldridge, and singer—"The Black Swan"—Elizabeth Greenfield. In effect, Smith places Douglass within a community, and a history, that one struggles to find even in more recent biographies, the community and history of global black struggle and achievement.

WHEN A MAN RAISES himself from the lowest condition in society to the highest, mankind pay him the tribute of their admiration; when he accomplishes this elevation by native energy, guided by prudence and wisdom, their admiration is increased; but when his course, onward and upward, excellent in itself, furthermore proves a possible, what had hitherto been regarded as an impossible, reform, then he becomes a burning and a shining light, on which the aged may look with gladness, the young with hope, and the down-trodden, as a representative of what they may themselves become. To such a man, dear reader, it is my privilege to introduce you.

The life of Frederick Douglass, recorded in the pages which follow, is not merely an example of self-elevation under the most adverse circumstances; it is, moreover, a noble vindication of the highest aims of the American antislavery movement. The real object of that movement is not only to disenthrall, it is, also, to bestow upon the Negro the exercise of all those rights, from the possession of which he has been so long debarred.

But this full recognition of the colored man to the right, and the entire admission of the same to the full privileges, political, religious and social, of manhood, requires powerful effort on the part of the enthralled, as well as on the part of those who would disenthrall them. The people at large must feel the conviction, as well as admit the abstract logic, of human equality; the Negro, for the first time in the world's history, brought in full contact with high civilization, must prove his title first to all that is demanded for him; in the teeth of unequal chances, he must prove himself equal to the mass of those who oppress him—therefore, absolutely superior to his apparent fate, and to their relative ability. And it is most cheering to the friends of freedom, today, that evidence of this equality is rapidly accumulating, not from the ranks of the half-freed colored people of the free states, but from the very depths of slavery itself; the indestructible equality of man to man is demonstrated by the ease with which black men, scarce one remove from barbarism—if slavery can be honored with such a distinction—vault into the high places of the most advanced and painfully acquired civilization. Ward and Garnet, Wells Brown and Pennington, Loguen and Douglass, are banners on the outer wall, under which abolition is fighting its most successful battles, because they are living exemplars of the practicability of the most radical abolitionism; for, they were all of them born to the doom of slavery, some of them remained slaves until adult age, yet they all have not only won equality to their white fellow citizens, in civil, religious, political and social rank, but they have also illustrated and adorned our common country by their genius, learning and eloquence.

The characteristics whereby Mr. Douglass has won first rank among these remarkable men, and is still rising toward highest rank among living Americans, are abundantly laid bare in the book before us. Like the autobiography of Hugh Miller, it carries us so far back into early childhood, as to throw light upon the question, "when positive and persistent memory begins in the human being." And, like Hugh Miller, he must have been a shy old-fashioned child, occasionally oppressed by what he could not well account for, peering and poking about among the layers of right and wrong, of tyrant and thrall, and the wonderfulness of that hopeless tide of things which brought power to one race, and unrequited toil to another, until, finally, he stumbled upon his "first-found Ammonite," hidden away down in the depths of his own nature, and which revealed to him the fact that liberty and right, for all men, were anterior to slavery and wrong. When his knowledge of the world was bounded by the visible horizon on Col. Lloyd's plantation, and while every thing around him bore a fixed, iron stamp, as if it had always been so, this was, for one so young, a notable discovery.

To his uncommon memory, then, we must add a keen and accurate insight into men and things; an original breadth of common sense which enabled him to see, and weigh, and compare whatever passed before him, and which kindled a desire to search out and define their relations to other things not so patent, but which never succumbed to the marvelous nor the supernatural; a sacred thirst for liberty and for learning, first as a means of attaining liberty, then as an end in itself most desirable; a will; an unfaltering energy and determination to obtain what his soul pronounced desirable; a majestic self-hood; determined courage; a deep and agonizing sympathy with his embruted, crushed and bleeding fellow slaves, and an extraordinary depth of passion, together with that rare alliance between passion and intellect, which enables the former, when deeply roused, to excite, develop and sustain the latter.

With these original gifts in view, let us look at his schooling; the fearful discipline through which it pleased God to prepare him for the high calling on which he has since entered—the advocacy of emancipation by the people who are not slaves. And for this special mission, his plantation education was better than any he could have acquired in any lettered school. What he needed, was facts and experiences, welded to acutely wrought up sympathies, and these he could not elsewhere have obtained, in a manner so peculiarly adapted to his nature. His physical being was well trained, also, running wild until advanced into boyhood; hard work and light diet, thereafter, and a skill in handicraft in youth.

For his special mission, then, this was, considered in connection with his natural gifts, a good schooling; and, for his special mission, he doubtless "left school" just at the proper moment. Had he remained longer in slavery—had he fretted under bonds until the ripening of manhood and its passions, until the drear agony of slave-wife and slave-children had been piled upon his already bitter experiences—then, not only would his own history have had another termination, but the drama of American slavery would have been essentially varied; for I cannot resist the belief, that the boy who learned to read and write as he did, who taught his fellow slaves these precious acquirements as he did, who plotted for their mutual escape as he did, would, when a man at bay, strike a blow which would make slavery reel and stagger. Furthermore, blows and insults he bore, at the moment, without resentment; deep but suppressed emotion rendered him insensible to their sting; but it was afterward, when the memory of them went seething through his brain, breeding a fiery indignation at his injured self-hood, that the resolve came to resist, and the time fixed when to resist, and the plot laid, how to resist; and he always kept his self-pledged word. In what he undertook, in this line, he looked fate in the face, and had a cool, keen look at the relation of means to ends. Henry Bibb, to avoid chastisement, strewed his master's bed with charmed leaves and *was whipped*. Frederick Douglass quietly pocketed a like *fetiche*, compared his muscles with those of Covey—and *whipped him*.

In the history of his life in bondage, we find, well developed, that inherent and continuous energy of character which will ever render him distinguished. What his hand found to do, he did with his might; even while conscious that he was wronged out of his daily earnings, he worked, and worked hard. At his daily labor he went with a will; with keen, well set eye, brawny chest, lithe figure, and fair sweep of arm, he would have been king among calkers, had that been his mission.

It must not be overlooked, in this glance at his education, that Mr. Douglass lacked one aid to which so many men of mark have been deeply indebted—he had neither a mother's care, nor a mother's culture, save that which slavery grudgingly meted out to him. Bitter nurse! may not even her features relax with human feeling, when she gazes at such offspring! How susceptible he was to the kindly influences of mother-culture, may be gathered from his own words, on page 57: "It has been a life-long standing grief to me, that I know so little of my mother, and that I was so early separated from her. The counsels of her love must have been beneficial to me. The side view of her face is imaged on my memory, and I take few steps in life, without feeling her presence; but the image is mute, and I have no striking words of hers treasured up."

From the depths of chattel slavery in Maryland, our author escaped into the caste-slavery of the north, in New Bedford, Massachusetts. Here he found oppression assuming another, and hardly less bitter, form; of that very handicraft which the greed of slavery had taught him, his half-freedom denied him the exercise for an honest living; he found himself one of a class—free colored men—whose position he has described in the following words:

> Aliens are we in our native land. The fundamental principles of the republic, to which the humblest white man, whether born here or elsewhere, may appeal with confidence, in the hope of awakening a favorable response, are held to be inapplicable to us. The glorious doctrines of your revolutionary fathers, and the more glorious teachings of the Son of God, are construed and applied against us. We are literally scourged beyond the beneficent range of both authorities, human and divine. * * * American humanity hates us, scorns us, disowns and denies, in a thousand ways, our very personality. The outspread wing of American christianity, apparently broad enough to give shelter to a perishing world, refuses to cover us. To us, its bones are brass, and its features iron. In running thither for shelter and succor, we have only fled from the hungry blood-hound to the devouring wolf—from a corrupt and selfish world, to a hollow and hypocritical church.—*Speech before American and Foreign Anti-Slavery Society*, May, 1854.

Four years or more, from 1837 to 1841, he struggled on, in New Bedford, sawing wood, rolling casks, or doing what labor he might, to support himself and young family; four years he brooded over the scars which slavery and semi-slavery had inflicted upon his body and soul; and then, with his wounds yet unhealed, he fell among the Garrisonians—a glorious waif to those most ardent reformers. It happened one day, at Nantucket, that he, diffidently and reluctantly, was led to address an anti-slavery meeting. He was about the age when the younger Pitt entered the House of Commons; like Pitt, too, he stood up a born orator.

William Lloyd Garrison, who was happily present, writes thus of Mr. Douglass' maiden effort; "I shall never forget his first speech at the convention—the extraordinary emotion it excited in my own mind—the powerful impression it created upon a crowded auditory, completely taken by surprise. * * * I think I never hated slavery so intensely as at that moment; certainly, my perception of the enormous outrage which is inflicted by it on the godlike nature of its victims, was rendered far more clear than ever. There stood one in physical proportions and stature commanding and exact—in intellect richly endowed—in natural eloquence a prodigy."[1]

It is of interest to compare Mr. Douglass's account of this meeting with Mr. Garrison's. Of the two, I think the latter the most correct. It must have been a grand burst of eloquence! The pent up agony, indignation and pathos of an abused and harrowed boyhood and youth, bursting out in all their freshness and overwhelming earnestness!

This unique introduction to its great leader, led immediately to the employment of Mr. Douglass as an agent by the American Anti-Slavery Society. So far as his self-relying and independent character would permit, he became, after the strictest sect, a Garrisonian. It is not too much to say, that he formed a complement which they needed, and they were a complement equally necessary to his "make-up." With his deep and keen sensitiveness to wrong, and his wonderful memory, he came from the land of bondage full of its woes and its evils, and painting them in characters of living light; and, on his part, he found, told out in sound Saxon phrase, all those principles of justice and right and liberty, which had dimly brooded over the dreams of his youth, seeking definite forms and verbal expression. It must have been an electric flashing of thought, and a knitting of soul, granted to but few in this life, and will be a life-long memory to those who participated in it. In the society, moreover, of Wendell Phillips, Edmund Quincy, William Lloyd Garrison, and other men of earnest faith and refined culture, Mr. Douglass enjoyed the high advantage of their assistance and counsel in the labor of self-culture, to which he now addressed himself with wonted energy. Yet, these gentlemen, although proud of Frederick Douglass, failed to fathom, and bring out to the light of day, the highest qualities of his mind; the force of their own education stood in their own way: they did not delve into the mind of a colored man for capacities which the pride of race led them to believe to be restricted to their own Saxon blood. Bitter and vindictive sarcasm, irresistible mimicry, and a pathetic narrative of his own experiences of slavery, were the intellectual manifestations which they encouraged him to exhibit on the platform or in the lecture desk.

A visit to England, in 1845, threw Mr. Douglass among men and women of earnest souls and high culture, and who, moreover, had never drank of the bitter waters of American caste. For the first time in his life, he breathed an atmosphere congenial to the longings of his spirit, and felt his manhood free and unrestricted. The cordial and manly greetings of the British and Irish audiences in public, and the refinement and elegance of the social circles in which he mingled, not only as an equal, but as a recognized man of genius, were, doubtless, genial and pleasant resting places in his hitherto thorny and troubled journey through life. There are joys on the earth, and, to the wayfaring fugitive from American slavery or American caste, this is one of them.

But his sojourn in England was more than a joy to Mr. Douglass. Like the platform at Nantucket, it awakened him to the consciousness of new powers that lay in him. From the pupilage of Garrisonism he rose to the dignity of a teacher and a thinker; his opinions on the broader aspects of the great American question were earnestly and incessantly sought, from various points of view, and he must, perforce, bestir himself to give suitable answer. With that prompt and truthful perception which has led their sisters in all ages of the world to gather at the feet and support the hands of reformers, the gentlewomen of England[2] were foremost to encourage and strengthen him to carve out for himself a path fitted to his powers and energies, in the life-battle against slavery and caste to which he was pledged. And one stirring thought, inseparable from the British idea of the evangel of freedom, must have smote his ear from every side—

> Hereditary bondmen! know ye not
> Who would be free, themselves must strike the blow?

The result of this visit was, that on his return to the United States, he established a newspaper. This proceeding was sorely against the wishes and the advice of the leaders of the American Anti-Slavery Society, but our author had fully grown up to the conviction of a truth which they had once promulgated, but now forgotten, to wit: that in their own elevation—self-elevation—colored men have a blow to strike "on their own hook," against slavery and caste. Differing from his Boston friends in this matter, diffident in his own abilities, reluctant at their dissuadings, how beautiful is the loyalty with which he still clung to their principles in all things else, and even in this.

Now came the trial hour. Without cordial support from any large body of men or party on this side the Atlantic, and too far distant in space and immediate interest to expect much more, after the much already done, on the other side, he stood up, almost alone, to the arduous labor and heavy expenditure of editor and lecturer. The Garrison party, to which he still adhered, did not want a *colored* newspaper—there was an odor of *caste* about it; the Liberty party could hardly be expected to give warm support to a man who smote their principles as with a hammer; and the wide gulf which separated the free colored people from the Garrisonians, also separated them from their brother, Frederick Douglass.

The arduous nature of his labors, from the date of the establishment of his paper, may be estimated by the fact, that anti-slavery papers in the United States, even while organs of, and when supported by, anti-slavery parties, have, with a single exception, failed to pay expenses. Mr. Douglass has maintained, and does maintain, his paper without the support of any party, and even in the teeth of the opposition of those from whom he had reason to expect counsel and encouragement. He has been compelled, at one and the same time, and almost constantly, during the past seven years, to contribute matter to its columns as editor, and to raise funds for its support as lecturer. It is within bounds to say, that he has expended twelve thousand dollars of his own hard earned money, in publishing this paper, a larger sum than has been contributed by any one individual for the general advancement of the colored people. There had been many other papers published and edited by colored men, beginning as far back as 1827, when the Rev. Samuel E. Cornish and John B. Russwurm (a graduate of Bowdoin college, and afterward Governor of Cape Palmas) published the *Freedom's Journal*, in New York City; probably not less than one hundred newspaper enterprises have been started in the United States, by free colored men, born free, and some of them of liberal education and fair talents for this work; but, one after another, they have fallen through, although, in several instances, anti-slavery friends contributed to their support.[3] It had almost been given up, as an impracticable thing, to maintain a colored newspaper, when Mr. Douglass, with fewest early advantages of all his competitors, essayed, and has proved the thing perfectly practicable, and, moreover, of great public benefit. This paper, in addition to its power in holding up the hands of those to whom it is especially devoted, also affords irrefutable evidence of the justice, safety and practicability of Immediate Emancipation; it further proves the immense loss which slavery inflicts on the land while it dooms such energies as his to the hereditary degradation of slavery.

It has been said in this Introduction, that Mr. Douglass had raised himself by his own efforts to the highest position in society. As a successful editor, in our land, he occupies this position. Our editors rule the land, and he is one of them. As an orator and thinker, his position is equally high, in the opinion of his countrymen. If a stranger in the United States would seek its most distinguished men—the movers of public opinion—he will find their names mentioned, and their movements chronicled, under the head of "BY MAGNETIC TELEGRAPH," in the daily papers. The keen caterers for the public attention, set down, in this column, such men only as have won high mark in the public esteem. During the past winter—1854–5—very frequent mention of Frederick Douglass was made under this head in the daily papers; his name glided as often—this week from Chicago, next week from Boston—over the lightning wires, as the name of any other man, of whatever note. To no man did the people more widely nor more earnestly say, *"Tell me thy thought!"* And, somehow or other, revolution seemed to follow in his wake. His were not the mere words of eloquence which Kossuth speaks of, that delight the ear and then pass away. No! They were *work*-able, *do*-able words, that brought forth fruits in the revolution in Illinois, and in the passage of the franchise resolutions by the Assembly of New York.

And the secret of his power, what is it? He is a Representative American man—a type of his countrymen. Naturalists tell us that a full grown man is a resultant or representative of all animated nature on this globe; beginning with the early embryo state, then representing the lowest forms of organic life,[4] and passing through every subordinate grade or type, until he reaches the last and highest—manhood. In like manner, and to the fullest extent, has Frederick Douglass passed through every gradation of rank comprised in our national make-up, and bears upon his person and upon his soul every thing that is American. And he has not only full sympathy with every thing American; his proclivity or bent, to active toil and visible progress, are in the strictly national direction, delighting to outstrip "all creation."

Nor have the natural gifts, already named as his, lost anything by his severe training. When unexcited, his mental processes are probably slow, but singularly clear in perception, and wide in vision, the unfailing memory bringing up all the facts in their every aspect; incongruities he lays hold of incontinently, and holds up on the edge of his keen and telling wit. But this wit never descends to frivolity; it is rigidly in the keeping of his truthful common sense, and always used in illustration or proof of some point which could not so readily be reached any other way. "Beware of a Yankee when he is feeding," is a shaft that strikes home in a matter never so laid bare by satire before. "The Garrisonian views of disunion, if carried to a successful issue, would only place the people of the north in the same relation to American slavery which they now bear to the slavery of Cuba or the Brazils," is a statement, in a few words, which contains the result and the evidence of an argument which might cover pages, but could not carry stronger conviction, nor be stated in less pregnable form. In proof of this, I may say, that having been submitted to the attention of the Garrisonians in print, in March, it was repeated before them at their business meeting in May—the platform, *par excellence*, on which they invite free fight, *a l'outrance*, to all comers. It was given out in the clear, ringing tones, wherewith the hall of shields was wont to resound of old, yet neither Garrison, nor Phillips, nor May, nor Remond, nor Foster, nor Burleigh, with his subtle steel of "the ice brook's temper," ventured to break a lance upon it! The doctrine of the dissolution of the Union, as a means for the abolition of American slavery, was silenced upon the lips that gave it birth, and in the presence of an array of defenders who compose the keenest intellects in the land.

"*The man who is right is a majority*" is an aphorism struck out by Mr. Douglass in that great gathering of the friends of freedom, at Pittsburgh, in 1852, where he towered among the highest, because, with abilities inferior to none, and moved more deeply than any, there was neither policy nor party to trammel the outpourings of his soul. Thus we find, opposed to all disadvantages which a black man in the United States labors and struggles under, is this one vantage ground—when the chance comes, and the audience where he may have a say, he stands forth the freest, most deeply moved and most earnest of all men.

It has been said of Mr. Douglass, that his descriptive and declamatory powers, admitted to be of the very highest order, take precedence of his logical force. Whilst the schools might have trained him to the exhibition of the formulas of deductive logic, nature and circumstances forced him into the exercise of the higher faculties required by induction. The first ninety pages of this "Life in Bondage," afford specimens of observing, comparing, and careful classifying, of such superior character, that it is difficult to believe them the results of a child's thinking; he questions the earth, and the children and the slaves around him again and again, and finally looks to "*God in the sky*" for the why and the wherefore of the unnatural thing, slavery. "*Yes, if indeed thou art, wherefore dost thou suffer us to be slain?*" is the only prayer and worship of the God-forsaken Dodos in the heart of Africa. Almost the same was his prayer. One of his earliest observations was that white children should know their ages, while the colored children were ignorant of theirs; and the songs of the slaves grated on his inmost soul, because a something told him that harmony in sound, and music of the spirit, could not consociate with miserable degradation.

To such a mind, the ordinary processes of logical deduction are like proving that two and two make four. Mastering the intermediate steps by an intuitive glance, or recurring to them as Ferguson resorted to geometry, it goes down to the deeper relation of things, and brings out what may seem, to some, mere statements, but which are new and brilliant generalizations, each resting on a broad and stable basis. Thus, Chief Justice Marshall gave his decisions, and then told Brother Story to look up the authorities—and they never differed from him. Thus, also, in his "Lecture on the Anti-Slavery Movement," delivered before the Rochester Ladies' Anti-Slavery Society, Mr. Douglass presents a mass of thought, which, without any showy display of logic on his part, requires an exercise of the reasoning faculties of the reader to keep pace with him. And his "Claims of the Negro Ethnologically Considered," is full of new and fresh thoughts on the dawning science of race-history.

If, as has been stated, his intellection is slow, when unexcited, it is most prompt and rapid when he is thoroughly aroused. Memory, logic, wit, sarcasm, invective pathos and bold imagery of rare structural beauty, well up as from a copious fountain, yet each in its proper place, and contributing to form a whole, grand in itself, yet complete in the minutest proportions. It is most difficult to hedge him in a corner, for his positions are taken so deliberately, that it is rare to find a point in them undefended aforethought. Professor Reason tells me the following: "On a recent visit of a public nature, to Philadelphia, and in a meeting composed mostly of his colored brethren, Mr. Douglass proposed a comparison of views in the matters of the relations and duties of 'our people'; he holding that prejudice was the result of condition, and could be conquered by the efforts of the degraded themselves. A gentleman present, distinguished for logical acumen and subtlety, and who had devoted no small portion of the last twenty-five years to the study and elucidation of this very question, held the opposite view, that prejudice is innate and unconquerable. He terminated a series of well dove-tailed, Socratic questions to Mr. Douglass, with the following: 'If the legislature at Harrisburgh should awaken, to-morrow morning, and find each man's skin turned black and his hair woolly, what could they do to remove prejudice?' 'Immediately pass laws entitling black men to all civil, political and social privileges,' was the instant reply—and the questioning ceased."

The most remarkable mental phenomenon in Mr. Douglass, is his style in writing and speaking. In March, 1855, he delivered an address in the assembly chamber before the members of the legislature of the state of New York. An eye witness[5] describes the crowded and most intelligent audience, and their rapt attention to the speaker, as the grandest scene he ever witnessed in the capitol. Among those whose eyes were riveted on the speaker full two hours and a half, were Thurlow Weed and Lieutenant Governor Raymond; the latter, at the conclusion of the address, exclaimed to a friend, "I would give twenty thousand dollars, if I could deliver that address in that manner." Mr. Raymond is a first class graduate of Dartmouth, a rising politician, ranking foremost in the legislature; of course, his ideal of oratory must be of the most polished and finished description.

The style of Mr. Douglass in writing, is to me an intellectual puzzle. The strength, affluence and terseness may easily be accounted for, because the style of a man is the man; but how are we to account for that rare polish in his style of writing, which, most critically examined, seems the result of careful early culture among the best classics of our language; it equals if it does not surpass the style of Hugh Miller, which was the wonder of the British literary public, until he unraveled the mystery in the most interesting of autobiographies. But Frederick Douglass was still calking the seams of Baltimore clippers, and had only written a "pass," at the age when Miller's style was already formed.

I asked William Whipper, of Pennsylvania, the gentleman alluded to above, whether he thought Mr. Douglass's power inherited from the Negroid, or from what is called the Caucasian side of his make up? After some reflection, he frankly answered, "I must admit, although sorry to do so, that the Caucasian predominates." At that time, I almost agreed with him; but, facts narrated in the first part of this work, throw a different light on this interesting question.

We are left in the dark as to who was the paternal ancestor of our author; a fact which generally holds good of the Romuluses and Remuses who are to inaugurate the new birth of our republic. In the absence of testimony from the Caucasian side, we must see what evidence is given on the other side of the house.

"My grandmother, though advanced in years, * * * was yet a woman of power and spirit. She was marvelously straight in figure, elastic and muscular." (p. 46.)

After describing her skill in constructing nets, her perseverance in using them, and her wide-spread fame in the agricultural way he adds, "It happened to her—as it will happen to any careful and thrifty person residing in an ignorant and improvident neighborhood—to enjoy the reputation of being born to good luck." And his grandmother was a black woman.

"My mother was tall, and finely proportioned; of deep black, glossy complexion; had regular features; and among other slaves was remarkably sedate in her manners." "Being a field hand, she was obliged to walk twelve miles and return, between nightfall and daybreak, to see her children." (p. 54.) "I shall never forget the indescribable expression of her countenance when I told her that I had had no food since morning. * * * There was pity in her glance at me, and a fiery indignation at Aunt Katy at the same time; * * * she read Aunt Katy a lecture which she never forgot." (p. 56.) "I learned after my mother's death, that she could read, and that she was the *only* one of all the slaves and colored people in Tuckahoe who enjoyed that advantage. How she acquired this knowledge, I know not, for Tuckahoe is the last place in the world where she would be apt to find facilities for learning." (p. 57.) "There is, in *Prichard's Natural History of Man*, the head of a figure—on page 157—the features of which so resemble those of my mother, that I often recur to it with something of the feeling which I suppose others experience when looking upon the pictures of dear departed ones." (p. 52.)

The head alluded to is copied from the statue of Ramses the Great, an Egyptian king of the nineteenth dynasty. The authors of the *Types of Mankind* give a side view of the same on page 148, remarking that the profile, "like Napoleon's, is superbly European!" The nearness of its resemblance to Mr. Douglass' mother rests upon the evidence of his memory, and judging from his almost marvelous feats of recollection of forms and outlines recorded in this book, this testimony may be admitted.

These facts show that for his energy, perseverance, eloquence, invective, sagacity, and wide sympathy, he is indebted to his Negro blood. The very marvel of his style would seem to be a development of that other marvel—how his mother learned to read. The versatility of talent which he wields, in common with Dumas, Ira Aldridge, and Miss Greenfield, would seem to be the result of the grafting of the Anglo-Saxon on good, original, Negro stock. If the friends of "Caucasus" choose to claim, for that region, what remains after this analysis—to wit: combination—they are welcome to it. They will forgive me for reminding them that the term "Caucasian" is dropped by recent writers on Ethnology; for the people about Mount Caucasus, are, and have ever been, Mongols. The great "white race" now seek paternity, according to Dr. Pickering, in Arabia—"Arida Nutrix" of the best breed of horses &c. Keep on, gentlemen; you will find yourselves in Africa, by-and-by. The Egyptians, like the Americans, were a *mixed race*, with some Negro blood circling around the throne, as well as in the mud hovels.

This is the proper place to remark of our author, that the same strong selfhood, which led him to measure strength with Mr. Covey, and to wrench himself from the embrace of the Garrisonians, and which has borne him through many resistances to the personal indignities offered him as a colored man, sometimes becomes a hyper-sensitiveness to such assaults as men of his mark will meet with, on paper. Keen and unscrupulous opponents have sought, and not unsuccessfully, to pierce him in this direction; for well they know, that if assailed, he will smite back.

It is not without a feeling of pride, dear reader, that I present you with this book. The son of a self-emancipated bond-woman, I feel joy in introducing to you my brother, who has rent his own bonds, and who, in his every relation—as a public man, as a husband and as a father—is such as does honor to the land which gave him birth. I shall place this book in the hands of the only child spared me, bidding him to strive and emulate its noble example. You may do likewise. It is an American book, for Americans, in the fullest sense of the idea. It shows that the worst of our institutions, in its worst aspect, cannot keep down energy, truthfulness, and earnest struggle for the right. It proves the justice and practicability of Immediate Emancipation. It shows that any man in our land, "no matter in what battle his liberty may have been cloven down, * * * no matter what complexion an Indian or an African sun may have burned upon him," not only may "stand forth redeemed and disenthralled," but may also stand up a candidate for the highest suffrage of a great people—the tribute of their honest, hearty admiration. Reader, *Vale!*

New York; May 23, 1855. JAMES M'CUNE SMITH

NOTES

1. Letter, Introduction to *Life of Frederick Douglass*, Boston, 1841. [Smith's note]
2. One of these ladies, impelled by the same noble spirit which carried Miss Nightingale to Scutari, has devoted her time, her untiring energies, to a great extent her means, and her high literary abilities, to the advancement and support of Frederick Douglass' Paper, the only organ of the downtrodden, edited and published by one of themselves, in the United States. [Smith's note]
3. Mr. Stephen Myers, of Albany, deserves mention as one of the most persevering among the colored editorial fraternity. [Smith's note]
4. The German physiologists have even discovered vegetable matter—starch—in the human body. See *Med. Chirurgical Rev.*, Oct., 1854, 339. [Smith's note]
5. Mr. Wm. H. Topp, of Albany. [Smith's note]

James McCune Smith, "Introduction," in *My Bondage and My Freedom*, by Frederick Douglass (New York: Miller, Orton & Mulligan, 1855), xvii–xxxi.

[Frederick Douglass, Religion, and Politics] (1870)

ISAIAH C. WEARS AND FREDERICK DOUGLASS

Douglass's prominence assured him a visible role in any concentrated effort to advance the rights and opportunities of African Americans, and his independence of thought regularly led him to controversial positions. In 1870, Douglass found himself rebuked for expressing his opinion that African Americans should not feel bound to the Republican Party but rather should vote for whomever they pleased. Many prominent African American leaders—who had worked for African American suffrage for many years and who had stayed faithful to the Republican Party, even when the party did not seem particularly faithful to African Americans—were upset by Douglass's comments, and one of them, Isaiah C. Wears, engaged Douglass in a series of public letters on the subject. But what is most interesting about this exchange is how prominently Douglass's views on religion enter into the debate. The following two articles give a taste of this very public debate and of the response Douglass received through much of his career to his principled rejection of churches, particularly to his objection to conventional religious rhetoric for explaining the social progress won by hard struggle. The Bishop Campbell mentioned by Wears is Jabez Pitt Campbell, eighth bishop of the African Methodist Episcopal Church, whose views tended to be much more conservative than Douglass's.

"Frederick Douglass"

SIR: Again I solicit the medium of your valuable paper, and I hope for the last time, on this subject of discussion. I am not of the opinion that some persons are, that Mr. Douglass desires not to meet me, but I shrewdly suspect that he means, by seeming to decline, to make it appear that he is forced into a discussion, and thereby secure the sympathy, if not the pity, of the community, at the expense of whoever shall be his adversary. In order to keep this wind from his sails, that seem to spread just to catch such breezes, I propose to state some of the history of this affair. He first at Horticultural Hall voluntarily, solitary and alone, arraigned, and without trial condemned not only the whole religious community and all the participants in the religious exercises of the day that we were then celebrating, but the very meeting before which he then stood, and which had just applauded to the echo the following resolutions:

Resolved, That the consummation of this glorious event is another evidence in the history of our nation that the Lord's hand is not shortened, that it cannot save.

Resolved, That He rules the destinies of nations and holds their future in the hollow of His hand, and that to Him in the highest we render due honor, glory, and thanksgiving.

Mr. Douglass, backed up by an "argument," as he said, threw down the gauntlet. Here is where the challenge is given; here is where the three classes of persons were criticized and arraigned: First, those who gave thanks to God for our deliverance; second, those who voted to retain the Bible in the schools; and third, those who denounce colored voters who are mean enough or stupid enough to vote the Democratic ticket under present circumstances. Now, if Mr. Douglass is right in these positions, there are a large number of his friends and admirers who are woefully in the dark on these subjects. And much and all as the matchless eloquence of which he is master, and the great prestige of his name, forbids the hope that I will not be severely handled by him. Nevertheless, I trust that he will not allow his desire to settle old scores with Bishop Campbell interfere in a matter in which he had challenged our community to discuss, long before Bishop Campbell was in any way connected with it. It must be plain to my friend Douglass that such a meeting as he proposes would (for the very reason that he seems to desire it) be fruitful of recrimination and bitterness, while on the other hand our friendliness should insure us against the lugging in of any extraneous and unpleasant matters, thereby allowing our interchange of views to be (to the extent that we might be able to make them) both interesting and instructive. Come, then, my dear friend, get away from behind the Bishop, and let some one to whom you delivered those theories in public, "with an argument," have a crack at them. If you are afraid of soiling your hands or garments with a disciple (as you are disposed to nominate me), let me ask when did you become a bishop, that none but a bishop can be your peer; when did you cease to be the disciple that you announced yourself to be of the Rev. Samuel R. Ward, who had converted you, as you said, to the belief of his political and reformatory doctrines? Mr. Douglass must take care, therefore, that in ignoring disciples he does not ignore himself. It will be noticed that I have forborne to write one word in defense of my views on the three original propositions to be discussed, preferring to wait until we are surrounded by such circumstances as will allow us to correct, on the spot, any misrepresentations made by either party. I am justified in this course by the last letter of Mr. Douglass in which he asks me: "Why will you misrepresent me? What is gained by repeating what I did not say? I did not question the right of Bethel Church to criticize my utterances, I merely exposed the character and value of such criticism." I did not claim the honor of the victory of refuting Mr. Douglass. I rather gave him the credit of doing that neat little thing for himself, which the following quotation from his first letter against the meeting at Bethel Church will show: "I spoke for myself, and for nobody else. It is difficult, therefore, to perceive any special reason why the preachers of Bethel should lead off in the war upon my 'dangerous sentiments.' I am not a member of that church, and never was. Why then should they disclaim my views and denounce me in solemn meeting?" All that I say is that in the same letter in which he announced that years ago he denounced the same Bethel Church, he not being a member thereof, is found a protest against the same church denouncing him. Now, where is the misrepresentation? But, further, as the protest is now before us in quotation, let us call attention to another of its features: "I spoke for myself, and for nobody else." Now, if we are not mistaken, Mr. Douglass was invited there to speak for that meeting and to join in its congratulations. Men have the right to do and say many things when alone, which the presence of company peremptorily forbids. There is not one of the proprieties of life which could not be violated with impunity if this cheap offset of acting for one's self, and for nobody else, is a sufficient excuse, explanation, or justification. However, I shall not say all even of this quotation that might be said, for I really do not desire to damage any one, and especially one whom I yet esteem so highly, and who says in his first letter that he holds "no opinions which he is not ready to abandon when convinced of their unsoundness."

And now let me say to him that if he comes back to Philadelphia, nobly acknowledges his error, he will be received with the same glowing cordiality that met him years ago when he came back to our city, and like a noble specimen of humanity recanted errors that he had propagated, abandoned the impracticable party and persons he had stood with, commenced a new life as a political activist and was qualified thereby to do more, and did do more, in the right direction than could have been done by his pursuing any other course. Now, in conclusion, my dear friend, let me reiterate that you, on the occasion of our celebration, April 26, challenged us (to use your own words) "with an argument." You are now called to defend that argument with all that wonderful power and polish which nature and practice have so lavishly bestowed upon you. But, for my own part, I confess to having grave doubts whether one who has been so long engaged in propagating and defending successfully the right can at all do justice to his great name in defense of error and wrong. Isaiah C. Wears.

Isaiah C. Wears, "Frederick Douglass," *Christian Recorder*, June 25, 1870.

"A Letter by Frederick Douglass"

In a speech delivered at the celebration of the fifteenth amendment, in Philadelphia, Frederick Douglass gave no little offence to some of his colored brethren by remarks which they construed as "dangerous," in that they were not sufficiently respectful of the church. A meeting of those aggrieved was held in Bethel church (colored,) at which condemnatory resolutions were adopted and sent to the newspapers for publication. Mr. Douglass replied to his accusers through the Philadelphia *Press*, and from that reply we copy as follows:

Trials for heresy in our day and country, where liberty of thought and speech are conceded to the humblest member of society, are usually deemed farcical; if not harmless. It was once, indeed, a fearful thing to fall into the hands of the church. History proves that there is no malice and cruelty so bitter and unrelenting as that malice and cruelty which clothes itself in saintly robes, and professes to be "contending for the faith once delivered to the saints." A few centuries ago the weapons of religion against heresy were carnal enough. "Cord and steel," "fire and sword," "halter and rack," were the chosen instruments. Thanks, not to faith, but to the enlightenment of the age and the growth of rational ideas among men, to differ with the church to-day does not bring torture and physical death. The worst that bigotry can now do is to assail reputation and fill the mouths of the vulgar crowd with meaningless epithets. There is no doubt that religious malice is the same to-day as three hundred years ago. It would bite, sting, and devour now, as then, if it only had the power. It would crush living flesh to-day with the same sanctimonious ferocity as it does reputation. The will to do is manifest; the power only is wanting. The church and the street are about the same in point of authority and in point of excellence. Both are ever on the side of popular wrong, and both are against unpopular right. The condemnations, maledictions, and denunciations of the church, whether Bethel or St. Peter's, to the outside world, have no more significance than the vulgar curses of the crowd. It may be said of Bethel as of other religious bodies, they are "naught but men and women," and no wiser or better than other men and women.

Without consulting the confused, incoherent, illogical, and strangely-worded resolutions, so characteristic of Bethel, by which the attempt is made to degrade me among the colored people, I will here give the substance of what I did say on the evening of the 29th of April, in Horticultural Hall, and which I take to be the very head and front of my offending.

I regarded, received, and treated the deliverance of the colored people of this country from bondage, their elevation to citizenship, and enfranchisement under the Fifteenth Amendment, not as a miracle, nor due to any special interposition of Divine Providence but as resulting from the certain operation of natural causes inherent in the very constitution of human nature. As slavery was created by human selfishness, so slavery was abolished by human justice, wisdom, benevolence. Such was my view, and such is the "dangerous sentiment" to which I gave utterance. Had I come out with some "ram's horn" story, some dream or vision, or presumptuous assertion as to the ways of Divine Providence, about which men speculate forever and settle nothing, I might have escaped the censures of my Bethel brothers, and perhaps passed along for a very pious man. If I had said that God had abolished slavery in answer to the prayers of the American Church and pulpit, a body which has done more to protect slavery and give it respectability than all other influences combined; if I had said that foremost among the instrumentalities which gave liberty to the American bondman were the sermons and prayers of "Big Bethel," a church which closed its doors against abolition in the hour of its extremest need, I should have spoken against fact, but should have received a cheering amen from Bishop Campbell. I, however, professed no knowledge of the agency of prayer in the great revolution which has taken place; but spoke simply of the natural moral forces of human society, and their tendency to the noble, the true, and the good. I spoke only as a reformer, understanding the wisdom of adapting means to ends, and believing, if this sin-cursed earth is ever to be made better, it is to be made so by faithful exertion and wise application of human energies. Moral, not less than physical evils are under the control of man. When anything is to be done in this world, some denizen of this world has got to do it, or it will go undone. We are under inexorable law, unchangeable and eternal, and "whatever a man soweth that shall he reap." The American people violated the law of justice, love, and liberty; and in due time that law, written in the human soul, vindicated itself, through war, blood, and pestilence.

But why could I not join in the loud hallelujahs and thanksgiving on the 26th of April, and thus have escaped the dreadful censures which have since been heaped upon me? I will tell you. Because I would not stultify myself. During the forty years of moral effort to overthrow slavery in this country, that system, with all its hell-black horrors and crimes, found no more secure shelter anywhere than amid the popular religious cant of the day. One honest Abolitionist was a greater terror to slaveholders than whole acres of camp-meeting preachers shouting glory to God.

Years ago, when denouncing the pro-slavery attitude of the church (the Bethel among the rest, for it too was in the South, preaching, "Servants, obey your masters!") it was predicted that the day would come when the churches of this country would claim the honor of abolishing slavery. They already do so. Knowing your time-serving and cowardly subserviency to slavery, and knowing Bethel to be like unto the rest, I could give no countenance to its pretensions. Hence I declare, what I believe the literal truth, that the abolition of slavery is due to natural causes.

Again, if we may venture upon such a question, admit, if we must, that God abolished slavery (and we must concede that He did that important work only as he does all things else) one act of His must be esteemed to be as wise and as beneficial as another. A finite creature has no right to discriminate between the acts of an infinite God. Do not all His acts accord with an infinite purpose? And is not this purpose eternally right? Who shall therefore sit in judgment upon the works of God? Unless we are prepared for this, have we not the same duty to thank God for slavery as for the abolition of slavery? Our divines, North and South, a few years ago, told us that slavery was of Divine appointment. Did "Big Bethel" then thank God for slavery? Did she call upon the slave in his chains to praise the Lord for the bloody lash that tore his quivering flesh? Why not, if God established slavery? If we assume to thank God for one of His acts, we must thank Him for all.

Very evidently, Mr. Editor, my Bethel brethren have opened up a large subject—far too large, I fear, for the limits of your paper, if not for the limits of Bethel intellect and theological learning. Being no theologian myself, I confine my public utterances to things more comprehensible. When a wrong thing has been done, I know that men have done it, and that somebody is to blame for it. I know, too, that when a right thing has been done somebody has done it—somebody to whom praise and blame are of some consequence, and that awarding or withholding it may in some degree affect the conduct of other responsible beings for good. The way is clear to do this, since it is natural, and involves no doubt, darkness, nor contradiction. If I am wrong in this, I shall be very glad to be set right, and will even return thanks to my Bethel brethren for enlightenment. But I warn them that hard names, threats, and denunciations, even though they should drive me outside their ranks and take from me the title of "leader of the colored people"—a title I never assumed and do not claim—will only leave me just where I am.

Frederick Douglass, "A Letter by Frederick Douglass," *National Era*, July 11, 1870.

"Frederick Douglass in the West" (1873)

"M"

Like Abraham Lincoln, to whom he is sometimes compared, Frederick Douglass was a master storyteller, famous for the impressions of slaveholders and others that he would integrate into his lectures. He was probably pleased, too, that many accounts of his stories involved his ability to win over a hostile audience. Such is the case with the following story from the land of Lincoln, where Douglass was invited to speak, where crowds prepared to give him trouble, and where he overcame the trouble to such an extent that his next visit met with a much warmer welcome. But it was not until his third visit that he was able to stay in a hotel during his visit. In its tone and in its accounting for a gradual social progress, this story is representative of many that both anticipated and followed Douglass in his extensive travels.

A WESTERN PROFESSOR, whose personal recollections of Lincoln and the part which Illinois took in the late war, gave us recently an evening of rare entertainment, contributed also some reminiscences of Frederick Douglass which were racy and characteristic. Speaking of Mr. Douglass as an intellectual man the Professor said that with the gravity, dignity, and breadth of mind that would qualify him for a senator, Mr. Douglass combined the finest conversational powers and a marvelous adroitness in handling an audience. Some years before the war when Southern Illinois was bitterly southern in its hostility to the negro, Frederick Douglass was invited to lecture by the College students before their Lyceum. They were not particularly friendly to abolitionists; but they wished to make a good speculation and so invited a lecturer whom they knew would draw well. Not a hotel in town would receive Mr. Douglass, and he became the guest of our Professor. When the hour for his lecture arrived, the clergy and the officials who should introduce Mr. Douglass to the audience and sit with him on the platform were all missing. Mortified at their recreancy our Professor stepped forward and introduced Mr. Douglass, and sat by him during the lecture. The house was a perfect jam, more than half the audience having come for the purpose of getting up a row. In half an hour Douglass had them perfectly in hand, thoroughly fascinated by his eloquence and knowledge of human nature. The more savage the audience, the more he sparkled and rippled and fairly overflowed with wit and good humor. In this lecture he introduced the anecdote of the elder Dumas—who when accosted by a diminutive dandy of a Frenchman with, "Is it true, Monsieur Dumas, that your father was a negro?" replied, "Yes Monsieur, my father was a negro, and my grandfather was an ape! My pedigree begins where yours ends!" There was no row, and the audience went home laughing. The next time that Frederick Douglass came to lecture the hotels were still closed against him and he made his home as before with the Professor. But on his third visit he found the popular feeling changed. The war had purged Illinois of much of its colorphobia and Frederick Douglass found ready admittance to the best hotel in town. In his lecture he slyly alluded to the circumstance that he was now stopping for the first time at one of their hotels—adding, "And a very excellent hotel it is, too." The subject in this lecture was Self-Culture. When nearly through, he said in a serio-comic way that "he had hoped to be able to get through with one lecture without bringing in the everlasting negro—but no—go where he would, and speak on what subject he might, he always had to lug in the negro." As a closing hit he told in his droll style of the Irishman who asked his comrade on his way home from one of his lectures, "And faith! Pat, what did ye think of the nager?" "Nager? did ye say he was a nager?" "Arrah, he's half nager any way." "Be jabers if half a nager can do like that I should like to know what a whole nager could do!"

"M," "Frederick Douglass in the West," *Oneida Circular*, October 13, 1873, 10, 42.

"Frederick Douglass" (1874)

WILLIAM WELLS BROWN

Far removed from his public disagreement with Douglass in 1855 is this admiring sketch from Brown's *The Rising Son; or, The Antecedents and Advancement of the Colored Race.* Perhaps the most ambitious of Brown's many books, *The Rising Son* begins with a memoir of Brown; turns to a number of historical chapters that take the reader through African, Caribbean, and South American history, and from ancient times to the American Civil War; leading finally to a long series of biographical sketches under the title "Representative Men and Women." This series of sketches, or collective biography, was then and remains today a popular and important approach to African American history, particularly in emphasizing the number of black men and women, in the United States and across the world, who have risen to great prominence. Douglass was of course an important member of this gathering of great men and women.

THE CAREER OF THIS distinguished individual whose name heads this sketch, is more widely known than that of any other living colored man. Born and brought up under the institution of slavery, which denied its victims the right of developing those natural powers that adorn the children of men, and distinguish them from the beasts of the forest,—an institution that gave a premium to ignorance, and made intelligence a crime, when the possessor was a negro,—Frederick Douglass is, indeed, the most wonderful man that America has ever produced, white or black.

His days of servitude were like those of his race who were born at the South, differing but little from the old routine of plantation life. Douglass, however, possessed superior natural gifts, which began to show themselves even when a boy, but his history has become too well known for us to dwell on it here. The narrative of his life, published in 1845, gave a new impetus to the black man's literature. All other stories of fugitive slaves faded away before the beautifully-written, highly-descriptive, and thrilling memoir of Frederick Douglass. Other narratives had only brought before the public a few heart-rending scenes connected with the person described. But Mr. Douglass, in his book, brought not only his old master's farm and its occupants before the reader, but the entire country around him, including Baltimore and its shipyard. The manner in which he obtained his education, and especially his learning to write, has been read and re-read by thousands in both hemispheres. His escape from slavery is too well understood to need a recapitulation here.

He took up his residence in New Bedford, where he still continued the assiduous student, mastering the different branches of education which the accursed institution had deprived him of in early life. His advent as a lecturer was a remarkable one. White men and black men had talked against slavery, but none had ever spoken like Frederick Douglass. Throughout the North the newspapers were filled with the sayings of the "eloquent fugitive."

He often traveled with others, but they were all lost sight of in the eagerness to hear Douglass. His traveling companions would sometimes get angry, and would speak first at the meetings; then they would take the last turn; but it was all the same—the fugitive's impression was the one left upon the mind. He made more persons angry, and pleased more, than any other man. He was praised, and he was censured. He made them laugh, he made them weep, and he made them swear. His "Slaveholders' Sermon" was always a trump card. He awakened an interest in the hearts of thousands who before were dead to the slave and his condition. Many kept away from his lectures, fearing lest they should be converted against their will. Young men and women, in those days of pro-slavery hatred, would return to their fathers' roofs filled with admiration for the "runaway slave," and would be rebuked by hearing the old ones grumble out, "You'd better stay at home and study your lessons, and not be running after the nigger meetings."

In 1841, he was induced to accept an agency as a lecturer for the Anti-slavery Society, and at once became one of the most valuable of its advocates. He visited England in 1845. There he was kindly received and heartily welcomed; and after going through the length and breadth of the land, and addressing public meetings out of number on behalf of his countrymen in chains, with a power of eloquence which captivated his auditors, and brought the cause which he pleaded home to their hearts, he returned home, and commenced the publication of the "North Star," a weekly newspaper devoted to the advocacy of the cause of freedom.

Mr. Douglass is tall and well made. His vast and fully-developed forehead shows at once that he is a superior man intellectually. He is polished in his language, and gentlemanly in his manners. His voice is full and sonorous. His attitude is dignified, and his gesticulation is full of noble simplicity. He is a man of lofty reason; natural, and without pretension; always master of himself; brilliant in the art of exposing and abstracting. Few persons can handle a subject, with which they are familiar, better than he. There is a kind of eloquence issuing from the depth of the soul as from a spring, rolling along its copious floods, sweeping all before it, overwhelming by its very force, carrying, upsetting, ingulfing its adversaries, and more dazzling and more thundering than the bolt which leaps from crag to crag. This is the eloquence of Frederick Douglass. One of the best mimics of the age, and possessing great dramatic powers; had he taken up the sock and buskin, instead of becoming a lecturer, he would have made as fine a Coriolanus as ever trod the stage.

As a speaker, Frederick Douglass has had more imitators than almost any other American, save, perhaps, Wendell Phillips. Unlike most great speakers, he is a superior writer also. Some of his articles, in point of ability, will rank with anything ever written for the American press. He has taken lessons from the best of teachers, amid the homeliest realities of life; hence the perpetual freshness of his delineations, which are never over-colored, never strained, never aiming at difficult or impossible effects, but which always read like living transcripts of experience.

Mr. Douglass has obtained a position in the front rank as a lyceum lecturer. His later addresses from manuscripts, however, do not, in our opinion, come up to his extemporaneous efforts.

But Frederick Douglass's abilities as an editor and publisher have done more for the freedom and elevation of his race than all his platform appeals. Previous to the year 1848, the colored people of the United States had no literature. True, the "National Reformer," the "Mirror of Liberty," the "Colored American," "The Mystery," the "Disfranchised American," the "Ram's Horn," and several others of smaller magnitude, had been in existence, had their run, and ceased to live. All of the above journals had done something towards raising the black man's standard, but they were merely the ploughs breaking up the ground and getting the soil ready for the seed-time. Newspapers, magazines, and books published in those days by colored men, were received with great allowance by the whites, who had always regarded the negro as an uneducated, inferior race, and who were considered out of their proper sphere when meddling with literature.

The commencement of the publication of the "North Star" was the beginning of a new era in the black man's literature. Mr. Douglass's well-earned fame gave his paper at once a place with the first journals in the country; and he drew around him a corps of contributors and correspondents from Europe, as well as all parts of America and the West Indies, that made its columns rich with the current news of the world.

While the "North Star" became a welcome visitor to the homes of whites who had never before read a newspaper edited by a colored man, its proprietor became still more popular as a speaker in every State in the Union where abolitionism was tolerated.

"My Bondage and My Freedom," a work published by Mr. Douglass a few years ago, besides giving a fresh impulse to anti-slavery literature, showed upon its pages the untiring industry of the ripe scholar.

Some time during the year 1850, we believe, his journal assumed the name of "Frederick Douglass's Paper." Its purpose and aim was the same, and it remained the representative of the negro till it closed its career, which was not until the abolition of slavery.

Of all his labors, however, we regard Mr. Douglass's efforts as publisher and editor as most useful to his race. For sixteen years, against much opposition, single-handed and alone, he demonstrated the fact that the American colored man was equal to the white in conducting a useful and popular journal.

William Wells Brown, "Frederick Douglass," in *The Rising Son; or, The Antecedents and Advancement of the Colored Race* (Boston: A. G. Brown, 1874), 435–440.

"Occasional Notes" (1877)

Grace Greenwood [Sara Jane Lippincott]

Grace Greenwood, the pseudonym under which Sara Jane Lippincott wrote, was widely known as a poet, a writer of both fiction and nonfiction, a lecturer, an editor, and, as in the example below, a journalist who served as an occasional correspondent for the newspapers and magazines of the day. Over the course of her long and varied career, she worked for the abolitionist newspaper *National Era*, and she was the first woman reporter with the *New York Times*. She was a strong advocate for women's rights and also for the abolition of slavery—and she was famous among antislavery sympathizers for her poem "The Leap from the Long Bridge," which plays a central role in William Wells Brown's 1853 novel *Clotel*, a poem based on an incident that Douglass himself recounted in an 1846 speech that he included in his appendix to *My Bondage and My Freedom*. Here, Greenwood surveys the post–Civil War social landscape, the March 18, 1877, vote by the Senate to confirm his appointment as U.S. marshal for the District of Columbia.

Washington, Monday, March 19, 1877.

At last "all is quiet on the Potomac." Our Democratic friends would perhaps put the gratifying announcement in the words used by the French writer in proclaiming the downfall of Poland, "Order reigns in Warsaw." It is unspeakably dull here after the roar of much speaking. We hardly know what to do with ourselves. The salt of life hath lost its savor. Last week we had a supplementary excitement over the news of the President's intention to bestow on Frederick Douglass the Marshal's truncheon. One would have thought that the "Black Douglass" had come again. If the appointment was a sop to the Cerberus of Radicalism, it roused scarcely less formidable animals—the surly mastiff of conservatism, the "dog Diogenes" of Democracy, rough and ready, and always barking at the enemy around the corner, and the "mongrel grim" of Liberal Republicanism. Then there were the bitter society dogs, "Tray, Blanche, and Sweetheart," that yelped themselves hoarse and fell into spasms of color-phobia. The choice of Mr. Hayes, and the confirmation by the Senate, were mostly protested and intrigued against by fastidious gentlemen and ladies of the old school of politics, prejudices, and proprieties, and by office-seekers and hangers-on of no school at all. It was not denied that Mr. Douglass was a good citizen, that he was esteemed in the community to a reasonable degree, and owned property to a respectable amount—being a colored man—that he had faithfully served the Republican Party; and yet, as soon as he was brought forward for a position of honor and emolument there was a sudden eruption of angry hostility—a "cutaneous eruption," for it is idle to say that the real objection is more than skin-deep. The chief element of fitness he lacks is the Caucasian element. If he had been a white man, even by complaisance, like, for instance, Senators Hamlin and Logan, his ability to perform the duties of his office would never have been questioned, and the mighty and mystic nature of those duties would hardly have been discovered. I have been amused by the tributes to the head and heart of Mr. Douglass from certain Washington journalists and memorialists, disinterested friends, who would have dissuaded him, for his own sweet sake, from a rash attempt to climb to such a dizzy height of power and responsibility. They all generously acknowledged his talent as an orator and his possession of some scattering literary culture, but they denied him all executive ability. Now, I hold that the man who took himself out of slavery in the watchful latter years of the jealous old institution, who escaped from master, overseer, marshals, and bloodhounds by the help alone of the polar star and his own good legs, and who, in the compromising North, kept himself out of the clutches of the active and zealous United States Commissioner and his posse of slave-catchers, and who asserted his manhood in the face of great constitutional lawyers and doctors of divinity, has shown will and courage enough to command a man-of-war or conduct a campaign, and sufficient executive ability to manage a Marshalship—with the aid of a decent deputy. One journal says: "Mr. Douglass is as honest and guileless as a child, but he has no more knowledge of business than a child." What are the facts? Frederick Douglass began the world with nothing—not even himself. Escaped from bondage, he soon realized a little income from what nature meant to be his very self—his mind, his soul, his impassioned eloquence, his grand, and, melodious voice, like a mighty wind blowing through a forest of pines. But he was liable at any moment to lose both income and principal, and lived always in peril—slept always the troubled sleep of dread. About a quarter of a century ago he was born into the life of self-ownership—and he is now in the first vigor of his youth, though he seems "declined into the value of years," like the rest of us. He has educated himself without the aid of colleges or sewing-circles; he has educated and supported his family without the help of donation parties; he has conducted journals without subsidies and without disaster; he has lectured with great success, for many years, without resorting to buffoonery or balloonery, without the aid of a grievance or a scandal. In short, he has hewn his own way through "the Forest of Difficulty" by good hard blows, and built his own bridges over "sloughs of discouragement." "Honest" he doubtless is, as honesty goes, in the best regulated political families, nowadays,—but "guileless" I should not call him, in the "child-like and bland" sense. A Pickwickian simplicity is not his strong point. The expression of his peculiar, long eyes, sleepy but wary—Moorish, or Malayan eyes—is shrewd to subtlety. Among other things which men of brains learned in the hard primal school of slavery were craft, reserve, circumvention, and repression. If these valuable acquirements, joined to even an irregular course of finesse, address, adroitness, mental reservation, and moral irresponsibility, pursued in Freedom's High School of politics, will not fit a man for an important Federal office, I don't know what will.

Certain citizens are terrified at the prospect of having the new Marshal as master of the ceremonies of presentation at the White House. Could he be dressed in a gaudy livery and stand at the door of the Blue Room to announce them, it would be all right. Such dainty souls would have been shocked at seeing the great Napoleon present to the Directory the mulatto, Gen. Dumas, as "the Horatius Cocles of the Tyrol." I do not think that Mr. Douglass is ambitious for the honor of introducing the average White House mob to a beleaguered President. He is seldom seen in such places himself—not that he need say:

> Haply, for I am black,
> And have not those soft parts of conversation
> That chamberers have,

for he is a gentleman of almost courtly grace of manner and more than courtly wit, but because he is almost sure to encounter in a crowd that unchristian prejudice that resents the fact that he is a man, and not a chattel, and that envious vulgarity that sees in his genius and culture only opportunities to wound and insult him the more deeply and grossly. One not only sees "Othello's visage in his mind," but his mind in his visage. The face of Frederick Douglass is one of great power and individuality. In youth it expressed a tropical intensity of passion, a fierce love for freedom, a noble rage against oppression, relieved by harmless heat-lightning flashes of wit and humor. Now it has a gentler and sadder look—a something of philosophic patience. He is a man of good sense and just ideas. The hue of his skin does not color his views—the kinks of his hair are not repeated in his brain. The blood of the two races is so mingled in his veins that he cannot be one-sided in his sympathies. He is neither savage in his resentment of old wrongs nor servile in his gratitude for new rights.

Grace Greenwood, "Occasional Notes," *New York Times*, March 24, 1877, 4.

"The Second Marriage of Frederick Douglass" (1884)

FRANCIS J. GRIMKÉ

Douglass's escape from slavery was aided by Anna Murray, who was born free but lived in the South. Following Douglass's escape, Anna moved north, and the couple were soon married, a union of nearly forty-four years that produced five children. Anna died in 1882, and in 1884 Douglass married his former secretary, Helen Pitts, a white woman. The ceremony was performed by the author of this piece, the Reverend Francis J. Grimké, a black Presbyterian minister and advocate for the rights of African Americans. In attendance were Senator Blanche Bruce, one of the first African Americans to serve in the U.S. Senate, and his wife and also the wife and daughter of J. Sella Martin, a pastor who had, like Douglass, risen from slavery. The marriage was opposed by Helen's parents, though they had been abolitionists, and it was criticized by many others as well, both black and white. The couple held firm, though, and were married for the rest of Douglass's life. Grimké's inside view, recalled many years later, indicates how dramatically controversial this interracial union was at the time. Grimké would later be part of the interracial group who founded the National Association for the Advancement of Colored People (NAACP).

IN CONNECTION WITH the last anniversary of Mr. Douglass' birthday, I became reminiscent, and recalled many events, and among them the marriage of Mr. Douglass. While he was Recorder of Deeds, one day, while I was in the neighborhood of his office I thought I would drop in and pay my respects to him. When I entered the room he was seated at his desk eating his lunch, and by his side was a lady seated in conversation with him. In a few minutes she left the room. On seeing me, Mr. Douglass said, "You are just the man that I want to see. I was just thinking about calling on you." To which I said, "Well, what's up?" He said, "I am thinking about getting married, and I want you to perform the ceremony." I said, "I will be delighted to do so."

I then said to him, "and who is the fortunate lady?" There were rumors afloat in the community that he was interested in one of two prominent women of the race, and that one or the other, if he ever got married, would be his choice. I was curious to know which of them. But to my surprise, neither of them was mentioned. He said, "Did you see the lady that was sitting by me when you came into the room?" I said, Yes. "She is the one."

And then he went on to tell me her name, Miss Helen Pitts. He said also that he had known the family for years. The father was a well-to-do farmer in Western New York, and was a staunch abolitionist. He had often been at her father's house; and remembered her well, little dreaming, that in the years to come, she was to be his wife. The time fixed for the wedding was January 24, 1884. Mr. Douglass was sixty years of age, and she was forty-six.

On the evening set for the wedding, two carriages drove up to my door, 1608 R Street, N. W. The bell rang, and Mr. Douglass, Miss Pitts, and Senator and Mrs. B. K. Bruce entered. After bidding them welcome, and chatting for a few minutes, the ceremony was performed. Miss Pitts became Mrs. Douglass.

Senator and Mrs. Bruce were the only parties that were invited to witness the ceremony. Mrs. Grimké, of course, was present, and also Mrs. J. Sella Martin and daughter, Josie, not, however, by invitation, but living with us at the time, were present. The contracting parties left the house, after being warmly congratulated, all radiant and joyful.

That night after we had all retired, there came a violent ring at the door bell. The news had gotten out, and the reporters were in search of the particulars. All I said to them, without coming down to the door, was, "Yes, it is true that Mr. Douglass and Miss Pitts were married by me here this evening."

The next day the papers, of course, were full of it. One of the incidents connected with it, was that shortly afterwards I received a letter from a white southerner denouncing me for having performed the ceremony. He, evidently, thought that I was white, for he said, "Any white minister who would marry a Negro to a white woman ought to be tarred and feathered." I was not, however, tarred and feathered, but lived to spend many pleasant days with Mr. and Mrs. Douglass in their beautiful home at Cedar Hill, Anacostia.

The colored people, generally, did not approve of his marriage to a white woman. They said it was showing contempt for the women of his race; and that he had married only a common, poor white woman. Mr. Douglass was the last man in the world to feel any contempt for the women of his race. He had come in contact with too many splendid women of the race to give ground for any such feeling. Why he decided, in his second marriage, to select a white woman as his helpmate, was a matter which concerned him only. If he wanted to marry a white woman, and she wanted to marry him, it was a matter between them only. It was nobody else's business. The intermarriage of the races may not be a wise thing, in this country, in view of present conditions, but the right to marry if they want to is inherent, God-given. No one may rightfully forbid it.

As to Mr. Douglass's marrying only a common, poor white woman, I want to say, and say emphatically, and, as one who knew Mrs. Douglass well, there is not a word of truth in the statement, which is intended as a slur upon her. That she was poor, in the sense that she had to work as a clerk to earn her living, as the best women of the colored race have to do, as teachers, clerks, stenographers, etc., is true; but that was no dishonor to her. It was to her credit that she was not ashamed to work for her living.

As to his marrying a common, ordinary white woman, I want to say that this is also false. She came from a highly reputable family, a family that respected themselves, and that were respected by all who knew them. Helen Pitts was no common, ordinary white woman. She was educated, a graduate of one of the best colleges in the country, and well read, refined and cultivated, a lady in the best sense of the term. Those who speak of her, as some colored people do, do so because they knew nothing of her personally, had no contact with her.

As to the standing of her family, the fact may also be mentioned, that one of her sisters was a highly valued teacher in the white high school in Washington, D.C., for years, and her brother was a prominent lawyer in the West. I had the pleasure also of meeting her mother who came, some time after the marriage, to Cedar Hill to live with her daughter, where she died. She was a refined and lovely old lady. There was nothing common about her, as there was nothing about her daughter, Mrs. Douglass.

And just here, let me say, had it not been for Helen Pitts, the white woman who has been spurned by so many colored people, Cedar Hill, now the pride of the Negro race and preserved as a perpetual memorial to Frederick Douglass because of what he was as a man, and of the great services which he rendered humanity, would have been lost to the race.

Mr. Douglass by his will left Cedar Hill to Mrs. Douglass. It turned out after his death that the will was defective, not having the requisite number of witnesses in the case of realty. When Mrs. Douglass found out that the will was defective, and that the property was not hers, she called the members of the family together, and suggested to them, that they should all agree to set Cedar Hill apart as a perpetual memorial to their father, and to appoint a board of trustees to whom the property should be deeded to be held as such. But they declined to do it, insisting that it should be left as a part of the estate and sold, and divided among the heirs. This was done. And Mrs. Douglass, determined if possible to save it as a memorial to Mr. Douglass, bought it in. She took what money she had, with what she could borrow on the place and secured money enough to satisfy the claims of the heirs, and other members of the family.

Mrs. Douglass had her heart set on saving to the race the place where Mr. Douglass had lived for some twenty-five years. She saw what it would mean in the coming years to a struggling race to have such a mecca to come to, which would be a constant reminder to them of the great struggle through which they had passed and were still passing, and of the spirit necessary, if ultimately success is to crown their efforts. She saw that Cedar Hill, the home of Douglass, great Douglass, would be a great educational force, a center from which could radiate influences that would keep the race steadily pressing on. She had great ideas as to the significance, the value to the race of such a memorial. It was the saving of it for this purpose, that more than anything else engaged her thought during her last days. It possessed her, she could not throw it off.

I remember, during the last year of her life, when her health was rapidly failing, and when funds were slow in coming in, we talked to her of how difficult it was to raise money for memorials of any kind. We called to her attention the difficulty of raising funds for the completion of the Washington Monument in our city. Though it had back of it some of the most influential people in the country, it remained unfinished for years until Congress was obliged to come to the rescue, and appropriated sufficient money to complete it. We spoke also of the hard struggle there was to complete it. We spoke also of the hard struggle there was to complete the monument to General Grant in New York City. And finally got her to agree, that if ultimately the money could not be raised to lift the mortgage, that the property be sold, and two scholarships be established in some reputable university as memorials to herself and Mr. Douglass. She finally agreed to this arrangement only on the condition that the scholarship should be named for Mr. Douglass only, as she wanted nothing for herself. It was not of herself that she was thinking, but of Mr. Douglass and the colored race only.

We supposed that the matter was settled, and that her will would be drawn to that effect. But as she grew weaker, as the end was approaching, she sent for us, and said, that she had changed her mind; that she had cut out the provision in her will about selling the property and establishing a scholarship. She said, with considerable emphasis, "If the colored people think so little of Mr. Douglass and his great services, as to be unwilling to raise the comparatively small sum to pay off the mortgage, it will be lost as a memorial to Mr. Douglass, but would stand as an everlasting disgrace and reproach to the race."

Among the very last things that she said, as she lay on her dying bed, was: "See to it that you do not allow my plan for Cedar Hill to fail." That was her dying admonition. I can see the look in her eyes now, and hear afresh the touching tones of her voice as she uttered those words. And it is gratifying to be able to say, "It has not failed."

When she died, after living a life of great self-denial for the sake of saving Cedar Hill, there was a mortgage of fifty-five hundred dollars on it. This was afterwards cut down to four thousand. It was at that juncture, that the National Association of Colored Women, meeting in Baltimore, came gloriously to the rescue under the enthusiastic and masterful leadership of Mary B. Talbert, of Buffalo, who was then the president of the organization. In a very short time the money was raised and the mortgage wiped out.

This is the way Cedar Hill came to be saved to the race. It was by the self-sacrificing devotion and tenacity of purpose on the part of a white woman, and the prompt and energetic support on the part of a group of loyal, race-loving women. All honor to them. It is a monument to Mr. Douglass, made possible by the joint effort of this one white woman, and the great National Association of Colored Women in this country.

It should also be said, in making this record, that Mr. Douglass's family had no part in it, took no interest whatever in the movement, but, on the contrary, did everything they could to defeat the project. Mrs. Talbert, under whose leadership the money was raised, told me herself, how everywhere she was hindered through the influence of some member of the family.

I may be permitted to say also before leaving this matter, that, very naturally, I felt complimented in being selected by Mr. Douglass out of all the ministers then living in Washington, and, being comparatively a young man and not quite seven years in the ministry, to officiate on this occasion. Why I was selected, how, in what way I had commended myself to him, I do not know; but all I know is that I was selected. Naturally, as a young man, I felt flattered, and have regarded it ever since, as an honor that I was selected by the greatest man of the race to play this part in his illustrious career. It is thus that I have become linked up with the history of this great man.

Francis J. Grimké, "The Second Marriage of Frederick Douglass," *Journal of Negro History* 19, no. 3 (July 1934): 324–329.

From *Life of Rev. Thomas James, by Himself* (1886)

Thomas James

"Among my first concerns on reaching New Bedford," Douglass remembers in *My Bondage and My Freedom*, "was to become united with the church, for I had never given up, in reality, my religious faith." Having been associated with the Methodist Church during his enslavement, Douglass attended the Methodist church in New Bedford, only to discover that the church practiced racial segregation even for "the sacrament of the Lord's Supper, that most sacred and most solemn of all the ordinances of the christian church." First the white congregants were served, and only afterward did the pastor invite the black congregants to the altar, assuring them that "God is no respecter of persons." "The colored members—poor, slavish souls—went forward," Douglass reports; "I went *out*, and have never been in that church since, although I honestly went there with a view to joining that body."[1] Douglass then turned to the African Methodist Episcopal Zion (AMEZ) Church, and even became a preacher, but finally left that church as well, believing it and all churches implicated in the maintenance of the system of slavery. For this, and for the convictions he expressed throughout his career, he was often accused of rejecting his Christian beliefs, a subject addressed in this piece by the Reverend Thomas James. Like Douglass, James had escaped slavery, after which he became a preacher and a devoted abolitionist. The two men met in New Bedford, the home of James's ministry at the time.

It was at New Bedford that I first saw Fred. Douglass. He was then, so to speak, right out of slavery, but had already begun to talk in public, though not before white people. He had been given authority to act as an exhorter by the church before my coming, and I some time afterwards licensed him to preach. He was then a member of my church. On one occasion, after I had addressed a white audience on the slavery question, I called upon Fred. Douglass, whom I saw among the auditors, to relate his story. He did so, and in a year from that time he was in the lecture field with Parker Pillsbury and other leading abolitionist orators. Not long afterwards a letter was received from him by his fellow church members, in which he said that he had cut loose from the church; he had found that the American church was the bulwark of American slavery.

We did not take the letter to mean that Mr. Douglass had repudiated the Christian religion at the same time that he bade good-by to the churches.

It was soon after this that great excitement arose in New Bedford over the action of Rev. Mr. Jackson, a Baptist minister, who had just returned from a Baltimore clerical convention, which sent a petition to the Maryland Legislature in favor of the passage of a law compelling free negroes to leave the state, under the plea that the free colored men mingling with the slaves incited the latter to insurrection. Rev. Mr. Jackson was a vice-president of that convention and a party to its action. Printed accounts of the proceedings were sent to me, and at a meeting called to express dissent from the course taken by the minister named and his brethren, I introduced a resolution, of which the following is a copy:

"*Resolved*, That the great body of the American clergy, with all their pretensions to sanctity, stand convicted by their deadly hostility to the Anti-Slavery movement, and their support of the slave system, as a brotherhood of thieves, and should be branded as such by all honest Christians."

The tone and tenor of this resolution now carry an air of extravagant injustice, but there was at that time only too much truth in the charge it contains. The resolution was tabled, but it was at the same time decided to publish it, and to invite the ministers of the town to appear at an adjourned meeting and defend their course, if they could. Nearly thirty ministers of New Bedford and vicinity appeared at the next meeting, and with one voice denounced the obnoxious resolution and its author. The result was that a strong prejudice was excited against me, a prejudice that was increased by an event which took place soon afterwards—the whole due to the fact that the respectable and wealthy classes, as well as the lower orders, at that time regarded abolitionists with equal aversion and contempt. The conscience of the North had not yet been fairly awakened to the monstrous wrong of human bondage.

NOTE

1. Frederick Douglass, *My Bondage and My Freedom* (1855), in *Frederick Douglass: Autobiographies*, ed. Henry Louis Gates Jr. (New York: Library of America, 1994), 360–361.

From Thomas James, *Life of Rev. Thomas James, by Himself* (Rochester, NY: Post Express Printing, 1886), 8–9.

“Frederick Douglass in Paris” (1887)

THEODORE STANTON

Douglass and his wife visited Paris in 1887 on a trip that included visits to England, Ireland, Switzerland, Italy, Egypt, and Greece, as well as France. Theodore Stanton was the son of abolitionist parents, and his mother, Elizabeth Cady Stanton, was an important figure in the women's rights movement and a source of support for Douglass and his wife as they dealt with the criticism over their marriage. Like his father, Theodore Stanton was a journalist, at one time the Berlin correspondent for the *New York Tribune*. Stanton would later bring his career to Paris, the site of the following sketch of Douglass and his wife during their travels. Throughout his life, Douglass regularly viewed the character of nations and institutions by considering the character of the individuals he encountered, particularly as revealed by the individuals' responses to him. Here, we see him at a convention in Philadelphia, where he encounters the American statesman, future vice president, and fierce opponent of slavery Henry Wilson, who seems uncomfortable; and General Benjamin Butler, formerly Union army, U.S. congressman, eventually governor of Massachusetts, and an untiring advocate of African American rights. In Paris, Douglass encounters the French abolitionist Victor Schoelcher and Charles Jean Marie Loyson, better known as Père Hyacinthe, a well-known French preacher and theologian.

DURING THE RECENT sojourn of Mr. and Mrs. Frederick Douglass in Paris it was my good fortune to meet the celebrated orator and reformer on many and different occasions, and I propose in this letter to report discreetly some of his sayings and doings.

Mr. Douglass, even amidst the new attractions of an European capital, never seems to forget that he is the champion of an oppressed race. “One of the reasons why I so much like France and the French,” he said to me one day, “is because the negro is not the butt of ridicule here as he is in the United States. There are no minstrel shows in Paris, and at the Louvre and Luxembourg Galleries and elsewhere I find that the public treats the African as an equal fellow-being. The occasional bandana is here considered one of the picturesque features of the boulevards and classed with the becoming headgear of the natty peasant girls from the provinces. No Frenchman ever snickers at the black face that sets off the parti-colored handkerchief." When Mr. Douglass stood in front of Gustave Doré's statue of Alexandre Dumas, on the Place Malesherbes, the artistic qualities of the monument failed to move him. He remembered how this son of a negress had never spoken a word or written a line in defense of his mother's race. "Let us go and see the statue of Lamartine," he exclaimed one afternoon; "he said some fine things." And when we reached the Place Lamartine Mr. Douglass cared but little for the masterly way in which the sculptor has grouped the legs of the chair, dog and man; his mind was dwelling on the fact that the poet-President signed in 1848 the decree that freed all the slaves of the French colonies, and his eyes were attracted by the resemblance of Lamartine's face to that of Lincoln.

Probably his two meetings with M. Victor Schoelcher, the William Lloyd Garrison of France, left a deeper impression on Mr. Douglass' mind than any other event that happened to him while in Paris, for it was Senator Schoelcher's long and indefatigable efforts that finally secured the abolition of negro servitude in the French possessions. I was present when this grand old octogenarian recounted the history of his life work, which seemed to carry Mr. Douglass back to the *ante bellum* struggle in the United States. M. Schoelcher then asked many questions about the anti-slavery conflict in our country, with which he is remarkably well acquainted, and criticized severely Mr. Lincoln's course. Thereupon Mr. Douglass defended Mr. Lincoln, explained to M. Schoelcher the difficult position in which the President was placed, and closed his apology with these words: "Mr. Lincoln was better inside than outside."

Mr. Douglass tells many interesting anecdotes of Lincoln. The following one he very naturally enjoys recounting: During the war Mr. Douglass was paying his respects to the President at the White House, when Governor Buckingham, of Connecticut, was announced. Mr. Lincoln thereupon called out to the servant in his high-pitched tone: "Tell Governor Buckingham to wait; I want to have a good talk with Mr. Douglass." "And we did have a good talk," said Mr. Douglass as he told us the anecdote the other day, "for Mr. Lincoln kept me half an hour longer. This circumstance made an impression on me, for not often in my life have I kept a Governor waiting, and a 'War Governor' at that."

"The delegates to the famous Union Convention held in August, 1866," continued Mr. Douglass, "didn't treat me like Mr. Lincoln. I was sent to that Philadelphia gathering to represent the city of Rochester, but before reaching my destination I was met by a committee that boarded the train and begged me not to enter the convention. They dwelt upon an important election then pending in Indiana, spoke of the conservative delegates to the convention, and expressed fear that the presence of a colored man would give Indiana to the Democrats and send home a certain number of the members. But I declined to return to Rochester, being convinced that the fears of the committee were not well founded, and results proved that I was correct. When we were forming in procession to march to the hall, I noticed that everybody was afraid of me. Even Henry Wilson was reserved. General Butler was almost the only man who gave me a hearty welcome. As the delegates paired off and fell into line, it looked for a moment as though I should have to walk by myself, but it was not the first time that I had stood alone and so I was not troubled on this score. As the band struck up and the volume moved an arm was suddenly locked in mine and I found Theodore Tilton at my side. And I must add that all through the streets of Philadelphia it was Theodore Tilton and his humble companion who awakened the most enthusiasm and cheers."

When Mr. Douglass came to Paris it was but natural, therefore, that he should hunt up his old friend, and the tall forms and silvered hair of Frederick Douglass and Theodore Tilton have, during the past autumn, attracted scarcely less attention on the boulevards of the French capital than their well-known faces did just twenty years ago on the streets of the Quaker City. They have gone together to St. Cloud, and to many of the other interesting spots in and around Paris. "You should have seen our astonished Frederick on the top of Notre Dame," wrote Mr. Tilton to me last November. "Coming unexpectedly into the grotesque presence of the grinning gargoyles! In fact these fantastic figures are the merriest company of imps, demons, goblins and good devils that I have met in this cheeriest of all cities. The true Comédie Francaise is on top of Notre Dame!"

Although Mr. Douglass holds liberal views on religion, he did not confine his church-going while in Paris to visits paid to the outside of his edifices. He was present at a grand mass in Saint Eustache, but felt forced to leave before the end of the ceremony. "The superstition made me sad," he remarked, in extenuation of his conduct. He could, however, sit through

Father Hyacinthe's service Sunday after Sunday, probably because he was held by the fascinating oratory of this wonderful divine. "I think I am Father Hyacinthe's most attentive listener," Mr. Douglass said to me after his first Sabbath in the little chapel in the Rue d'Arras; "and he appears to be of the same mind, for I notice that he keeps his eyes on me throughout most of his sermon. I apprehend his thoughts, although I do not understand his language, which proves that he is a true orator." Father Hyacinthe finally learned who was this rapt worshiper, and invited him to tea. The next morning we were seated in M. Schoelcher's study waiting for the senator, when Mr. Douglass arose, stood behind his chair, and began to develop his views on revealed religion with a clearness of thought and a flow of language that was really remarkable. My only regret was that the audience was so small. "I cannot understand," he said, among other things, "how Father Hyacinthe stopped half way in his religious evolution, and when I see him still going through the service of the Roman Church, I reluctantly ask myself, can it be that he believes in this?" "No, of course he doesn't," interrupted M. Schoelcher, who entered at this point; "it is only a sentiment, just like Victor Hugo's idea of immortality. We were standing one day at his front window discussing this question of a future life," continued M. Schoelcher, who is a confirmed atheist, and was a close friend of the dead poet, "when I said to him: 'Now, what would be the use of saving the soul of that stupid cabman passing there?' 'None, whatever,' answered Victor Hugo; 'it is only such as you that I expect to see in the next world.' I venture to say that Father Hyacinthe holds much the same view, if he were to express what is in the bottom of his heart." "Father Hyacinthe said to me yesterday," interrupted Mr. Douglass, "when I told him that I was coming to see you this morning, 'Well, you are going to meet a man who doesn't believe in heaven himself, but makes other people believe in it.' "

Mr. Douglass delights to revert to the anti-slavery struggle, and his anecdotes of Phillips, Garrison and the other leaders in the abolition movement are very entertaining. We were crossing the Pont St. Michel one afternoon, when Mr. Douglass stopped in the middle and looking down into the Seine, said: "When I came up North from slavery I found the abolitionists declaring the federal constitution to be a covenant with the Evil One. But, as soon as I got my eyes open to the situation, I felt that we could make out a case standing on the constitution. So I differed with them and immediately found that I had got myself into trouble. Mr. Garrison was especially hard on me. If you once agreed with Garrison and then differed with him, your position was a difficult one. But later we became good friends again, and I also had the satisfaction of seeing the abolitionist come round to my way of thinking."

We were passing through the Passage de Choiseul one evening, feasting our eyes on the rare books that abound in the little shops when Mr. Douglass espied a second-hand violin exposed for sale in one of the windows. We entered, he asked the price of the instrument, looked at it carefully, twanged the strings and, as we went out, thanked the merchant for his politeness. "Why, do you know anything about the violin?" I asked of Mr. Douglass. "Certainly," was his reply; "I have a good violin at home and often play on it. I must tell you the first time I ever took up this instrument. It was during my sojourn in London directly after my escape from slavery. I was in very low spirits, and as I was walking the streets of the vast English capital in a most dejected mood, I noticed a violin in a shop window just as I did that one a moment ago. In the former instance, however, I purchased the instrument, returned to my hotel, where I remained four days, shut up in my room, striving to become familiar with my new friend. And when I came forth again, I had played myself in tune."

A few nights after this conversation I met Mr. Douglass at a little musical party where an amateur quartette [*sic*] performed. Having never seen him with a violin under his chin, and remembering what had happened and what was said in the Passage de Choiseul, I hinted that Mr. Douglass be invited to play something. He at first declined, but, being pressed by the company, finally took up the violin and rendered some plaintive Scotch airs with much spirit and feeling. Before we separated, one of the guests struck up the "Marseillaise," and then it was that Mr. Douglass' passion for music displayed itself. He rose from the sofa, made his way to the piano, and joined in this majestic national anthem just as he must have done in the war days when "John Brown" was being sung.

Mr. Douglass left Paris with considerable regret, for he had found here many appreciative friends, both among the English-speaking exotics and the indigenous French. And he had begun to take a strong liking to its people, its customs, its streets and its public monuments. In fact, so deep is this attachment for the French capital that he intends to return here in the spring, when he shall have completed his tour in Egypt, where he now is, and have visited Northern, as he has just done Southern, Italy.

Mr. Douglass has seen Paris in its somber autumnal and winter dress, and now he quite naturally wishes to look upon it in its proverbial summer brightness.

Theodore Stanton, "Frederick Douglass in Paris," *The Open Court, a Quarterly Magazine* 1, no. 6 (April 28, 1887): 151.

“The North Star” (1891)

I. Garland Penn

On March 16, 1827, an editorial in the first issue of *Freedom’s Journal*, the first newspaper owned by and directed to black Americans, announced the central mission of the newspaper—to be the voice of the community and to thereby exercise some influence in the representation of African American character. “We wish to plead our own cause,” the editorial stated; “too long have others spoken for us. Too long has the public been deceived by misrepresentations, in things which concern us dearly, though in the estimation of some mere trifles; for though there are many in society who exercise towards us benevolent feelings; still (with sorrow we confess it) there are others who make it their business to enlarge upon the least trifle, which tends to the discredit of any person of color; and pronounce anathemas and denounce our whole body for the misconduct of this guilty one.”[1] Throughout the nineteenth century, African Americans would echo this complaint and call for the further development of a black press. One of the great champions of that cause was I. Garland Penn, who wrote the first history of African American newspapers and their editors. Penn was himself a newspaperman, but his career was mostly devoted to education and to his service to the Methodist Episcopal Church. In the following piece, one can see his deep admiration for Douglass’s work as editor, even as Penn tries to maintain the dry tones of a historian working to establish a comprehensive record.

THE NORTH STAR was conducted on a much higher plane than any of the preceding publications. Mr. Douglass had, by his eloquent appeals in behalf of the Abolition cause, created a wide-spread sentiment, and he was known as an orator. While much of his time was spent on the rostrum in behalf of Abolition, yet many say his best and most effective work for freedom was as editor, in the publication of *The Star* at Rochester, New York.

Mr. Douglass was what is hard to find in any one man,—a good speaker, as well as an effective, able, and logical writer. There is no man to-day who is a Douglass with the quill and upon the rostrum.

Previous to this publication, Mr. Douglass was not known as a writer; but he was afterward recognized as a great man in more than one sphere.

No writer ever expressed truth in better and more fitting language than did the man who said—"His (Mr. Douglass') boldness and superior journalistic ability won for him a world-wide reputation."

His power as a writer was large, while his ready and vigorous use of the English language was always effective and good.

We clip the following from *The Rising Sun*: "Frederick Douglass' ability as an editor and publisher has done more for the freedom and elevation of his race than all his platform appeals."

The commencement of the publication of *The North Star* was the beginning of a new era in the black-man's literature. Mr. Douglass' great fame gave his paper at once a place among the first journals of the country; and he drew around him a corps of contributors and correspondents from Europe, as well as from all parts of America and the West Indies, that made his columns rich with the current literature of the world.

While *The North Star* became a welcome visitor to the homes of the whites who had never before read a paper edited by an Afro-American, its proprietor became still more popular as a speaker in every state in the Union where Abolitionism was tolerated.

Of all his labors, we regard Mr. Douglass' efforts as publisher and editor the most useful to his race.

For sixteen years, against much opposition, single-handed and alone, he demonstrated the fact that the Afro-American was equal to the white man in conducting a useful and popular journal.

The paper was continued under the title of *The North Star* until, in 1850, its name was changed, and it was afterwards known as "*Frederick Douglass' Paper.*"

But there was only a change in name; for the same principles, the same ability, and fight for Abolition, characterized its every movement.

In the publication and work incident to the paper, Mr. Douglass was assisted by his sons. This accounts, in a great measure, for their love of newspapers at this writing, and their connection, from time to time, with many different journals. *Fred Douglass' Paper* continued to be published until it was able to chronicle the emancipation of the slaves. It was then gathered into the arms of its promoters, having triumphed in the cause for which it so vigorously fought.

NOTE

1. "To Our Patrons," *Freedom's Journal*, March 16, 1827, 1.

I. Garland Penn, "The North Star," in *The Afro-American Press and Its Editors* (Springfield, MA: Willey, 1891), 67–70.

"An Account of the Tuskegee Institute Commencement" (1892)

E. W. Blake

Founded on July 4, 1881, as the Tuskegee Normal School for Colored Teachers, Tuskegee quickly developed into an important educational and political center for African Americans, largely because of the enormous influence of its first principal, Booker T. Washington. Established through the efforts of Lewis Adams, a former slave, and George W. Campbell, a former slaveholder, and built, largely by the students themselves, on the site of a former plantation, Tuskegee was an imposing symbol of African American self-determination. Douglass came to Tuskegee to present this commencement speech—a version of his established "Self-Made Men" address—at a time when African Americans were facing a world characterized by new hope and newly invigorated oppression. In a commencement speech presented at Atlanta University on May 23, 1892, Douglass had briefly commented on the lynching of black men in Memphis before presenting a message of hope and determination to the graduating students. Douglass at this time was an elder statesman, revered for all that he had done but carefully negotiating the increasingly threatening political world of African American leadership.

ON MAY 26TH occurred the Eleventh Annual Commencement of the Tuskegee Normal and Industrial School, at Tuskegee, Alabama. This notable institution does more than send out its annual quota of colored teachers to the field; its very presence is an inspiration and an education to the neighborhood. This is evidenced by the multitudes who assemble to witness its annual Commencement exercises. The sight was a most picturesque one. Early in the morning the visitors began to arrive; in wagons, in carts, in ox-teams, on horse-back, on mule-back and on foot. Gray-headed men and bright-eyed children marched along, eager to see what was being done by the sons and daughters of their people. From miles and miles away they came; and by noon the School grounds were filled almost to overflowing. A moderate estimate places the number of visitors at five thousand. The mule teams and other vehicles lined the road many deep for a quarter of a mile.

After a morning spent in the inspection of classes and in examining products from the School farm and workshops, the vast throng of spectators assembled in the "Pavilion," a rough temporary structure, to listen to the Hon. Frederick Douglass, of Washington, D.C., who delivered the annual address. His subject was "Self-made Men," and he spoke, in spite of his three score and fifteen years, with all the eloquence, spirit and humor of youth. The tenor of the speech, so far as it touched upon race questions, was calm and dispassionate. He urged economy, thrift and common sense, and declared that the Negro had no right to live unless he could live honestly, giving a fair equivalent for everything he received. "Let us alone, and give us a fair chance," said he. "But be sure you *do* give us a fair chance. That's very important."

A graduates' reception in the evening concluded the exercises of the day. The Senior Class this year numbers fifteen; six girls and nine boys. It is safe to say that they will do all in their power to help their people in the line of practical progress, and do what they can to leaven that great mass of ignorance and superstition in which their work will be cast.

E. W. Blake, "An Account of the Tuskegee Institute Commencement," *Southern Workman* 21 (July 1892): 122.

"Frederick Douglass: One of the Most Remarkable of All Living Men—a Nice Tribute" (1893)

[Anonymous]

The critic quoted in the following piece remains unidentified, but this short entry from the March 30, 1893, issue of the Milwaukee *Northwestern Recorder* is a good example of the circulation of stories about Douglass by those who saw him, heard him speak, and read his writings. Less a review than an appreciation of *Life and Times of Frederick Douglass* (which title it gets wrong), the anonymous critic speaks to the presence of the man behind the pages. Along the way, the critic, addressing the lessons of Douglass's life, mentions *Let Him First Be a Man*, a book by William Henry Venable, a respected white educator and poet from Cincinnati.

In reviewing the "Life and Work of Frederick Douglass," the critic for the *Inter-Ocean* has the following to say of the greatest of Afro-Americans:

To say that Frederick Douglass is one of the most remarkable living men is to state the truth mildly. For forty-five years he has been before the American people, and today an old, gray-headed man, full of honor, sums up the events of his life in a volume of 752 pages, and every chapter more profoundly interesting than the best romance. For twenty-three years a slave; then a fugitive, protected by no law, and a member of a hated and despised race, shut out by public opinion from every personal right. Life indeed seems hopeless to such a wanderer, yet Fred Douglass was a man, and he overcame all his besetments, and year by year arose, until to-day he stands as the peer of the best among the Nation's grand men. By nature, and not by the refinements of education, did Douglass reach out for honors. The writer of this knew him more than forty years ago and listened to his impassioned appeals for his down-trodden race; upon one occasion, in 1852, at a meeting in one of the great halls in Philadelphia, Douglass spoke for two hours to an audience which filled every seat and packed the aisles. Ten o'clock came and he stopped amid the cries "Go on! go on!" He stopped and said: "I don't often have a chance to talk to such an audience of friends. You who are standing are certainly wearied. We will take a five-minute recess and allow any to retire." The time was up and he spoke for another hour and a quarter, and not a man or woman left the audience. We mention the incident as illustrating the power of the man who then had but recently purchased his own freedom, and had comparatively begun his education which has fitted him for the high posts of honor to which he has since been called, and to be the counselor and adviser of the wisest statesmen of his time. As a biography none ever written has in it more of inspiration for every young man, whether his skin be white or black. Last week we noticed Dr. Venable's book, "First be a Man," and it was just that maxim that made Frederick Douglass. That motherless boy (slave children were often not honored with a father), driven to the fields of Tuckahoe, and worked from daylight to dark, does not give out any large hope of manhood. But nevertheless the manhood was there, and brutality and persecution and starvation could not obliterate it. The story of slavery he recites to a multitude of younger readers will be a revelation, and will serve to awaken a new interest in this poor, despised race, which for generations has been the unpaid chattels of the white man. That the pictures of slavery are as true as if drawn by a camera none can doubt, and in keeping with the forgiving spirit of the black man—no spirit of revenge crops out in any line. No race so long misused and abused ever so fully demonstrated in their acts the prayers of Christ—"Forgive them, they know not what they do"—as the black race during the late war. Had their places been filled by Italians, or Chinese, or Frenchmen or Englishmen, or even Americans, hundreds of plantations and villages of the South would have witnessed horrible scenes of disorder and bloodshed. It was not because the black man did not understand fully the situation. He did. We note this same spirit of forgiveness in the story of Mr. Douglass. But no brief notice in the space allowed can do justice to the book. Its illustrations are pointed. It is written, as we have observed, in the best spirit, and its elegant literary style is well nigh faultless. The volume, truthful in its history, and covering some of the most eventful periods of history, enriches the best biographical literature, and deserves, as it will doubtless receive, a wide reading.

"Frederick Douglass: One of the Most Remarkable of All Living Men—a Nice Tribute," *Northwestern Recorder*, March 30, 1893, 4.

From *Frederick Douglass the Orator* (1893)

James M. Gregory

In the introduction to James M. Gregory's engaging and instructive study of Douglass, *Frederick Douglass the Orator*, one encounters a great symbolic representation of African American intellectual history. Gregory, a graduate of Howard University, became a professor at his alma mater. The introduction to his book was written by William Sanders Scarborough, a man born in slavery who later in life became the first African American classical scholar and, for many years, the president of Wilberforce University. And at the center of both men's attention is Frederick Douglass, whose own rise from enslavement and subsequent efforts made the lives of the other two men possible. What follows are two chapters from Gregory's book that offer a thoughtful assessment of Douglass as orator and pioneering public intellectual. Gregory places Douglass within a gallery of great American and British orators (including William Johnson Fox of England and Patrick Henry, Henry Clay, and Daniel Webster of the United States), public figures (David Garrick, the eighteenth-century British playwright and actor, and Joseph Jefferson, an American actor), and iconic statesmen, including Benjamin Franklin and Presidents James A. Garfield and Ulysses S. Grant. When Gregory takes the reader to Douglass's house, we encounter a similar but different gallery of great men: Toussaint L'Ouverture, leader of the Haitian Revolution (1791–1804); Joseph Cinqué, leader of the revolt on board the *Amistad* in 1839; John Brown, the white abolitionist who led a raid at Harpers Ferry in 1859 in hopes of initiating a large-scale slave revolt; President Abraham Lincoln; and Florvil Hyppolite, president of Haiti from 1889 to 1896. Douglass, in effect, is the man who bridges the two revolutionary and political heritages in one determined mission.

As Orator and Writer

By whatever standard judged Mr. Douglass will take high rank as orator and writer. It may be truly said of him that he was born an orator; and, though he is a man of superior intellectual faculties, he has not relied on his natural powers alone for success in this his chosen vocation. He is called a self-made man, but few college bred men have been more diligent students of logic, of rhetoric, of politics, of history, and general literature than he. He belongs to that class of orators of which Fox of England and Henry and Clay in our own country are the most illustrious representatives. His style, however, is peculiarly his own.

Cicero says, "The best orator is he that so speaks as to instruct, to delight, and to move the mind of his hearers." Mr. Douglass is a striking example of this definition. Few men equal him in his power over an audience. He possesses wit and pathos, two qualities which characterized Cicero and which, in the opinion of the rhetorician Quintilian, gave the Roman orator great advantage over Demosthenes. Judge Ruffin of Boston, in his introduction to Mr. Douglass' autobiography, says: "Douglass is brimful of humor,—at times of the driest kind; it is of a quaint kind; you can see it coming a long way off in a peculiar twitch of his mouth; it increases and broadens gradually until it becomes irresistible and all-pervading with his audience." The humor of Mr. Douglass is much like that of Mr. Joseph Jefferson, the great actor, who never makes an effort to be funny, but his humor is of the quiet, suppressed type. Like Mr. Jefferson, now he excites those emotions which cause tears, and now he stirs up those which produce laughter. Grief and mirth may be said to reside in adjoining apartments in the same edifice, and the passing from one apartment to the other is not a difficult thing to do.

The biographer of Webster gives the following amusing anecdote to show the simplicity of expressing thought for which that Colossus of American intellect is distinguished in his speeches: "On the arrival of that singular genius, David Crockett, at Washington, he had an opportunity of hearing Mr. Webster. A short time afterwards he met him and abruptly accosted him as follows: 'Is this Mr. Webster?' 'Yes, sir.' 'The great Mr. Webster of Massachusetts?' continued he, with a significant tone. 'I am Mr. Webster of Massachusetts,' was the calm reply. 'Well, sir,' continued the eccentric Crockett, 'I had heard that you were a great man, but I don't think so; I heard your speech and *understood every word you said.*' "

President Lincoln gave this reply to the question asked, to what secret he owed his success in public debate: "I always assume that my audiences are in many things wiser than I am, and I say the most sensible things I can to them. I never found that they did not understand me."

The power of simple statement is one of the chief characteristics of Mr. Douglass' style of speaking, and in this respect he resembles Fox, the great British statesman, who, above all his countrymen, was distinguished on account of plainness, and, as I may express it, homeliness of thought which gave him great power in persuading and moving his audience.

Mr. Douglass' influence in public speaking is due largely to the fact that he touches the hearts of his hearers—that he impresses them with the belief of his sincerity and earnestness. His heart is in what he says. "Clearness, force, and earnestness," says Webster, "are the qualities which produce conviction. True eloquence, indeed, does not consist in speech; it cannot be brought from far; labor and learning may toil for it, but they will toil for it in vain. Words and phrases may be marshaled in every way, but they cannot compass it; it must exist in the man, in the subject, and in the occasion."

There have been those of brilliant minds who have gained some reputation as speakers; they have been successful in pleasing and amusing those they addressed, but their success stopped here. They could not reach the depths of the heart, because their own hearts were not touched. The poet Horace admirably enforces this thought when he says: "If you wish me to weep, you must first yourself be deeply grieved."

But to be fully appreciated, Mr. Douglass must be seen and heard. This was also true of Henry Clay. One could form but a faint conception of his eloquence and grandeur by reading his speeches, and yet, as reported, they were both logical and argumentative. The fire and action of the man could not be transferred to paper. Mr. Douglass in speaking does not make many gestures, but those he uses are natural and spontaneous. His manner is simple and graceful, and there is nothing about his style artificial or declamatory. Much of an orator's success depends upon his delivery. The younger Pitt said that he could not discover where lay his father's eloquence by simply reading his speeches. It is related of Garrick that he was asked by a clergyman why it was that he could produce greater effect by a recital of fiction than the clergy by the presentation of the most important truths. Garrick replied: "Because you speak truths as if they were fictions; we speak fictions as if they were truths."

Mr. Douglass, as an extemporaneous speaker, was much more impressive than he has been since he began to write out his speeches and deliver them from manuscript. He remarked to the writer one day that he thought he had made a mistake in thus writing out his lectures; he imbibed the idea that his extemporaneous speeches would be defective and subject him to criticism. He had by so doing lost much power in delivery. "For," said he,

"I never was a good reader." The first address he wrote out in full was the paper before the Western Reserve College in 1854. Ever since his return from England in 1860 he has steadily followed the habit of writing what he has to say and reading from manuscript. His former style is what we call extemporaneous, but we do not wish to convey the idea that he spoke without preparation. On the contrary, he gave much thought to the topics which he intended to discuss, and then prepared notes under the different divisions of his subject. By not being confined to his manuscript, he caught the inspiration of his audience. This inspiration, so essential to true eloquence in the orator, can never be secured by the essayist, however finished and perfect he may be.

While Mr. Douglass may have lost much of his eloquence in using manuscript, yet some important advantages have resulted from this practice. He was led to investigate more extensively the subjects on which he wrote, and to take more time for preparation; and thus made his speeches more complete. Formerly, many of his best extemporaneous efforts were never fully reported, and consequently much that he said has been lost. His later lectures and speeches have been preserved in manuscript form, and when published together, as they will be one day, will prove a valuable contribution to literature.

Some of his best lectures are The Mission of the War, The Sources of Danger to the Republic, Self-made Men, Recollections of the Anti-slavery Contest, William the Silent, Santo Domingo, The National Capital, Abraham Lincoln, John Brown.

The discourses of Mr. Douglass when reviewed, will bear the test of criticism, and will be found to contain the requisites of a correct and finished style. His language is pure, his words are choice, and in accordance with the best usage. His sentences are constructed in the English idiom, and have the elements of strength because preference is given in their formation to short Anglo-Saxon words, rather than to those derived from Latin and Greek. So carefully is the rule of propriety observed by him that one would think he had thoroughly mastered the principles of grammar and rhetoric under the most competent instructors. From the discrimination he uses in the selection of words to express the idea he wishes to convey, we conclude he must have been for many years a diligent student of the dictionary. His writings are remarkably free from obscurity and affectation, which Macaulay regards as "the two greatest faults in style," and they may, therefore, be taken as models of perspicuity, so essential to one who would become eminent as an essayist. This excellence to which we allude, is due, no doubt, to the fact that the first forms clear and distinct conceptions of the truth he wishes to illustrate, and then making use of simple language to express the ideas arranged in his mind in logical order, writes freely as if under inspiration. Since he has followed the practice of writing his speeches his style has become more argumentative and massive, similar to that of Webster and Burke. In all he says, like these great masters, whom none have surpassed, there is so much beauty of expression, elegance of diction, dignity of thought, and elevation of moral feeling that the most happy and lasting effect is produced upon the mind of the reader.

In the preparation of his speeches and addresses, Mr. Douglass at times requires greater privacy than his library affords, where he is liable to interruption by members of his household and visitors. In order that he may wholly give his attention to the literary work which he has in hand, he retires to his "den," as he calls it, a small, one-room building, situated in the rear of his dwelling, and used by former owners as a storehouse, but now with certain interior alterations made into a cozy study. It is a pleasant retreat in summer, for it is protected from the heat of the sun by trees and vines, and in winter is made comfortable by a glowing fire in the old-fashioned fireplace found within. The study is furnished simply with a lounge, a high desk, and a stool. It is the practice of Mr. Douglass to write standing, when in this room, where he will remain for hours at a time, denying himself to all visitors. While composing, he thinks accurately and correctly, and on this account his composition requires but little correction. His manuscript is always neat, not marred by erasures and alterations. We mention this fact because it proves that correct writing is the result of care exercised by the writer in the beginning, which in time becomes a fixed habit.

His Home.—Personal Traits and Characteristics

The home of Mr. Douglass is at Anacostia, about three miles northeast from the city of Washington. Its situation is extremely beautiful. His house stands upon an elevation called Cedar Hill, which overlooks the Potomac and commands a fine view of the city and surroundings. The house of modest pretensions, commodious withal, is of Southern style of architecture, and, as all such houses are, was constructed with a view to comfort and convenience. You enter the front hall from a veranda extending the entire length of the house in front. From this veranda one has a view of the sunsets, which in this latitude are unparalleled for grandeur and beauty. On either side of the hall is a parlor, and back of the east parlor is a library of well-selected books. This latter is Mr. Douglass' workshop where he prepares those lectures which delight and thrill so many audiences. Adjoining the front hall and west parlor is his dining room, where from time to time he has entertained many distinguished guests. In the front hall hang portraits of Charles Sumner and ex-Senator Blanche K. Bruce. There are also two portraits, one in either parlor, of Mr. Douglass. The first represents him in the early days of his anti-slavery career, the other in more mature life. In the west parlor over the mantel is a beautiful picture in water colors of Othello wooing Desdemona. This picture Mr. Douglass values very highly. On the walls of the library hang portraits of the African Cinque, of Toussaint L'Ouverture, John Brown, Abraham Lincoln, Hyppolite, and other illustrious men. The same simplicity which is characteristic of Mr. Douglass in his manner, in his dress, in his conversation, in his speeches, may be seen in the appointments of his house. All the rooms are tastefully but not extravagantly furnished.

That portion of the ground not reserved for an orchard and a garden is beautifully laid off in walks and drives. In the rear of the house is an extensive level tract which he has converted into a fine croquet ground. Here he may be seen any evening, when the weather permits, playing croquet with his wife and friends from the city. He is extremely fond of the game, and is usually the victor however skillful in play his antagonist may be.

Mr. Douglass is an excellent conversationalist. He expresses himself with correctness, ease, and elegance. He rivals Mr. Lincoln in telling anecdotes.

His stock of humor is an unending source of entertainment. When he has laid aside the restraints of office and public duty, he gives himself up freely to the pleasures and enjoyments of home. The writer remembers one evening when he and other friends spent several hours in social converse with Mr. and Mrs. Douglass. Mr. Douglass seemed to be in one of his happiest moods. The presence of his guests called forth many reminiscences of his past life, and happy remarks of practical wisdom. Referring to the discouragements which young men encounter, he said that a man cannot ordinarily expect to rise to the topmost round of successful achievement by a single bound without taking the intermediate steps. He observed in the time of the California fever that those who took money with them brought back nothing; but those who went empty handed, depending on diligence and economy, returned in possession of wealth. Referring to his own early experience he said that in the first few years of his public life, having then a wife and four children, he received a salary of only three hundred and fifty dollars a year, but managed to lay by a portion of this for future use.

Speaking of the A. M. E. Church *Review* published by Dr. Tanner, of Philadelphia, which he had recently read, he praised it in glowing terms, and said that while it made no pretension to excellence in artistic skill, it nevertheless contained valuable information set forth in well written articles. As the first literary magazine of the colored race, it is most creditable and we have reason to be proud of it. Twenty years ago a like production would have been impossible. He said he was engaged in reading the writings and speeches of Rome's ancient senators and statesmen, referring to his book-strewn table. In his reading he observed one thing in particular—the profundity and incisiveness of their style. Such laconic brevity is scarcely observable in the utterances of modern statesmanship. The Roman senator cracks the nut and gives you the kernel. We have not made much progress in these matters since that time. In answer to the suggestion as to the desirableness of an authentic publication of his lectures and speeches, he said it was his hope at some time to arrange them for publication, along with a collection of his letters. He wished something to be left as a memorial of his work, humble though it was. It might, in some way, help to weaken the force of the criticism some one has made that, "If the negro were sunk in the depth of the sea, all that the negro has done and the negro himself would be forgotten within twenty years."

During their visit, the company were served with tea, Mrs. Douglass presiding. The members of the party were deeply impressed with the generous hospitality of the host, and realized that they were in the presence of a man of varied experience, having a mind stored with useful knowledge; and the success of whose life illustrates the difference between mere knowledge and practical wisdom. On the departure of the company Mr. and Mrs. Douglass followed them to the door, and all were delighted with the charming beauty of the view of Washington and the Potomac illumined with the glory of the setting sun.

He is fond of music and often plays the violin accompanied on the piano by Mrs. Douglass. It is related that in earlier days while an exile in Scotland, passing along the street in a despondent mood he saw a violin hanging out at a store door, and going in bought it. He then went home, shut himself up, played for three days until he was in tune himself and again went out into the world—a cheerful man.

Mr. Douglass is of a bright and buoyant disposition at home as well as in public. An indication of his vivacity is shown in the fact that when confined in the Easton jail, with liability of being sold to New Orleans, he unraveled his socks and made a ball with which he played.

He is a man of temperate habits and strict in his business engagements: In Washington, as elsewhere, his word is his bond. He has accumulated a competency, the result of industry and economy. He has made it a principle of his life to save something out of his earnings, small though those earnings be. With all his habits of economy he has been a generous man, giving freely to every worthy cause. Numerous instances could be mentioned which would show how Mr. Douglass' purse has always been open to relieve misery and distress. He is often sought by persons, some seeking pecuniary aid and others employment. He seems always to have a due regard for the feelings and rights of others, even in the smallest matters. It is natural for him to be polite; it is not that artificial politeness which comes from studying books of etiquette, but it springs from his soul.

He is frank and fearless in expressing his views even though they bring him into sharp antagonism with those who hold different opinions. This was evidenced by his antagonizing his lifelong friends, the Garrisonians, upon the interpretation of the constitution, they holding that the constitution was pro-slavery in character and he that it was anti-slavery. Vials of wrath, so to speak, were poured out upon his head by the Garrisonian abolitionists when he proclaimed his views to the country, but Mr. Douglass was not driven from his position on that question. A man of ordinary courage would have been utterly overwhelmed by the great force of the opposition. Through a long and eventful life, he has never been known to deny his principles through fear or timidity or for the sake of temporary advantage. No one is ever long in doubt on which side of any important question he stands. Having satisfied himself which side is the *right* side, his course is neither vacillating nor uncertain.

He is a man of great force of will, and is very much like Mr. Garrison in this respect, who, it will be remembered, placed at the head of the *Liberator*, when he first began to publish it, these words, "I am in earnest, I will not equivocate, I will not excuse, I will not retreat a single inch—I will be heard." The success of the anti-slavery cause required that men of such force of character and determination should be its champions. Without them there could have been no success.

Mr. Douglass is one of the best examples the country affords of what a man of character and ability may become by energy and industry. Franklin, Henry Clay, Webster, Lincoln, Wilson, Garfield, and Grant are given as illustrations of the developing influences of our country. These men all rose from poverty and obscurity to high places in the government, but Mr. Douglass sprang from depths which these men never knew in their experience. With them it was possible to obtain the highest honor in the gift of the people, and three of the men named did reach that exalted position. How different it was with Mr. Douglass, the slave, the fugitive, the exile. Twice was he compelled to flee his native land and seek shelter and safety under the flag of a foreign power. Not till the war ended was his freedom actually made secure. Even at this late day color stands as a bar against social recognition and political preferment in this country. If Mr. Douglass had enjoyed the same advantages enjoyed by his white contemporaries, and if the same opportunities for advancement had been open to him, what public position in this country might he not have filled, not even excluding the presidency? Had he like Clay and Webster been brought up in the profession of the law and afterwards transferred to the United States Senate, he would have become the peer of any in that body; for he has powers of mind which eminently fit him to grapple with the great questions that engage the attention of statesmen.

His influence on the colored race has been greater than that of any other man. He is endeared to them on account of his early struggles. They point with pride to his achievements and success; they reverence him because of his sterling qualities and spotless character. They recognize him as their most prominent leader, whose opinion they have always respected and whose advice they have in most cases followed. But his influence is not limited to the colored race. He will always be an inspiration to struggling youth who are ambitious to win distinction, and he will always be regarded as a model of true eloquence. History, because of his excellence and achievements, will accord him a place in the galaxy of worthies whose fame is confined to no particular race or country. His is

> One of the few, the immortal names,
> That were not born to die.

From James M. Gregory, chapters 8 and 13 of *Frederick Douglass the Orator. Containing an Account of His Life; His Eminent Public Services; His Brilliant Career as Orator; Selections from His Speeches and Writings* (Springfield, MA: Willey, 1893), 89–96, 207–215.

"Frederick Douglass's Character and Career" (1895)

J. E. RANKIN

Frederick Douglass died on February 20, 1895, and the following remarks were presented in Washington, D.C., on February 25, the day of Douglass's funeral. Rankin, the white president of Howard University, was a minister and social reformer who is today best remembered for his service to Howard and for the hymns "God Be with You 'Til We Meet Again" and "Tell It to Jesus." Rankin and Douglass had regularly corresponded in life, and one can only wonder how Douglass might have responded to his friend's deeply religious interpretation of his enslavement and post-emancipation career. At this point in Douglass's life, one can hardly be surprised to encounter him in the company of a number of celebrities and statesmen—in this case, Lord Brougham and Daniel O'Connell, whom we encountered earlier; and other notable British statesmen, Lord John Russell, Richard Cobden, John Bright, and Benjamin Disraeli.

HE SENT A MAN before them. He was sold for a servant. His feet they hurt with fetters. He was laid in chains of iron. Until the time that His word came to pass, the word of the Lord tried him. Psalm cv. 17–19.

There is but one parallel to the life of Frederick Douglass, and this is found in the Bible; the Bible, which surpasses all other literature. There is no narrative which in natural pathos and eloquence so reminds me of the history of the favorite son of Jacob as the story of Frederick Douglass. And I find God in one as much as the other. And I think, of all the men in his generation, so momentous of great events, so influential upon the future of humanity, no man is more to be congratulated—could human congratulations reach him—than this man who now sleeps in death's marble before us. God made him great; yes, but God also gave him a great opportunity. And that opportunity began when he was born a slave.

I feel the pathos of it, in every fiber of my being, when this boy, without father, without mother, save as once or twice in his memory she walked twenty-four miles, between sunset and sunrise, to give her son a few clandestine kisses—yes, without beginning of days, for Mr. Douglass never knew the day of his birth, was in that prison-house of bondage, slowly emerging to consciousness of himself and to consciousness of his surroundings. But that was his schooling for the years to come. It was the only way in which he could become a swift witness against the great wrong which was crushing the bodies and souls of millions. It was the secrets of that prison-house of despair which the world needed to know. And God had given him the tongue of the eloquent to tell them. Fascinating as is the masterpiece of Harriet Beecher Stowe, beautiful and touching as are the scenes depicted, dramatic as are the movements, powerful as are the delineations, we all know it is fiction. It is founded on fact. But this narrative is fact.

And I say, that just as God sent Joseph down into Egypt preparatory to great events which were to follow; to save much people alive; just as His word tried him in the house of Potiphar and in the dungeons of Egypt, so it was with the boy, the young man Douglass. When he was praying there with Uncle Lawson, God was girding him for that day when he was to go from town to town, from state to state, a flaming herald of righteousness; to cross oceans, to gain admission to palaces, lifting up that great clarion voice, which no one who ever heard can forget or forget its burden. So that I say Frederick Douglass was fortunate in the misfortune of his birth. If he had not been born of a slave-mother, one potent factor in the great work put upon the men and women of his generation would have been wanting. God wanted a witness. After Dante wrote his "Inferno," the people of Florence said as he walked their streets, "There goes the man who has been in hell!" What the cause of freedom wanted was a man who had been in hell; in the hell of human slavery, an eyewitness of the dark possibilities and experiences of the system into which he was born; who had felt the iron enter his own soul; who knew what it was to be compelled to yearn in vain for mother-love; to fight his way inch by inch, into the simplest rudiments of human speech, of human knowledge; into any of the prerogatives of manhood.

The Beginning of the End

I do not at all underrate the work done by those magnificent champions of freedom, who took this young man at twenty-five into the charmed coterie of their fearless eloquence; who gave him the baptism of their approval; who laid their hands upon his head, William Lloyd Garrison, Wendell Phillips and their associates. But they needed him as much as he needed them. After their cool and eloquent logic, after their studied irony and invective, which, mighty as it was, was wanting in the tremolo of the voice of one that has suffered, of one whose very modulations signified more than their words; when this man arose, as one rises from the dead, as the ghost of one, the crown and scepter of whose manhood has been stolen away, while he goes from land to land proclaiming the wrong and asking for justice, then the climax was reached. This man made the work of such men as Garrison and Phillips and Sumner and even Lincoln possible. I do not wish to use the language of exaggeration. It is not fitting the occasion. It is not in keeping with the dignified manner and methods of the man whom we commemorate, or the providential movement of which he was so long a part. But I believe that the birth of Frederick Douglass into slavery was the beginning of the end; and that this was just as needful to his anti-slavery associates as to himself. God planted a germ there, which was to burst the cruel system apart. It was as though He said, "Go to, now, ye wise men of the Great Republic, ye Websters and Clays. I will put this Samson of freedom in your temple of Dagon, and his tawny arms shall yet tumble its columns about the ears of the worshipers. I will put the ark of my covenant in the soul of this man, and the time shall come when your idol-god shall be toppled over upon his nose in his presence."

I think Frederick Douglass is to be congratulated on the kind of tuition that came to him; no, that God had provided for him, through these anti-slavery associates. They were regarded as the offscouring of the earth, and yet many of them received their culture in the choicest New England schools and they sprang from the noblest New England stock. And when he went abroad, it was his privilege to hear such men as Cobden and Bright and Disraeli and O'Connell and Lord John Russell and Lord Brougham. These men Mr. Douglass studied, admired, analyzed. His more elaborate addresses, too, show the influence of that first and greatest of New England orators—Daniel Webster. But even beyond the great American orator, whose model orations are in all our school-books, was Mr. Douglass in the quality of fervor and fire.

Ah! that was a day when the runaway slave heard the great statesman at Bunker Hill. And he once told me that he owed a great debt to the poems of Whittier. To converse with Mr. Douglass, to hear him in public, one who knew his humble origin and limited opportunities, might well ask, "How knoweth this man letters?" But, in the art of which he himself had such mastery, he had the best teachers and examples the Anglo-Saxon schools could afford, while not one of the great men mentioned had such a theme as his. How carefully he improved his intercourse with such men, his observation of them, one has only to read his life to discover. Howard University, I believe, gave this man the degree of doctor of laws, and there were some laws that no man knew better how to doctor than he. But there was not an official of the University who could reach high enough to put a wreath on his brow. It had to be done from above, by the winged genius of the University.

Contrasts of His Life

Then, in the third place, Mr. Douglass is to be congratulated on the wonderful contrasts and antitheses of his life. If we go on in the Psalm from which I have quoted, we read: "The king sent and loosed him; even the ruler of the people, and let him go free; he made him lord of his house and ruler of all his substance; to bind his princes at his pleasure and teach his senators wisdom." The King that loosed this man was the King of Kings, and not Pharaoh, even as of old, till after the angel of war had smitten the first-born of the land. It was as though God said, "I shall need this man born of a slave-woman, ay, this woman's seed, to set his heel on the serpent's head. I shall need him among my great princes in the regeneration, when my heroes have come up from their great battles, when Gog and Magog drew apart from their last encounter." If we except this prime minister of Pharaoh, perhaps no man who ever lived ever had such extremes and vicissitudes of experience as Mr. Douglass. There is probably no civilized nation on earth that has not been made acquainted with this wonderful story.

Perhaps he never saw a prouder day than when, as United States Marshal—an official once so offensive to the sensibilities of a few people, because of his participation in the arrest and return of fugitive slaves—he accompanied President-elect Garfield from the Senate chamber to the platform of the portico, where he took the oath of office and delivered his inaugural address. This was a man who ran away from the neighboring state of Maryland, whose territory was once the ground on which the Capitol stands; who had twice exiled himself from his native land to escape arrest, first as a fugitive slave, and then as in complicity with the John Brown conspiracy; whose friends had actually paid the sum of $100—I have this morning read the bill of sale again—to purchase his freedom from bondage, and who now acted as the representative of the United States in the moment of transition from the term of one President to that of another.

And if we turn from his public to his private career, what more striking and unusual scene, save, perhaps, Joseph's forgiveness to his brethren, ever was introduced into the lot of man than his visit to his old and dying master, so many years after his escape from bondage? Was there ever an experience more pathetic? Was there ever forgiveness more generous? We pray, "Forgive us our debts as we forgive our debtors." This our great Teacher has taught us. The spirit of forgiveness is the basis on which we stand before God, who has so much to forgive in us; is the spirit which fits us for the kingdom of heaven.

Mr. Douglass' Eloquence

I come now to the last ground on which I think Mr. Douglass should be congratulated. By many it would be thought of first. Mr. Douglass was fortunate in his endowments as an orator. Eloquence is a virtue. This the Germans have taught us. That is, there must be virtuous character, genuine truth and manliness behind all eloquent speech. A crafty, deceitful, dishonest, dishonorable man cannot be an eloquent one. He can deceive only the groundlings. His eloquence is all a sham and mockery. Mr. Douglass had a commanding figure, a commanding presence, a commanding voice. In all these there is leadership. There was something more there. When he rose to his feet, when an audience saw that dignified and serious but kindly face, that venerable and seer-like aspect; when they heard that voice, it arrested attention and hushed everyone to silence and expectation. Utterance with him was the considerable and judicious gathering of great forces; like the gathering of a storm in the sky; now and then a distant mutter, then the marshaling of the winds and the sweeping of the clouds across the horizon; then the descending thunderbolt and the lightning flash; then the rolling back of the clouds as a curtain, the return of the sunshine and the song of birds and the laughter of children. Mr. Douglass' voice was of unequaled depth and volume and power. And back of all this was a great-hearted, generous, forgiving-natured soul, who feared not the face of man and believed in the living God.

Mr. Douglass never lost his sense of the proportion of things; never was unduly elated by his successes and achievements. He was uncompromising in his opinions, and yet a patient waiter. He had a sagacious, a long patience for the result.

When a great man is gone, for the last time we begin to see the space he filled, as though a mountain peak had been removed from our moral horizon. It will take a long time to measure the conservative and yet progressive influence of this great man. For he was great, and great in the period of great men. He was greater than his eloquent speech; he was greater than his life. If you write the history of the anti-slavery movement, he was great there; it centered in him and around him; of the Civil War and the reconstruction period, he was a man to whom presidents and senators, to whom millions of enfranchised people looked for counsel. He taught the senators wisdom. Shakespeare makes Marc Antony say over the form of the dead Caesar: "My heart is in the coffin there with Caesar." I know what that means to-day. Mr. Douglass had qualities that won the heart. No younger man could know him without having for him a reverence that was filial. And wise will it be for the young men, whom he tenderly addressed as a father, if they heed his counsels, read his life, study his example, live as he lived.

Douglass, Lincoln and Grant

Mr. Douglass was a consistent man. He had no erratic moods or vagaries. There were men, great men, who drew away from Abraham Lincoln because carrying on his shoulders, like Atlas, this great American world, he seemed to move so slow. They were lighter-loaded and could dance and cut capers along such a rugged pathway. But not Frederick Douglass. He saw where God was walking on that field, and believed that Mr. Lincoln was walking with God. There were men, great men, who broke with President Grant. But not Frederick Douglass. He believed in the man who had fought the nation's battles through. And of Santo Domingo he said: "Since liberty and equality have become the law of the land, I am for extending our dominion whenever and wherever such extension can peaceably and honorably be accomplished." A wiser saying to-day than when it was uttered. If any man had a right to criticize and break down, if he could, the public policy of our great leaders and executives, on the subject of human freedom, it was Mr. Douglass. But he had not so learned the duty of a citizen; nor the art of statesmanship. It was his to suggest and counsel and then patiently wait. Lord Beaconsfield has said, "Everything comes, if a man will only wait," and Philip II., "Time and I against any two"; and Mr. Douglass has often quoted, if he did not originate, that greater proverb, "One with God is always a majority." In that majority he was contented. For he knew that in His own time God would show himself, moving on His great affairs. It was this that made all his methods noble. There was no meanness in this man. He did not conspire and intrigue and backbite and undermine. He was no such mole as that. He was always above ground, always acting in the open day. He did not poison his weapons and give the thrust of the assassin. But, standing in God's light, he fought what he believed to be God's battles against principalities and powers, with the weapons of a man. He gave hard blows, but he never hit below the belt.

His Death

In his autobiography, Mr. Douglass describes the anxiety with which millions watched the breaking of that day when President Lincoln had promised to let loose the thunderbolts of war against the system of slavery, and give the watchword, "Freedom for all!" to our gallant soldiers in blue, to see if it would be done. True as the movement of the stars, the mandate came. No such watching was his, when a few days since he was delivered from the entanglements and infirmities of this mortal prison-house, somewhat shattered in its walls by seventy-seven years' occupancy, where we all await the emancipation act of our great Captain, of Him who was broken through the bars of death, and brought light and immortality to light in the Gospel. The summons came as came the horsemen and chariots of Israel to Elijah, straight from the excellent glory, and before we could say, "My Father," the splendid retinue of heaven had returned with their delivered guest, leaving only dust and ashes. It was natural for Mr. Douglass to come back here to the bosom of the Methodist Church. Here he sat in that draped pew, as said Professor Shedd, after resigning his chair, "getting ready to die"; saying to his old mother-church, "that all the past was forgiven"; repeating the words of Ruth to her mother, Naomi, "Thy people shall be my people, and thy God my God," hiding himself anew, as he loved to sing, in the cleft of the rock that was smitten on Calvary. She long ago had made him a preacher before he became an orator. This was the expectation and prayer of Uncle Lawson, while he was yet a slave. The secret of the Lord is with them that fear Him. So that here, again, like a vessel that has made many a rough voyage, but now comes back to final anchorage, Mr. Douglass each Lord's Day sat with his dearly cherished companion, in this sanctuary of God. Call this man irreligious, an infidel? This man, whose foundations of truth and righteousness were established in God! This man, with whom one with the form of the Son of Man had so often walked in a hotter than a Nebuchadnezzar furnace! This man, with the spirit of God's kingdom, as the angels sang it, deep within him! Nay, call him father, brother, husband, friend! Have we forgotten the words of our own great Liberator, in the synagogue of Nazareth, "The spirit of the Lord God is upon me, because He hath sent me to preach deliverance to the captive?" Have we forgotten the epithets that were thick in the air about the Master? "Beelzebub! This man casteth out devils through the prince of the devils!" Gentle with a womanly gentleness, wise with a wisdom beyond that of the universities, patient, long-suffering and kind, always ready to forgive, always ready with the word of cheer; this was the man we mourn! Lips from which have fallen such golden eloquence, eyes from which have flashed such radiance, heart with such great throbs of sympathy for all God's downtrodden ones, hands which were always open and outstretched toward the wretched; these were his, these belonged to that man whom we call Frederick Douglass. Through the changes of the greatest and most eventful period in American history, not once did he lose his footing; not once did he forfeit the companionship of our greatest; ay, not once did he lose his hold upon God!

Here is thy greatest son, my Maryland! Rise up to greet him, as he passes through. Seventy-seven years ago thou gavest him the birth of the bondman. But thou has lost him. The nation has claimed him; the wide world. Thou great Virginia Planter, sleeping by the Potomac, let the river bear thee these tidings: "What thou didst with thy bondmen, we have done with ours. They are free." And thou martyr-soul, beneath God's throne, to whom was given to speak the fiat of freedom to millions of men and women, whose lot was like this man's; who were thus "cabined, cribbed and confined," though God's image was in them, take this martyr-spirit to thy celestial companionship. And thou, the great Empire State, who gavest to this man a home, when he had not where to lay his head, and by whose great river sleeps the dust of freedom's great captain, take to thy central heart, and bear on thy bosom, as the ages sweep more and more into the sunlight of the Man Christ Jesus, the battle-scarred form of Frederick Douglass. Sleep, freedom's great herald, in the land of the free-born. Thine exile is over. Thou art dowered with the freedom of the city of God. All hail and farewell!

J. E. Rankin, "Frederick Douglass's Character and Career," *Our Day: The Altruistic Review* 14, no. 82 (April 1895): 171–175.

“Frederick Douglass as Orator and Reformer” (1895)

William Lloyd Garrison Jr.

The tensions between Douglass and his old friend and ally William Lloyd Garrison were eventually left in the past. When Garrison died in 1879, Douglass acknowledged their troubles, saying, “Speaking for myself I must frankly say I have sometimes thought him uncharitable to those who differed from him. Honest himself, he could not always see how men could differ from him and still be honest.” Clear in his criticism, Douglass was clear also in his admiration of the great abolitionist. “In the death of William Lloyd Garrison,” he stated, “we behold a great life ended, a great purpose achieved, a great career beautifully finished, and a great example of heroic endeavor nobly established. For our own good and the good of those who come after us, we cannot let this event sink too deep into our hearts, we cannot too often recur to this noble life and thrilling history, or too closely copy this great example.”[1] After Douglass’s death in 1895, Garrison’s son, also named William Lloyd Garrison, returned the sentiment in his reflections on Douglass’s life and career.

FREDERICK DOUGLASS was born a slave, in the State of Maryland, probably about 1817, although, as no records of the birth of slaves were kept, the exact date is not known. His father was a white man, but who he was even the son never surmised. Mr. Douglass said: “Of my father I know nothing. Slavery had no recognition of fathers, as none of families. That the mother was a slave was enough for its deadly purpose. By its law the child followed the condition of its mother. The father might be a white man, glorying in the purity of his Anglo-Saxon blood, and the child ranked with the blackest slaves.” In 1838 he escaped from Boston [*sic*] to New York City, and then went to New Bedford, where there was a large colored settlement. There he lived about three years, getting what odd jobs he could. Although a caulker, the white workers in that trade would not tolerate a colored man.

So, instead of earning two dollars a day, as he might have done, he was forced to saw wood and take anything that offered.

His mother had given him the high-sounding name of Frederick Augustus Washington Bailey; but his friends persuaded him, for the sake of safety, to change it to Frederick Douglass, the last name having been the choice of a Quaker, who had recently been reading Scott's "Lady of the Lake," and thought Douglass a fine name. Meantime he sent to Baltimore for the free young colored woman to whom he was attached. They were married, and settled down, as he thought, to a life of common toil. It happened, however, that his natural powers of speech induced him to take part in the Methodist meetings for prayer and exhortation; and this brought him into notice. He had also seen and subscribed for the *Liberator*, and became deeply interested in the anti-slavery movement.

In 1841 there happened to be an anti-slavery convention held at Nantucket, which Douglass was tempted to attend. He had no thought of speaking, and did not suppose any one there would know him. An abolitionist from New Bedford, however, named Coffin, who had heard him talk in the little school-house where the colored people worshiped, recognized him, and prevailed upon him to come upon the platform. He tells in his story that it was with the utmost difficulty that he could stand erect, or could command and articulate two words without stammering. He trembled in every limb. He says: "The audience sympathized with me at once, and from having been remarkably quiet, became much excited. Mr. Garrison followed me, taking me as his text. Whether I had made an eloquent speech in behalf of freedom or not, his was one never to be forgotten."

When his unusual powers as a public speaker were discovered, Mr. Douglass was at once put into the lecturers' field by the Anti-slavery Society, and went about from town to town preaching abolition. It was an occupation that brought him into the company of earnest and devoted people, and often into scenes of danger and persecution. For abolition was everywhere unpopular, and those who denounced slavery were themselves denounced by society as fanatics and disturbers of the peace. Meetings were frequently mobbed and broken up, and lecturers greeted with missiles. Arrest and imprisonment were not uncommon. Boston was as bitter against the free negro then as South Carolina is now, and for one to avow himself an abolitionist was to lose caste in society, religion and business. The churches permitted the colored people to occupy only the "nigger pew," as it was called. They were shut out of the theaters, except in a portion of the upper gallery set apart for them, and known as "nigger heaven." Hotels denied them entrance, save as servants; and to only one grammar school in this city, the Smith School, were they admitted. In my boyhood's day it was the custom to insult colored people as they passed along the street. On the railroad they must ride in a "Jim Crow car" or with the baggage.

Frederick Douglass, after leaving New Bedford, went to live for a time in Lynn. The president of the Eastern Railroad, a prominent Quaker of Salem, was, nevertheless, a bitter pro-slavery man, and decreed that no negro should ride in the common cars. But Douglass, who was a man of courage, with a stalwart frame and strength of muscle, undertook to test his rights one day. His white friend, James N. Buffum, a staunch and earnest abolitionist, in later years mayor of the city, went with Douglass to defend him. Together they took seats in the forbidden car. The conductor ordered the colored man to leave at once. Buffum protested, and Douglass refused to budge. The brakemen were called, and in spite of Mr. Buffum's remonstrance and Mr. Douglass' resistance, the latter was carried out by force, taking with him the back of the seat, to which he had clung. He finally was forced to ride in the baggage-car; and Mr. Buffum stayed with him, refusing to go back to his seat when his friend could not.

My earliest recollection of Frederick Douglass was about 1845, when I was seven years old, and he used occasionally to come to my father's house. The story of his early life and the interest attaching to his personality made a great impression upon me. In the anti-slavery meetings his eloquence always attracted, especially as he spoke of slavery with an interior knowledge and experience that no white abolitionist could possess. The iron had entered his soul, and his burning words were most effective. He was a natural speaker, having a fine presence, a powerful voice, admirably in control, an ease and force of expression, without that fatal fluency so often the bane of ready speakers, a native wit and gift of sarcasm, and, behind all, an intellectual quality that weighted every sentence. Other colored orators have attained great success upon the platform and in the pulpit, but it is no disparagement to them to say that Frederick Douglass towers above them all, like Saul among his brethren. My own conviction is that had he been thrown as a white man into the nation's councils, even when Webster, Clay and Calhoun were in the ascendent, with equal early advantages, he would not have been dwarfed by their companionship.

The abolitionists were very few in those days. In Boston only three or four houses were ready to entertain colored people or anti-slavery advocates. Of those who kept open houses, I can recall only Francis Jackson, Joseph Southwick and my father. At any time, day or night, they were liable to be called upon to shelter fugitive slaves on their way to Canada, or receive itinerant lecturers or others who had suffered for the cause. The fugitives came to our house as a natural refuge, and the feelings of the household were harrowed up by the details of cruelty which the poor terrified creatures told. But more impressive than any words were the scarred backs and maimed limbs, the welts made by the driver's lash being most often in evidence. Sometimes white men who had tried to help slaves escape were brutally dealt with. A noble man, Captain Jonathan Walker, allowed some slaves to escape on his vessel. He was a Down-East skipper, and his vessel was in the coasting trade. He was arrested, imprisoned, and sentenced to have his right hand branded. I remember the astonishment with which my brothers and myself examined the ridged letters on his palm, "S.S." They were supposed to stand for slave-stealer, but the abolitionists insisted that their true meaning was "Slave Savior." He was a gentle and brave man. The story of his experience is preserved in a book, which contains a picture of the branded hand.

In 1846 Mr. Douglass was sent to England on an anti-slavery mission, his old friend James N. Buffum accompanying him. There he lectured to enormous and enthusiastic audiences, making a host of friends for life. The color prejudice did not exist in Europe, and the man who was dragged out of the Lynn car, and barred out of American churches and theaters, was received on equal terms in fashionable drawing-rooms and in the houses of the nobility in Great Britain. It was a grateful contrast from the persecution and malignity to courtesy, appreciation and respect. It is strange that any colored person, once feeling the difference, was ever tempted to come back to the land of chains.

Samuel J. May, in his delightful "Recollections of the Anti-slavery Conflict," tells of Mr. Douglass' reception in Great Britain: "He was treated with great attention by the abolitionists of the United Kingdom, was invited to lecture everywhere, and rendered most valuable services to the cause of his oppressed countrymen. So deeply did he interest the philanthropists of that country that they paid $750 to procure from his master a formal, legal certificate of manumission, so that on his return to the United States he would be no longer liable to be sent back into slavery."

Douglass' own delight in the sudden transition from a region of prejudice and persecution to an atmosphere of equality and respect was expressed in an eloquent letter to his friend Mr. Garrison, to be found in "The Life and Times of Frederick Douglass."

Mr. Douglass moved to Rochester, New York, and established a paper of his own about the year 1847, and on account of differences with his old friends, no longer visited them as was his wont. But wherever he lived or went, the marked personality of the man, his eloquence and intellect, and, added thereto, a tact and judgment that allayed social antagonisms, and never unnecessarily aroused them, made him a center of force and attraction. It was the tendency of many colored men who felt deeply the degradation inflicted upon them, simply on account of color, to emphasize their sensitiveness, and be quick to resent the least appearance of a slight. Not so with Frederick Douglass. He never looked for insult, nor showed a consciousness that he was different from other men. To meet him and converse, one would forget that he was of a despised race, and think only of the charming qualities which this interesting human being possessed. It was an evidence of his magnanimity and greatness of spirit.

I remember a story of Douglass and Sojourner Truth, a character as remarkable in her way as Douglass was in his. She was a thorough African, of unmixed blood, gaunt and black. She was born a slave in New York, and emancipated when slavery was abolished in the state. She could neither read nor write, whereas Douglass had educated himself, and was the peer of any so-called self-made white man. At an anti-slavery meeting, when the aspect of affairs was particularly dark, Douglass was speaking, and indulging in a gloomy view of the situation. Sojourner, who was a listener, and was possessed with an intense religious faith, was disturbed at the tone of despondency, and in a moment relieved her feelings, and those of the meeting as well, by saying in her deep voice, "Is God dead, Frederick?" Nobody could appreciate the hit better than himself, and the closing remarks were in a more hopeful strain.

John Brown, when contemplating his raid on Harper's Ferry, took Douglass into his confidence. After the tragedy, Douglass was sought by Governor Wise, of Virginia, who issued a requisition for his arrest, to escape which he went again to England, staying till the danger had blown over. Of the wealth and honors that came naturally to Frederick Douglass in his later years I do not propose to speak. They happen in the lives of all successful men. Of course, it was noteworthy for an ex-slave to be Marshal of the District of Columbia, under both a Republican and a Democratic administration, and be received and honored at the White House in a high official capacity. His last representative distinction was at the World's Fair, where during its existence he was a conspicuous and attractive personality. Since the war he has lived on a fine estate at Anacostia, Washington D.C., where he died so suddenly the other day.

He took a sympathetic interest in reforms, notably that of woman suffrage. The day of his death he attended the great convention of women in Washington, and was escorted in honor to the platform by two ladies, one of whom was his old Rochester anti-slavery friend and neighbor, Miss Susan B. Anthony. With Frederick Douglass has passed away a life as full of romance and wonder as can be found in the world of fiction. His career is an incentive and encouragement to all downtrodden and unfortunate human beings.

NOTE

1. Frederick Douglass, "Speech on the Death of William Lloyd Garrison," in *The Frederick Douglass Papers, Series One: Speeches, Debates and Interviews*, ed. John W. Blassingame and John R. McKivigan (New Haven, CT: Yale University Press, 1991), 4:506, 505.

William Lloyd Garrison Jr., "Frederick Douglass as Orator and Reformer" (reprinted from *Christian Register*), *Our Day: The Altruistic Review* 14, no. 82 (April 1895): 182–185.

"Frederick Douglass Loved Music" (1895)

[Anonymous]

Douglass's great love of music was well known to his friends but is often forgotten by those who remember him only for his social activism. But Douglass's activism was directed toward realizing a world where the arts could be enjoyed and pursued by all. Douglass's grandson Joseph became one of the first African American violinists to attain international recognition, and he was the first to make transcontinental tours. In the following notice from the magazine *Musical Record*, we are afforded a brief but revealing glimpse into this important part of Douglass's life.

FREDERICK DOUGLASS was a great lover of music, and quite a performer on the violin.

During a visit to Boston, he became much interested in the violins of a violin-maker in that city, and visited his workshop several times, in company with his grandson Joseph, who has only recently graduated from the New England Conservatory of Music, and is preparing to study in Paris. They both played upon these violins, in duets and solos, pronouncing them excellent.

After a comparison with a fine Cremona instrument which Mr. Douglass had bought in Rome, he selected one worth seventy-five dollars.

Upon his return to Massachusetts a month later he sent the maker of the violin a testimonial.

"Frederick Douglass Loved Music," *Musical Record* 406 (November 1895): 13.

From *Sonnets to the Memory of Frederick Douglass* (1895)

Theodore Tilton

Many poems have been written about Douglass over the years, enough to fill a volume. The following are taken from a sonnet sequence "written in Paris, France, immediately after his funeral," as the author notes in a short preface. Theodore Tilton was a white abolitionist and poet who for many years had served as the assistant to Henry Ward Beecher, brother of the famous Harriet Beecher Stowe. That relationship ended in 1874 when Tilton filed criminal charges against Beecher for "criminal intimacy" with Tilton's wife. Following Beecher's acquittal, Tilton moved to Paris and after Douglass's death composed the following tribute. Douglass and Tilton had caused a stir many years earlier, in 1866, at the National Union Convention in Philadelphia, when they walked down the aisle arm in arm to make a point about social equality across racial lines. They remained friends and correspondents.

A Career Unique

I.

I knew the noblest giants of my day,
　　And he was of them—strong amid the strong:
　　But gentle too: for though he suffered wrong,
Yet the wrong-doer never heard him say
"Thee also do I hate!" . . .
. . . .
How does it happen that, in every clime,
　　When any groaning nation of the earth
　　　　Hath need of some new leader of a race,
Or some true prophet of a better time.
　　The Heavens elect him for his lowly birth,
　　　　Ere they uplift him to his lofty place?

III.

I answer: He must first be taught to know—
(I say to *know* and not to *guess*)—how real
Is all the misery which he hopes to heal!
The high may show a kindness to the low:
Some wealthy lord is generous—be it so:
Yet *who* except the poor and pinched can feel
Their pang of poverty ? . . .
So for their weal,
They need a champion who has borne their woe!

. . . .

O tardy Nation, slow agen to learn!
Let not thy former lesson now be lost!
For now thy Northern millions toil in vain!
Beware! Deny them not the bread they earn!

VI.

Shall there be Hunger in a Land of Corn?
Then if—(shut out from idle mill and mine)—
Come the bold beggars forth in battle-line,
Armed and in fury, answering scorn with scorn—
Oh *who* shall lead them in their Hope Forlorn?
How shall they know him? How shall they divine
Their true deliverer ? I will tell the sign!
Let him be like the man whom now we mourn!—
A hero high above revenge or greed,
Forbidding bloodshed and restraining hate,
Chiding and shaming every threat of crime—
Not rash, but patient, knowing well indeed
That Justice, being blind, must therefore wait
And cannot come except as led by Time!

. . . .

Chief of his tribe, he centered in his soul—
As their evangel—all their hopes and fears!
—Through all his lifetime, as their wisest head,
He planned to lead them to some happy goal!
(How they will lack him in the coming years,
And wish him back among them, from the dead!)

X.

I knew his latch-string—it hung always out!
I knew his books, on which he loved to pore:
His Bible—(*no* man ever read it more![1])—
His Izak Walton on Religious Doubt
(And how to settle it by catching trout!)—
His Shakespeare (with a bust above the door[2])—
His Talmud—and the never-tiring lore
Which takes a Thousand Nights to tell about.

And much he loved to con the Concord Sage,
And Hawthorne's Hester, and the Quaker Bard,
And Uncle Tom (the "Cabin" and the "Key")—
And sometimes he would even read a page
From this poor pen of mine—not for regard
Of my dull verses, but for love of me!

XI.

A wistful loneliness was in his look;
For thus he ever bore upon his face
(As in his heart) the sorrows of his race:
And yet he gaily—in the walks we took—
Would stop and chatter to a chattering brook,
And mimic all the creatures of the place.
And buzz in sharps, and croak in double bass,
And caw in semi-quavers like the rook!
Not one of Nature's voices (he declared)—
Whether of beast, or bird, or wind, or wave—
Had ever chid him for his sable hue!
His fellow-men—and these alone—had dared,
With cruel taunt, to say to him "Thou Slave!"
(And were the only brutes he ever knew!)

XII.

He oft would bask, through all a winter's eve.
Before his yule-log, till the fire was low;
And in his talk, with all his mind aglow.
What wit and wisdom he would interweave!
It was a hearthstone I was loth to leave!—

Alack ! I thither nevermore shall go!—
So, though my song is not a wail of woe.
Yet such a thought is sombre—and I grieve.

Keen was his satire; but the flashing blade.
Instead of poison on the biting steel,
Bore on its edge a balsam of a kind
Whereby the very wound the weapon made
Was at the very moment sure to heal.
And nevermore to leave a scar behind.

XIII.

If love of music be a mortal sin
(As certain of the saints are wont to say),
He was a sinner to his dying day!
For like the rest of his melodious kin
A song was what his soul delighted in,—
Especially some soft and plaintive lay
Which in the old and weird plantation way
He loved to echo on his violin.

He touched the strings with more than rustic art;
For oft a sudden supernatural power
Would swell within him—till he gave a vent
To all the pent-up passion of his heart!—
So his Cremona in a troubled hour
Beguiled for him a care to a content.[3]

XIV.

He came to Paris; and we paced the streets
As if we twain were truants out of school!
We clomb aloft where many a carven ghoul
And grinning gargoyle mocked our giddy feats;
We made a sport of sitting in the seats
Where Kings of France were wont to sit and rule!
"A throne," quoth he, "is a pretender's stool—
For kingship is a fraud, and kings are cheats!"

He loved a hero. Nor can I forget
How with uncovered head, in awe profound,
He hailed Coligny's all-too-tardy stone;[4]
And how, before the tomb of Lafayette,[5]
He said, "This place is *doubly* sacred ground—
This patriot had *two* countries for his own!"

XV.

I here might crowd this empty rhyme of mine
With tales of how my travel-eager friend
(Who wished to see the world from end to end)
Sped southward from the many-castled Rhine
To languid Italy—a land supine,
Yet soon to rouse herself (as signs portend),
Though why she waits is hard to comprehend:
Thence to the country of the Muses Nine—
To Marathon, and to the Academe:
Thence to the Sphinx at Ghizeh—whom with awe
He answered—and his answer may be guessed:
For there—in Egypt—by her classic stream.
He said that every famous land he saw
Taught him the more to love his own the best!

XVI.

For though his own had been a cruel land,
Wherein, through many a long and groaning year.
Oppression had been bitter and austere
(As harsh as under Pharaoh's iron hand)—
Yet such a slave could never be unmanned;
But ever with a sweet and secret cheer
He felt the day of freedom to be near.
So when it came, he well could understand
That his dear Country, long herself a thrall,
Self-chained and self-degraded in the past—
Till, smiting off her shackles with her sword,
She too!—she too!—the chiefest slave of all—
Self-freed and self-uplifted, had at last
Stood forth redeemed, and lovely, and adored!

XVII.

His form was like Apollo's, and his brow
Like what the sculptors carve for Zeus's own—
As godlike as was ever cut in stone!
For if the old god Thor were living now,
With his dark visage, with his frosty pow,
And with his awe-inspiring thunder-tone,—
Such a resembling pair (could both be known)
Would pass for twin-born brothers, I avow!

The gods are dead,—and all the godlike men
Are dying too! How fast they disappear!
For Death seems discontent to fill the grave
With common bones, but downward to his den
Drags, like a greedy monster, year by year
The men most missed—the good, the wise, the brave!

XVIII.

Spake I of goodly giants in the land?
And did I boast that I had known them well?
I was a stripling: so I live to tell.
In these degenerate days, how great and grand,
How plain and simple, were the noble band
Who cried to Heaven against that crime of Hell
Which to the auction-block brought Babes to sell,
And which on Women burnt a market-brand!

Who were those heroes? Since the roll is known
I need not call it: Lincoln was the chief:
The rest were legion— name them whoso can:
But whoso counts the list of Freedom's Own
Must name the Chattel whom, with pride and grief,
We buried yesterday and called a Man!

XIX.

What final wreath of olive, oak or bay
(Which to withhold would do the dead a wrong)
Is due him for the fetter, yoke and thong
Which, as a Slave, he bore for many a day?

If to his wintry burial blooming May
Had come herself, chief-mourner of the throng,
And stopt his bier as it was borne along,
And laid a million lilies on his clay,—
Not one of all these fading funeral-flowers
Would have survived the frost! . . . So—(since, alas!
Such honours fade)—my Country, hark to *me*!
Let us, in yonder Capitol of ours.
Mould him a statue of enduring brass
Out of the broken chains of slaves set free!

NOTES

1. Speaking of his slave-life in Baltimore, he says in his Autobiography, "I have gathered scattered pages of the Bible from the filthy street-gutters, and have washed and dried them, that in moments of leisure I might get a word or two of wisdom from them." [Tilton's footnote]

2. This house was in Rochester, N.Y., and was burned in 1872—with all the books and busts. [Tilton's footnote]

3. "Of all the interesting objects in the Museum of Genoa," he wrote, "the one that touched me most was the violin of Paganini—a precious object in my eyes." [Tilton's footnote]

4. Admiral de Coligny was murdered in the St. Bartholomew massacre, on the night of August 24, 1572. [Tilton's footnote]

5. Lafayette lies in the Picpus Cemetery, rue Picpus, Paris. [Tilton's footnote]

From Theodore Tilton, "A Career Unique," in *Sonnets to the Memory of Frederick Douglass* (Paris: Brentano's, 1895), 1, 2–3, 4, 6–12.

"Frederick Douglass" (1897)

CORDELIA RAY

Born in New York City in 1852, Henrietta Cordelia Ray was the daughter of a blacksmith, minister, and abolitionist who became a teacher and poet. Ray graduated from the University of the City of New York in 1891 and went on to teach in the city's public school system. Her reputation as a poet was established in 1876 when her ode to Lincoln was read (by William E. Matthews) at the unveiling of the Freedmen's Monument in Washington, D.C. Frederick Douglass delivered the keynote address at that event, and when Douglass died nearly twenty years later, the following was one of the poems chosen for the memorial book put together by Douglass's wife. Ray wrote a biography of her father and published her collected poetry in 1893 and 1910, work for which she achieved a modest but important place in African American literary history.

One whose majestic presence ever here
Was as an inspiration held so dear,
Will greet us nevermore upon the earth.
The funeral bells have rung; there was no dearth
Of sorrow as the solemn cortege passed;
But ours is a grief that will outlast
The civic splendor. Say, among all men,
Who was this hero that they buried then,
With saddest plaint and sorrow-stricken face?
Ay! 'Twas a princely leader of his race!

And for a leader well-equipped was he;
Nature had given him most regally
E'en of her choicest gifts. What matter then
That he in chains was held? What matter when
He could uplift himself to noblest heights?
For with his native greatness, neither slights

Nor wrongs could harm him; and a solemn wrath
Burned in his soul. He well saw duty's path;
His days heroic purposes did know,
And could he then his chosen work forego?

Born to a fate most wretched, most forlorn!
A slave! alas! of benefits all shorn
Upon his entrance into life. What lot
More destitute of hope! Yet e'en that blot
Could not suffice to dim the glowing page
He leaves to History; for he could wage
Against oppression's deadliest blows a war
That knew no ending, until nevermore
Should any man be called a bondman. Ay!
Such was a conflict for which one could die!

Panting for freedom early, he did dare
To throw aside his shackles; for the air
Of slavery is poison unto men
Moulded as Douglass was; they suffer, then
Manhood asserts itself; they are too brave—
Such souls as his, to die content a slave.
So being free, one path alone he trod,
To bring to liberty—sweet boon from God—
His deeply injured race; his tireless zeal
Was consecrated to the bondman's weal.

He thought of children sobbing round the knees
Of hopeless mothers, where the summer breeze
Blew o'er the dark savannas. What of woe
In their sad story that he did not know?
He was a valiant leader in a cause,
Than none less noble, though the nation's laws
Did seem to spurn it; and his matchless speech
To Britain's sea-girt island shores did reach.
Our Cicero, and yet our warrior knight
Striving to show mankind might is not right!

He saw the slave uplifted from the dust,
A freeman! Loyal to the sacred trust
He gave himself in youth, with voice and pen,
He had been to the end. And now again
The grandest efforts of that brain and heart
In ev'ry human sorrow bore a part.
His regnant intellect, his dignity
Did make him honored among all to be;
And public trusts his country gladly gave
Unto this princely leader—born a slave!

Shall the race falter in its courage now
That the great chief is fallen? Shall it bow
Tamely to aught of injury? Ah, nay!
For daring souls are needed e'en today.
Let his example be a shining light,
Leading through duty's paths to some far height
Of undreamed victory. All honored be
The silv'ry bead of him we can no more see!
Children unborn will venerate his name,
And History keep spotless his fair fame.

The Romans wove bright leafy crowns for those
Who saved a life in battle with their foes;
And shall not we as rare a chaplet weave
To that great master soul for whom we grieve?
Yea! Since not always on the battle field
Are the best vict'ries won; for they who yield
Themselves to conquer in a losing cause,
Because 'tis right in God's eternal laws,
Do noblest battle; therefore fitly we
Upon their brows a victor's crown would see.

Yes! our great chief has fallen, as might fall
Some veteran warrior answering the call
Of duty. With the old serenity,
His heart still strung with tender sympathy,

He passed beyond our ken; he'll come no more
To give us stately greeting as of yore.
We cannot fail to miss him. When we stand
In sudden helplessness, as through the land
Rings echo of some wrong he could not brook,
Then vainly for our leader will we look.

But courage! no great influence can die
While he is doing grander work on high;
Shall not his deeds an inspiration be
To us left in life's struggle? May not we
Do aught to emulate him whom we mourn?
We are a people now, no more forlorn
And hopeless. We must gather courage then,
Rememb'ring that he stood man among men.
So let us give, now he has journeyed hence,
To our great chieftain's memory, reverence!

Cordelia Ray, "Frederick Douglass," in *In Memoriam: Frederick Douglass*, ed. Helen Pitts Douglass (Philadelphia: John C. Yorston, 1897), 161–163.

[Two Poems] (1897 and 1913)

Paul Laurence Dunbar

The first African American poet to enjoy national recognition and broad admiration, Paul Laurence Dunbar was of a later generation than Douglass, and he understood how much Douglass had done to make Dunbar's life and career possible—and how much Douglass's leadership was missed in the ongoing struggle. Dunbar and Douglass met at the World's Columbian Exhibition in Chicago, where Douglass, at that time the U.S. minister to Haiti, was the commissioner of the Haitian exhibition. Douglass hired Dunbar as a clerk at the Haitian Building, paying him from his own funds, and he also arranged for the poet to read his work at the Colored American Day celebration held there. When Douglass passed away in 1895, Dunbar stayed up through the night to write "Frederick Douglass." Years later, still feeling keenly the loss of Douglass's leadership, he wrote the second of the two poems that follow, which he included in *Lyrics of Love and Laughter.*

Frederick Douglass

A hush is over all the teeming lists,
And there is pause, a breath-space in the strife;
A spirit brave has passed beyond the mists
And vapors that obscure the sun of life.
And Ethiopia, with bosom torn,
Laments the passing of her noblest born.

She weeps for him a mother's burning tears—
She loved him with a mother's deepest love
He was her champion thro' direful years,
And held her weal all other ends above.
When Bondage held her bleeding in the dust,
He raised her up and whispered, "Hope and Trust."

For her his voice, a fearless clarion, rung
That broke in warning on the ears of men;
For her the strong bow of his pow'r he strung
And sent his arrows to the very den
Where grim Oppression held his bloody place
And gloated o'er the mis'ries of a race.

And he was no soft-tongued apologist;
He spoke straight-forward, fearlessly uncowed;
The sunlight of his truth dispelled the mist
And set in bold relief each dark-hued cloud;
To sin and crime he gave their proper hue,
And hurled at evil what was evil's due.

Thro' good and ill report he cleaved his way
Right onward, with his face set toward the heights,
Nor feared to face the foeman's dread array—
The lash of scorn, the sting of petty spites.
He dared the lightning in the lightning's track,
And answered thunder with his thunder back.

When men maligned him and their torrent wrath
In furious imprecations o'er him broke,
He kept his counsel as he kept his path;
'Twas for his race, not for himself, he spoke.
He knew the import of his Master's call
And felt himself too mighty to be small.

No miser in the good he held was he—
His kindness followed his horizon's rim.
His heart, his talents and his hands were free
To all who truly needed aught of him.
Where poverty and ignorance were rife,
He gave his bounty as he gave his life.

The place and cause that first aroused his might
Still proved its pow'r until his latest day.

In Freedom's lists and for the aid of Right
Still in the foremost rank he waged the fray;
Wrong lived; His occupation was not gone.
He died in action with his armor on!

We weep for him, but we have touched his hand,
And felt the magic of his presence nigh,
The current that he sent thro' out the land,
The kindling spirit of his battle-cry
O'er all that holds us we shall triumph yet
And place our banner where his hopes were set!

Oh, Douglass, thou hast passed beyond the shore,
But still thy voice is ringing o'er the gale!
Thou'st taught thy race how high her hopes may soar
And bade her seek the heights, nor faint, nor fail.
She will not fail, she heeds thy stirring cry,
She knows thy guardian spirit will be nigh,
And rising from beneath the chast'ning rod,
She stretches out her bleeding hands to God!

Paul Laurence Dunbar, *Lyrics of Lowly Life* (London: Chapman & Hall, 1897), 8–11.

Douglass

Ah, Douglass, we have fall'n on evil days,
Such days as thou, not even thou didst know,
When thee, the eyes of that harsh long ago
Saw, salient, at the cross of devious ways,
And all the country heard thee with amaze.
Not ended then, the passionate ebb and flow,
The awful tide that battled to and fro;
We ride amid a tempest of dispraise.

Now, when the waves of swift dissension swarm,
And Honor, the strong pilot, lieth stark,

Oh, for thy voice high-sounding o'er the storm,
For thy strong arm to guide the shivering bark,
The blast-defying power of thy form,
To give us comfort through the lonely dark.

Paul Laurence Dunbar, *Lyrics of Love and Laughter* (New York: Dodd, Mead, 1913), 127–128.

From *Eighty Years and More* (1898)

Elizabeth Cady Stanton

Earlier we encountered Theodore Stanton's memories of Frederick Douglass in Paris. Here, Theodore's mother, the famous abolitionist and women's rights activist Elizabeth Cady Stanton, recalls an incident from her younger days with Douglass. Stanton was a firm friend to Douglass when the latter faced public criticism and ostracism for marrying a white woman, though their friendship was tried mightily when Stanton refused to support the Fourteenth and Fifteenth Amendments to the Constitution, believing that suffrage for women needed to be a part of any redefinition of citizenship. Like Douglass, though, Stanton was an independent thinker, demonstrated in her controversial views on Christianity that led her to collaborate with others to produce *The Woman's Bible*, a theological challenge to the patriarchy of established religion. Stanton's cousin Gerrit Smith, whose mansion was the scene for the following event, was Douglass's primary white abolitionist ally after Douglass's split from Garrison.

The month of August, 1895, we spent in Peterboro, on the grand hills of Madison County, nine hundred feet above the valley. Gerrit Smith's fine old mansion still stands, surrounded with magnificent trees, where I had played in childhood, chasing squirrels over lawn and gardens and wading in a modest stream that still creeps slowly round the grounds. I recalled as I sat on the piazza how one time, when Frederick Douglass came to spend a few days at Peterboro, some Southern visitors wrote a note to Mr. Smith asking if Mr. Douglass was to sit in the parlor and at the dining table; if so, during his visit they would remain in their own apartments. Mr. Smith replied that his visitors were always treated by his family as equals, and such would be the case with Mr. Douglass, who was considered one of the ablest men reared under "The Southern Institution." So these ladies had their meals in their own apartments, where they stayed most of the time, and, as Mr. Douglass prolonged his visit, they no doubt wished in their hearts that they had never taken that silly position. The rest of us walked about with him, arm in arm, played games, and sang songs together, he playing the accompaniment on the guitar. I suppose if our prejudiced countrywomen had been introduced to Dumas in a French salon, they would at once have donned their bonnets and ran away.

From Elizabeth Cady Stanton, *Eighty Years and More* (New York: European Publishing, 1898), 453–454.

From *Frederick Douglass, a Biography* (1899)

Charles Waddell Chesnutt

Now recognized as one of the great American writers of the turn of the century, Charles Waddell Chesnutt was frustrated by the limitations and terms of his recognition in his own time. Of his life in the South, he once complained in his journal, "I occupy here a position similar to that of the Mahomet's Coffin. I am neither fish, flesh, nor fowl—neither 'nigger,' poor white, nor 'buckrah.' Too 'stuck-up' for the colored folks, and, of course, not recognized by the whites." And Chesnutt could be very critical of his fellow African Americans, as when he wrote in his journal when still a young man that "the Negro is yet to become known who can write a good book."[1] But as an educator and as a writer, Chesnutt had a clear commitment to black America. His early stories appeared in some of the top magazines in the country, including the *Atlantic Monthly*, and he was viewed as a promising writer. But many of his white readers were not ready for the harsh truths Chesnutt explored in his work. Known primarily for his fiction, Chesnutt wrote a biography on Douglass for the popular series Beacon Biographies of Eminent Americans. Although much of the biography is based on Douglass's own autobiographies, the following excerpts give a sense of Chesnutt's assessment of, and sense of affinity with, the great man. Of the many writers and other celebrities of the time with whom Chesnutt surrounds Douglass, especially notable are Fanny Kemble, a British actress who married an American who owned plantations in Georgia, and Thomas Wentworth Higginson, the Unitarian minister and abolitionist who served as a colonel of the first official African American regiment in the Civil War, the 1st South Carolina Volunteers. Kemble kept a journal of her experiences and observations on the plantations, which she later published as *Journal of a Residence on a Georgian Plantation in 1838–1839* (1863), a vivid testimonial against slavery. Higginson, active in some of the most famous abolitionist struggles of the time (and known as a supporter of John Brown), is remembered today primarily for his friendship with Emily Dickinson, whose poetry he helped bring to public notice. In such company, joined with many of the great orators we have encountered before, Chesnutt finds Douglass's greatness.

Preface

Frederick Douglass lived so long, and played so conspicuous a part on the world's stage, that it would be impossible, in a work of the size of this, to do more than touch upon the salient features of his career, to suggest the respects in which he influenced the course of events in his lifetime, and to epitomize for the readers of another generation the judgment of his contemporaries as to his genius and his character. Douglass's fame as an orator has long been secure. His position as the champion of an oppressed race, and at the same time an example of its possibilities, was, in his own generation, as picturesque as it was unique; and his life may serve for all time as an incentive to aspiring souls who would fight the battles and win the love of mankind. The average American of to-day who sees, when his attention is called to it, and deplores, if he be a thoughtful and just man, the deep undertow of race prejudice that retards the progress of the colored people of our own generation, cannot, except by reading the painful records of the past, conceive of the mental and spiritual darkness to which slavery, as the inexorable condition of its existence, condemned its victims and, in a less measure, their oppressors, or of the blank wall of proscription and scorn by which free people of color were shut up in a moral and social Ghetto, the gates of which have yet not been entirely torn down. From this night of slavery Douglass emerged, passed through the limbo of prejudice which he encountered as a freeman, and took his place in history. "As few of the world's great men have ever had so checkered and diversified a career," says Henry Wilson, "so it may at least be plausibly claimed that no man represents in himself more conflicting ideas and interests. His life is, in itself, an epic which finds few to equal it in the realms of either romance or reality." It was, after all, no misfortune for humanity that Frederick Douglass felt the iron hand of slavery; for his genius changed the drawbacks of color and condition into levers by which he raised himself and his people. The materials for this work have been near at hand, though there is a vast amount of which lack of space must prevent the use. Acknowledgment is here made to members of the Douglass family for aid in securing the photograph from which the frontispiece is reproduced. The more the writer has studied the records of Douglass's life, the more it has appealed to his imagination and his heart. He can claim no special qualification for this task, unless perhaps it be a profound and in some degree a personal sympathy with every step of Douglass's upward career. Belonging to a later generation, he was only privileged to see the man and hear the orator after his life-work was substantially completed, but often enough then to appreciate something of the strength and eloquence by which he impressed his contemporaries. If by this brief sketch the writer can revive among the readers of another generation a tithe of the interest that Douglass created for himself when he led the forlorn hope of his race for freedom and opportunity, his labor will be amply repaid.

Charles W. Chesnutt, Cleveland, October, 1899 [. . .]

If it be no small task for a man of the most favored antecedents and the most fortunate surroundings to rise above mediocrity in a great nation, it is surely a more remarkable achievement for a man of the very humblest origin possible to humanity in any country in any age of the world, in the face of obstacles seemingly insurmountable, to win high honors and rewards, to retain for more than a generation the respect of good men in many lands, and to be deemed worthy of enrolment among his country's great men. Such a man was Frederick Douglass, and the example of one who thus rose to eminence by sheer force of character and talents that neither slavery nor caste proscription could crush must ever remain as a shining illustration of the essential superiority of manhood to environment. Circumstances made Frederick Douglass a slave, but they could not prevent him from becoming a freeman and a leader among mankind.

The early life of Douglass, as detailed by himself from the platform in vigorous and eloquent speech, and as recorded in the three volumes written by himself at different periods of his career, is perhaps the completest indictment of the slave system ever presented at the bar of public opinion. Fanny Kemble's *Journal of a Residence on a Georgian Plantation*, kept by her in the very year of Douglass's escape from bondage, but not published until 1863, too late to contribute anything to the downfall of slavery, is a singularly clear revelation of plantation life from the standpoint of an outsider entirely unbiased by American prejudice. *Frederick Douglass's Narrative* is the same story told from the inside. They coincide in the main facts; and in the matter of detail, like the two slightly differing views of a stereoscopic picture, they bring out into bold relief the real character of the peculiar institution. *Uncle Tom's Cabin* lent to the structure of fact the decorations of humor, a dramatic plot, and characters to whose fate the touch of creative genius gave a living interest. But, after all, it was not Uncle Tom, nor Topsy, nor Miss Ophelia, nor Eliza, nor little Eva that made the book the power it proved to stir the hearts of men, but the great underlying tragedy then already rapidly approaching a bloody climax. [. . .]

Some of Douglass's friends, it must be admitted, were at times rather extreme in their language, and perhaps stirred up feelings that a more temperate vocabulary would not have aroused. None of them ever hesitated to call a spade a spade, and some of them denounced slavery and all its sympathizers with the vigor and picturesqueness of a Muggletonian or Fifth Monarchy man of Cromwell's time execrating his religious adversaries. And, while it was true enough that the Church and the State were, generally speaking, the obsequious tools of slavery, it was not easy for an abolitionist to say so in vehement language without incurring the charge of treason or blasphemy,—an old trick of bigotry and tyranny to curb freedom of thought and freedom of speech. The little personal idiosyncrasies which some of the reformers affected, such as long hair in the men and short hair in the women,—there is surely some psychological reason why reformers run to such things,—served as convenient excuses for gibes and unseemly interruptions at their public meetings. On one memorable occasion, at Syracuse, New York, in November, 1842, Douglass and his fellows narrowly escaped tar and feathers. But, although Douglass was vehemently denunciatory of slavery in all its aspects, his twenty years of training in that hard school had developed in him a vein of prudence that saved him from these verbal excesses,—perhaps there was also some element of taste involved,—and thus made his arguments more effective than if he had alienated his audiences by indiscriminate attacks on all the institutions of society. No one could justly accuse Frederick Douglass of cowardice or self-seeking; yet he was opportunist enough to sacrifice the immaterial for the essential, and to use the best means at hand to promote the ultimate object sought, although the means thus offered might not be the ideal instrument. It was doubtless this trait that led Douglass, after he separated from his abolitionist friends, to modify his views upon the subject of disunion and the constitutionality of slavery, and to support political parties whose platforms by no means expressed the full measure of his convictions. [. . .]

It is perhaps fitting, before we take leave of Douglass, to give some estimate of the remarkable oratory which gave him his hold upon the past generation. For, while his labors as editor and in other directions were of great value to the cause of freedom, it is upon his genius as an orator that his fame must ultimately rest.

While Douglass's color put him in a class by himself among great orators, and although his slave past threw around him an element of romance that added charm to his eloquence, these were mere incidental elements of distinction. The North was full of fugitive slaves, and more than one had passionately proclaimed his wrongs. There were several colored orators who stood high in the councils of the abolitionists and did good service for the cause of humanity.

Douglass possessed, in large measure, the physical equipment most impressive in an orator. He was a man of magnificent figure, tall, strong, his head crowned with a mass of hair which made a striking element of his appearance. He had deep-set and flashing eyes, a firm, well-moulded chin, a countenance somewhat severe in repose, but capable of a wide range of expression. His voice was rich and melodious, and of great carrying power. [. . .]

The poet William Howitt said of him on his departure from England in 1847, "He has appeared in this country before the most accomplished audiences, who were surprised, not only at his talent, but at his extraordinary information."

In Ireland he was introduced as "the black O'Connell,"—a high compliment; for O'Connell was at that time the idol of the Irish people. In Scotland they called him the "black Douglass [Douglas]," after his prototype in *The Lady of the Lake*, because of his fire and vigor. In Rochester he was called the "swarthy Ajax," from his indignant denunciation and defiance of the Fugitive Slave Law of 1850, which came like a flash of lightning to blast the hopes of the anti-slavery people.

Douglass possessed in unusual degree the faculty of swaying his audience, sometimes against their maturer judgment. There is something in the argument from first principles which, if presented with force and eloquence, never fails to appeal to those who are not blinded by self-interest or deep-seated prejudice. Douglass's argument was that of the Declaration of Independence,—"that *all* men are created equal; that they are endowed by their Creator with certain inalienable rights; that among these are life, liberty, and the pursuit of happiness. That, to secure these rights, governments are instituted among men, deriving their just powers from the *consent of the governed.*" The writer may be pardoned for this quotation; for there are times when we seem to forget that now and here, no less than in ancient Rome, "eternal vigilance is the price of liberty." Douglass brushed aside all sophistries about Constitutional guarantees, and vested rights, and inferior races, and, having postulated the right of men to be free, maintained that negroes were men, and offered himself as a proof of his assertion,—an argument that few had the temerity to deny. If it were answered that he was only half a negro, he would reply that slavery made no such distinction, and as a still more irrefutable argument would point to his friend, Samuel R. Ward, who often accompanied him on the platform,—an eloquent and effective orator, of whom Wendell Phillips said that "he was so black that, if he would shut his eyes, one could not see him." It was difficult for an auditor to avoid assent to such arguments, presented with all the force and fire of genius, relieved by a ready wit, a contagious humor, and a tear-compelling power rarely excelled.

"As a speaker," says one of his contemporaries, "he has few equals. It is not declamation, but oratory, power of description. He watches the tide of discussion, and dashes into it at once with all the tact of the forum or the bar. He has art, argument, sarcasm, pathos,—all that first-rate men show in their master efforts." His readiness was admirably illustrated in the running debate with Captain Rynders, a ward politician and gambler of New York, who led a gang of roughs with the intention of breaking up the meeting of the American Anti-slavery Society in New York City, May 7, 1850. The newspapers had announced the proposed meeting in language calculated to excite riot. Rynders packed the meeting with rowdies, and himself occupied a seat on the platform. Some remark by Mr. Garrison, the first speaker, provoked a demonstration of hostility. When this was finally quelled by a promise to permit one of the Rynders party to reply, Mr. Garrison finished his speech. He was followed by a prosy individual, who branded the negro as brother to the monkey. Douglass, perceiving that the speaker was wearying even his own friends, intervened at an opportune moment, captured the audience by a timely display of wit, and then improved the occasion by a long and effective speech. When Douglass offered himself as a refutation of the last speaker's argument, Rynders replied that Douglass was half white. Douglass thereupon greeted Rynders as his half-brother, and made this expression the catchword of his speech. When Rynders interrupted from time to time, he was silenced with a laugh. He appears to have been a somewhat philosophic scoundrel, with an appreciation of humor that permitted the meeting to proceed to an orderly close. Douglass's speech was the feature of the evening. "That gifted man," said Garrison, in whose *Life and Times* a graphic description of this famous meeting is given, "effectually put to shame his assailants by his wit and eloquence."

A speech delivered by Douglass at Concord, New Hampshire, is thus described by another writer: "He gradually let out the outraged humanity that was laboring in him, in indignant and terrible speech. . . . He was an insurgent slave, taking hold on the rights of speech, and charging on his tyrants the bondage of his race."

In Holland's biography of Douglass extracts are given from letters of distinguished contemporaries who knew the orator. Colonel T. W. Higginson writes thus: "I have hardly heard his equal, in grasp upon an audience, in dramatic presentation, in striking at the pith of an ethical question, and in single [signal] illustrations and examples." Another writes, in reference to the impromptu speech delivered at the meeting at Rochester on the death of Lincoln: "I have heard Webster and Clay in their best moments, Channing and Beecher in their highest inspirations. I never heard truer eloquence. I never saw profounder impression."

The published speeches of Douglass, of which examples may be found scattered throughout his various autobiographies, reveal something of the powers thus characterized, though, like other printed speeches, they lose by being put in type. But one can easily imagine their effect upon a sympathetic or receptive audience, when delivered with flashing eye and deep-toned resonant voice by a man whose complexion and past history gave him the highest right to describe and denounce the iniquities of slavery and contend for the rights of a race. In later years, when brighter days had dawned for his people, and age had dimmed the recollection of his sufferings and tempered his animosities, he became more charitable to his old enemies; but in the vigor of his manhood, with the memory of his wrongs and those of his race fresh upon him, he possessed that indispensable quality of the true reformer: he went straight to the root of the evil, and made no admissions and no compromises. Slavery for him was conceived in greed, born in sin, cradled in shame, and worthy of utter and relentless condemnation. He had the quality of directness and simplicity. When Collins would have turned the abolition influence to the support of a communistic scheme, Douglass opposed it vehemently. Slavery was the evil they were fighting, and their cause would be rendered still more unpopular if they ran after strange gods.

When Garrison pleaded for the rights of man, when Phillips with golden eloquence preached the doctrine of humanity and progress, men approved and applauded. When Parker painted the moral baseness of the times, men acquiesced shamefacedly. When Channing preached the gospel of love, they wished the dream might become a reality. But, when Douglass told the story of his wrongs and those of his brethren in bondage, they felt that here indeed was slavery embodied, here was an argument for freedom that could not be gainsaid, that the race that could produce in slavery such a man as Frederick Douglass must surely be worthy of freedom.

What Douglass's platform utterances in later years lacked of the vehemence and fire of his earlier speeches, they made up in wisdom and mature judgment. There is a note of exultation in his speeches just after the war. Jehovah had triumphed, his people were free. He had seen the Red Sea of blood open and let them pass, and engulf the enemy who pursued them.

Among the most noteworthy of Douglass's later addresses were the oration at the unveiling of the Freedmen's Monument to Abraham Lincoln in Washington in 1876, which may be found in his *Life and Times*; the address on Decoration Day, New York, 1878; his eulogy on Wendell Phillips, printed in Austin's *Life and Times of Wendell Phillips*; and the speech on the death of Garrison, June, 1879. He lectured in the Parker Fraternity Course in Boston, delivered numerous addresses to gatherings of colored men, spoke at public dinners and woman suffrage meetings, and retained his hold upon the interest of the public down to the very day of his death.

NOTE

1. Charles W. Chesnutt, *The Journals of Charles W. Chesnutt*, ed. Richard Brodhead (Durham, NC: Duke University Press, 1993), 164.

From Charles Waddell Chesnutt, *Frederick Douglass, a Biography* (Boston: Small, Maynard, 1899), vii–x, 1–3, 37–39, 107–108, 109–118.

From *Frederick Douglass: The Colored Orator* (1891)

FREDERIC MAY HOLLAND

This is the second time we have looked into Frederic May Holland's book on Douglass, the first at the end of the dramatic and contentious entries of "The Great Controversy," the divisive and acrimonious public exchanges over Douglass's turn toward political abolitionism and away from the Garrisonian camp. In his final autobiography, *Life and Times of Frederick Douglass*, Douglass himself recommends a turn to Holland for those who wish to be fair to the political abolitionists. Douglass notes that history seemed to favor the Garrisonians and to undervalue the political abolitionists, and he looks to the historian who would offer "an impartial history of this the grandest moral conflict of the century," adding that, in the meantime, he would find consolation in "the scrupulous justice done me in the biography of myself lately written by Mr. Frederick May Holland of Concord, Massachusetts."[1] Holland was the author of several books, some of which, like *Liberty in the Nineteenth Century*, demonstrated his deep connections to the group of reformers—from Ralph Waldo Emerson to the Alcotts to Theodore Parker—associated with Concord and Boston society.

A FULL ACCOUNT of his interview with Lincoln is given in his "Life and Times" (pp. 384–7): but it is interesting also to read what he said about it a few months afterward. On Friday, December 4, 1863, he was present at the Thirtieth Anniversary of the A. A. S. S., which was held in Philadelphia, in a hall ornamented with the American flag and the motto, "Union and Liberty." Many familiar speakers were heard from the platform, and several comparatively new ones. Among the latter was Senator Wilson, whose speech was so well suited to the times that a demand for three cheers was made by a colored man who had sat hitherto silent on the platform. He was now recognized; and as soon as the Senator had finished, there were cries from different parts of the hall of "Douglass! Douglass!" Then he spoke on the right of the Southern negro to the ballot. During his speech he referred to the time when he felt, on reaching Philadelphia, that he was rubbing against the wall of his prison and could go no farther. Now he was able to go back to Maryland, and even to Washington.

"I have been down there to see the President; and as you were not there, perhaps you may like to know how the President of the United States received a black man at the White House. I will tell you how he received me—just as you have seen one gentleman receive another" (great applause); "with a hand and a voice well-balanced between a kind cordiality and a respectful reserve. I tell you I felt big there." (Laughter.) "Let me tell you how I got to him; because everybody can't get to him. He has to be a little guarded in admitting spectators. The manner of getting to him gave me an idea that the cause was rolling on. The stair-way was crowded with applicants. Some of them looked eager; and I have no doubt some of them had a purpose in being there, and wanted to see the President for the good of the country. They were white; and as I was the only dark spot among them, I expected to have to wait at least half a day; I had heard of men waiting a week; but in two minutes after I sent in my card, the messenger came out, and respectfully invited 'Mr. Douglass' in. I could hear, in the eager multitude outside as they saw me pressing and elbowing my way through, the remark, 'Yes, d—n it, I knew they would let the nigger through,' in a kind of despairing voice—a Peace Democrat, I suppose." (Laughter.) "When I went in, the President was sitting in his usual position, I was told, with his feet in different parts of the room, taking it easy." (Laughter.) "Don't put this down, Mr. Reporter, I pray you; for I am going down there again to-morrow." (Laughter.) "As I came in and approached him, the President began to rise" (laughter), "and he continued rising, until he stood over me" (laughter); "and reaching out his hand, he said, 'Mr. Douglass, I know you; I have read about you, and Mr. Seward has told me about you'; putting me quite at ease at once.

"Now, you will want to know how I was impressed by him. I will tell you that, too. He impressed me as being just what every one of you have been in the habit of calling him—an honest man." (Applause.) "I have never met with a man who, on the first blush, impressed me more entirely with his sincerity, with his devotion to his country, and with his determination to save it at all hazards." (Applause.) "He told me, (I think he did me more honor than I deserve,) that I had made a little speech somewhere in New York and it had got into the papers, and among the things I had said was this; that if I were called upon to state what I regarded as the most sad and most disheartening feature in our present political and military situation, it would not be the various disasters experienced by our armies and our navies, on flood and field, but it would be the tardy, hesitating, vacillating policy of the President of the United States. And the President said to me, 'Mr. Douglass, I have been charged with being tardy, and the like';

and he went on, and partly admitted that he might seem slow; but he said: 'I am charged with vacillating; but, Mr. Douglass, I do not think that charge can be sustained; I think it cannot be shown that when I have once taken a position I have ever retreated from it.'" (Applause.) "That I regarded as the most significant point in what he said during our interview. I told him that he had been somewhat slow in proclaiming equal protection to our colored soldiers and prisoners; and he said that the country needed talking up to that point. He hesitated in regard to it, when he felt that the country was not ready for it. He knew that the colored man throughout this country was a despised man, a hated man, and that if he at first came out with such a proclamation, all the hatred which is poured on the head of the negro race would be visited on his administration. He said that there was preparatory work needed, and that that preparatory work had now been done. And he said, 'Remember this, Mr. Douglass; remember that Milliken's Bend, Port Hudson, and Fort Wagner are recent events; and that these were necessary to prepare the way for this very proclamation of mine.' I thought it was reasonable, but came to the conclusion that while Abraham Lincoln will not go down to posterity as Abraham the Great, or as Abraham the Wise, or as Abraham the Eloquent, although he is all three—wise, great, and eloquent, he will go down to posterity if the country is saved, as Honest Abraham" (Applause); "and going down thus, his name may be written anywhere in this wide world of ours, side by side with that of Washington, without disparaging the latter." (Renewed Applause.)

NOTE

1. Frederick Douglass, *Life and Times of Frederick Douglass*, in *Frederick Douglass: Autobiographies*, ed. Henry Louis Gates Jr. (New York: Library of America, 1994), 943.

From Frederic May Holland, *Frederick Douglass: The Colored Orator* (New York: Funk & Wagnalls, 1892), 303–306.

"A Tribute to Frederick Douglass" (1906)

MONROE ALPHEUS MAJORS

Born in Waco, Texas, in 1864, Monroe Alpheus Majors rose to a position of national leadership in the African American community. Having graduated from Meharry Medical College of Nashville, Tennessee, he became a prominent physician—and therefore a target among those whites who, in the late nineteenth century, threatened and sometimes lynched African Americans who achieved visible success. Majors worked with Douglass when he lived in Chicago, at which time Majors worked at the Provident Hospital while also editing the Texas *Searchlight*, one of several periodicals with which he was associated over the course of his career. The author of the book *Noted Negro Women* (1893), Majors appreciated deeply the importance of exemplary lives, and he naturally wanted to give voice to Douglass's, both in the biographical sketch that follows and in his *Epic Poem to Hon. Frederick Douglass* (1917). Here, Majors addresses Douglass's role in the 1893 World's Columbian Exhibition in Chicago, where Douglass served as the representative of Haiti.

THE MILLIONS WHO attended the great Chicago Fair saw it from many view points. Myriads of nationalities, coming around the globe to lend their presence to this emphasized world effort, to witness the aggregation of all the best, in the greatest effort of man, and to drink into gladdened eyes this conglomerate heap of huge achievement. The writer saw the World's Fair from his standpoint, and will name the narrative from the lessons it contains "The Strength of Honor."

The Fair with all of its indescribable grandeur, and almost limitless area of greatness, not to be confined within the narrow precincts of a large park—it was the world itself seen through a microscope, for nothing since the dawn of Christendom that man has ever attempted was found unfinished at this collective grouping of all age-effort. Strange as it may all appear in such a composite representation of human distinction of men and women honored, renowned, sung of in tender strains of melody, princes, princesses, foreign rulers, rajahs, high men in royal authority in countries where courtiers bow the knee as they pass, the Hon. Frederick Douglass to me was the greatest citizen in all that vast company of world celebrities. Appreciating keenly the inability on my part to do reverence to so noble a character, and contending that the race for which Mr. Douglass spent all of his active life has but poorly honored his greatness, and not very deeply respected his memory—words coming at such a belated period I trust will be placed on the credit side of the sum total of all that honor and respect has sincerely paid as tributes. Among the many things, his position as Commissioner General, representing the Haytian Government inspired in the American, was his "strength of honor." He had been humiliated by his own American fellow men. "He was not a bribe-taker," he could not rob men, by race his kinsmen, to suit a sentiment contrived in Wall street [*sic*], and did rather sever his honor from the office he held as Minister to Hayti. He kept his honor and allowed the papers of state to go with his official recall from duty. His representation of Hayti at the World's Fair accentuated the popular favor done them by Mr. Douglass, for which Hayti rewarded him. It was the most stalwart exoneration the world has ever witnessed. Thus the race in America for whom Mr. Douglass sacrificed his life has but poorly honored him. For say what you will, Mr. Douglass was the sole voice of the world's Negro, and represented that race in every conceivable way known to civilization. The Haytian Building was the capital for the world's Negro, and Mr. Douglass was the President in racial authority, greatness, and all that civilization appertains to the race.

There were other men, small in calibre, diminutive giants let us call them, but Mr. Douglass was in a class that never had but one pupil in it at a time. Statesmen have marveled at his imposing personality, thousands had been swayed by his matchless oratory, logical, argumentative, and strong, but at the White City during the World's Columbian Exposition hundreds of thousands were attracted around the Haytian Building by his rare charm of kindly grandeur, under which roof he presided with all the dignity and grace, like some great potentate, dispensing to all the courtesies of the peoples he personally represented. There were days upon days that he sought relaxation, and withdrew himself from the eager gaze of the multitude. At such times he might be seen taking in the sights along the Midway, or enjoying a ride in a gondolier, threading the extent of the waterway by Wooded Island, or sauntering the colossal isles of some magnificent exhibit hall. Paul Laurence Dunbar, Charles Morris, or some very dear attache of his department usually escorted him in such recreative jaunts. His Midway excursions portrayed the ripe spirit of extensive travels; he had seen many of these nationalities in their native haunts, and it was worth a great deal to hear him indulge his inquisitive aptitude among the Orientals. He delighted in the thought that the races of the earth, in spite of the civilization and history of conquest wrought by the haughty Caucasian, were here to add their quoto to the homogeneity of world acclamation.

In Festival Hall, on the occasion of the monstrous demonstration made by American Negroes, by their captivating song, entrancing music, elocution, and original odes, he said: "We are here as Negroes to applaud whatever feeble efforts we have made in the years of our citizenship and to thank the great American people for small favors."

On the occasion of the international meeting of World's Fair Commissioners, by some peculiar misunderstanding he was not put on the program as a Commissioner General representing a foreign power, but he was invited to be present and given a seat of honor among the princes, foreign generals, and representatives of all the crown heads. When the program was about to be concluded, and that mighty throng of seven hundred thousand people saw that Mr. Douglass was not to speak, pandemonium broke loose, and "Douglass, Douglass," went up from a hundred thousand throats simultaneously. No man in all Christendom before or since had ever received such merited honor from peoples of every nation, types and races of the entire world. It was the crowning moment of Mr. Douglass' eventful life—it was a tribute paid to his personality, unique in fame as well as singular in his cheerful individuality. He rose to be introduced. The eyes of that mighty throng were riveted to a single spot, and there before them stood that mighty champion of a struggling race, with hair white and long, beautifying his heavy head upon a giant's frame, well worn by time and the battles he had won, yet in the strength of eighty years "age had not wrecked nor time withered his infinite variety." He made a speech that wrung with philosophy, and saved the day of routine monotony. He said:

> It is great to represent a king, to be a potentate, and it is magnanimous to rule with a kindliness of heart a subordinate yeomanry, but my friends it is far greater to be a man, greater in the freedom which truth predicates, and grander in the loftiness of manly power to be a man untrammeled by the sordid love of sinister selfishness.

The great daily papers the next morning, throughout the world, in many languages spoke in one unanimous voice that the speech made by Hon. Frederick Douglass was the greatest effort in oratory and clean cut philosophy of the day. His apology to the audience that he did not come there to lift up his feeble voice where so weighty learning held sway, nor to mar so vast an occasion by the uplifted voice of one of the despised race, for there was not much his race could be thankful for, seemed to sharpen the keen ears of the audience, and two-thirds of a million voices of many peoples tore the air with "Douglass, go on; speak Douglass."

Upon other occasions, at the Ethnological Congress, at the national meeting of the Educational Association for the Colored Youths, and also in an answer to the Superintendent of Education of South Carolina, the writer heard the great sage of Anacostia each time with marked interest and always greatly charmed by his matchless oratory, which rang out to the thousands who eagerly listened to catch every word that fell from his lips.

Was Douglass great? Put him in the scale with others of his race, and that moment they sink into horrifying littleness. Stand him up by the side of any Negro on the earth—his size is huge, colossal are his proportions, diminutive are all others. Measure him with any method of measurement, with any Negro who has lived in the world since the remoteness of time, and the irrepressible magnetic orator of Tuckahoe will stand alone the one embodiment of greatness, the epitome of race hopes, the colossus of the Negro race, panoplied by the singularity and unique place he occupies in American history. Born at a time his race needed him, serving them throughout the ravage of a hostile sentiment against the oppressed, shedding honor in its full blaze of glory on the luckless members of his race to his dying day. Fighting for every inch of race attained freedom, and laying down his armor only when the Master called him away. The Negro has not reached that exalted place in its history when with one voice, like the Grecians, the Romans, the Jews, the Caucasians, they applaud their heroes, gladiators, poets, sculptors, artists and singers.

The hardships of ill-used races mark the pages of history with the ugly spirit of belated recognition and wholesome disregard. There will have to be given to the race a greater Dunbar, a greater Alberry Whitman, a greater Chesnutt and a greater Johnson in literature to brighten the literary world with their imaginative minds, whose intellectual excursions into the loftier magnitudes of thought will indeed win back to the Negro all the wasted greatness of racial worth. It will be at such a time when the Negro will have reached prettier heights in its race life of intellectual splendor—not merely bookish, but a plane of scholarly grandeur covering every field of science, art, mechanics and literature, all or either to serve the cause of a needy world.

It will be at such a time when the life of the race will support the earth-plane principles and live to prove its worthiness to die. Mr. Douglass used to say, "Make the most of this world because it comes first," and "Show your worthiness to be saved by living right in this world." For well nigh a century the Negro has had preached into his willing ears that heaven was a place of golden streets, where crowns were decked with stars, and the race has been church-ridden, religiously cursed by its over supply, that money-loving church officials might live on the fat of the land. Mr. Douglass took no stock in such nonsense. His position was non-sectarian as to church, and I believe he discarded religion as something that binds to this faith or to this doctrine. He was a Christian at heart, lived it and died it. Heaven is not a place, but a condition. This the Negro must learn, and more. He must learn that sinister motives are the emissaries of the church among races of the world, trust to religion less for this world and allow his judgment and common sense to rule with larger scope every affair which gives strength and vitality to his earthly existence, remembering with undiminished reverence that the gift of God is eternal life and that no bargains for heaven can be made over the collection table.

The history of Mr. Douglass is a treasure. His autobiography, his writings and speeches are a part of American history, interwoven with painstaking detail, legacies rich with the gems of race loftiness. His standard was so high in purpose, in accomplishment, his achievements so vast that the present age stands dumb in awe of his marvelous work. Some other age must sing of his glory. Some greater facilities will contrive the issue, a nobler race appreciate his marked personality, and at such a time color distinctions will war to claim him. We shall not see his like again.

Monroe Alpheus Majors, "A Tribute to Frederick Douglass," *Colored American Magazine* 11, no. 6 (December 1906): 387–390.

“Reminiscences of Frederick Douglass” (1916)

John P. Green

John P. Green was born of free parents in New Bern, North Carolina, in 1845. When his father died, his mother took him to Cleveland, Ohio, where he was educated in the public schools. In 1870, he was admitted to the bar of South Carolina, and he returned to Ohio, where he served as justice of the peace in Cleveland and, in 1881, was elected to the Ohio legislature, eventually serving three terms. Following his election in 1896, President McKinley appointed him postal stamp agent, the first time an African American was appointed to that post. Green was also a writer who published *Recollections of the Inhabitants, Localities, Superstitions and Ku Klux Klan Outrages of the Carolinas* (1880) and an autobiography, *Fact Stranger Than Fiction* (1920). Deeply involved in the Republican Party, Green was in a position to gather interesting anecdotes about Douglass while also placing him in the company of such prominent African Americans as Blanche K. Bruce, whom we have encountered before; John Mercer Langston, the first dean of Howard University's law school and the first president of Virginia Normal and Collegiate Institute, now known as Virginia State University; James M. Gregory, professor of Latin language and literature at Howard University; and Edward Wilmot Blyden, born in the West Indies but known mostly as an educator, writer, and diplomat from Liberia.

FREDERICK DOUGLASS was so great a man, and filled with so large a sphere in the activities of the world, during his eventful life, that, by your request, I give to you these anecdotes, as yet unpublished, that they may be preserved for future generations. The first, is by the courtesy of W. S. Kerruish, Esq., the Nestor of the Ohio bar.

First, in 1856, the senior class of the Western Reserve college, then located at Hudson, O., while casting about for an orator of country-wide fame, chose Frederick Douglass, notwithstanding he was a colored man. The president (not Dr. Thwing) and some of the professors demurred—said it would be bad policy to have a Negro speak for them. The students asserted their right; and on the eventful day, under a big tent, which was pitched on the campus, an immense crowd of the literary elite, listened enraptured, to his burning words of eloquence. During the course of his deliverance, he said, "They say the Negro is inferior to the white man, because he has a WEAK VOICE!!! Kerruish says, when Douglass stretched himself up to his towering height, shook his shaggy MANE and thundered forth those few words, WEAK VOICE, he nearly threw that concourse into hysteria. After that, nothing was said about the Negro's weak voice in that part of the country.

Second. In the summer of 1865, Mr. Douglass was orator of the day and the [cynosure] of all eyes, at Iron City Park (now built up), Pittsburgh. I called upon him at the nice home of old "Father Peck," whom some of our older citizens may remember. Although I was a mere youth, trying to raise means to go to school, yet, he kindly and cordially received me. He commended my efforts to improve my mind [and] told me to seek the association of educated men; to observe their conduct closely; and to try to copy their diction—their conversation. He told me, that, he owed the purity of his speech and elevation of his ideas and thoughts, more to this conduct on his part, than any other cause. He said he had never attended school a day to prepare himself for his great work. Speaking from an elevated platform at the park, in the afternoon, he said, "My friends, there is a young man on the grounds—a mere youth, trying to sell a little book he has written, to get money with which to go to school; patronize him—buy his book [text missing]."

Third. In the winter of 1882, the late Professor James M. Gregory arranged a great banquet in honor of Mr. Douglass, in Washington, D.C. On invitation, I went to Washington and paid $7 for a seat and plate at the banquet board. Dr. Blyden, John M. Langston, Senator Blanche K. Bruce, and many other distinguished colored men were present. When the great Douglass entered the spacious hall, where a hundred or more were eagerly awaiting his coming, we all, to a man, arose. Mr. Douglass towering above all the rest, was FACILE PRINCEPS, verily an uncrowned king amongst men.

Fourth. At the national Republican convention, in Chicago, 1884, when the late James G. Blaine, was nominated for president, by the Republicans, we were both present. Mr. Douglass was invited to a seat on the platform, amongst the August dignitaries of the G.O.P. and in other ways, he was highly honored by all. At night, in an immense hall, the colored citizens poured themselves out, to hear Mr. Douglass. This writer was the other speaker with him. I said to him, "Mr. Douglass, some are complaining because you have married a white lady"; he said quietly, "Yes; but, that is my own personal affair. My first wife was a black woman, and some took exception to that. Now, I have evened it up."

Fifth. Reverend Joseph Parker of the London City Temple, Holborn Viaduct—a great divine, said to me: "That countryman of yours, Frederick Douglass, I regard a great statesman and philosopher." Mr. Parker craved a copy of Douglass' autobiography, I gave him mine, which I happened to have with me—in the next mail, he sent me a "British Sovereign for that son and heir of yours," referring to my son, William. Dr. Parker related the following anecdote concerning Douglass, which had come to him, from an authentic source: "During the dark days between the execution of 'Old John Brown' and the Civil War, Douglass was, on an occasion, addressing an audience in Faneuil hall, Boston. It was easily seen that, he was not at his best, his heart was 'bowed down!' Up rose old Sojourner Truth, who exclaimed, in a thrill, piping voice, 'Frederick, is GOD dead?' Douglass awoke as from a dream, and thence forward acquitted himself, like a man!"

Sixth. Mrs. Eliza Wigham, since deceased, told me that when Douglass visited Edenborough [Edinburgh], Scotland, during the great Irish famine, nearly 70 years ago, he took a spade from the hands of a workman and cut in the green lawn, which spreads out from the foot of Arthur's Seat, these words: "Send the money back!" quoting the words of the great Daniel O'Connell, the champion of the rights of his countrymen. O'Connell said, referring to a large fund sent over to Ireland by slave holders in the United States, to relieve their distress during the famine, "Send the money back, we do not want blood money." An officer passing by was about to place Douglass under arrest, but, upon explanation, he was excused and commended.

Seventh. Referring to the Chicago platform of 1884, in which the rights of the freed men were relegated and the protective tariff was made prominent, Mr. Douglass wrote to me in the letter which I still have, in substance, "It used to be customary to use a red herring to kill the scent and lead the blood-hounds off the trail; the protective tariff, this year, is the red herring to divert the attention of the people from the welfare of the Negro who is being greatly abused in the Southland."

Cleveland, O., Feb. 18, 1915.

John P. Green, "Reminiscences of Frederick Douglass," *Cleveland Advocate* 2, no. 42 (February 26, 1916): 3.

From "Two Episodes of Anti-Slavery Days" (1925)

HORACE McGUIRE

Horace McGuire was a white man born to extreme poverty (a family abandoned by a father for the Gold Rush, from which he never returned) who worked in various printing offices in upstate New York—Binghamton, Elmira, and Horseheads—before moving to Rochester where, at age fifteen, he began working for Frederick Douglass. It was while working for *Frederick Douglass' Paper* that he witnessed Douglass's meeting with the fiery abolitionist John Brown, which he describes here. As other entries have indicated, Douglass's association with Brown was viewed with great suspicion, and Douglass had reason to worry about being implicated in the aftermath of Brown's raid on Harpers Ferry. Following Brown's arrest, Douglass fled to Canada to avoid being arrested and from there sailed to England, where he stayed for six months. He returned to the United States only when he received news of the death of his daughter Anna. McGuire would later become one of the white officers of African American troops in the Civil War, about which service he speaks movingly in his autobiography.

THE OTHER EPISODE to which I now refer briefly occurred in 1859. My family had removed from Syracuse, my birthplace, to Rochester, and I, a young man, was employed in the printing office of Frederick Douglass. The office was on Main Street in the old Wilder Arcade building or one that preceded it and adjoined the rooms of the *Rochester Democrat*. I had worked for a while on the *Democrat*, then owned and published by Alvah Strong, father of Rev. Augustus H. and Henry Strong. It was through the kindness of Alvah Strong that I obtained employment with Mr. Douglass. My duties were of a varied character. I was at the office at six-thirty, a.m., to make the fire and sweep out. I set type, did errands, and tried to make myself generally useful. It was no unusual thing to find colored persons, refugee slaves, sitting on the stairs as I came to open the office in the early morning. I became conversant with the location of the stations of the so-called "under-ground railroad." The house of Mr. Douglass on South Avenue was the principal station here. Trusted men and women did not hesitate to open their houses and secrete these fugitives from slavery. Among the friends in Rochester were Isaac Post, William Hallowell and Samuel D. Porter. At night these black people were taken on their way to Charlotte or Oswego or Lewiston, going as far as possible during the darkness and stopping at daylight to be again secreted in the houses or barns of men known to be of the Abolition Party. It is related that a family of five persons, colored fugitives, were hidden in the barn of Samuel D. Porter on the corner of Fitzhugh and Spring Streets. The officers had searched Mr. Porter's house and barn, but had failed to look under the hay.

The office consisted of but a single room, in one corner of which was Mr. Douglass' desk and around the sides of the room were the cases of type, where his son Frederick, Jr., and sometimes his daughter Rosa, with my help, set the type for the paper formerly *The North Star*, then *Frederick Douglass' Paper*. When the forms were locked up we carried them into the office of the *Democrat*, where the edition was printed. We then folded, single-wrapped and mailed the papers to the subscribers.

I remember the occasion of a call, early one morning when I was alone in the office. The visitor was a tall, white man, with shaggy whiskers, rather unkempt, a keen piercing eye, and a restlessness of manner:

> Like one who on a lonely road
> Doth walk in fear and dread,
> And having once turned round walks on
> And turns no more his head.

I asked the stranger to be seated and informed him Mr. Douglass would be in soon. As Mr. Douglass was out of town much of the time giving lectures, it did not occur to me then as strange that this white man did not inquire whether or not Mr. Douglass was in town. Since then I became convinced the interview was by appointment. This visitor was John Brown, whose soul is said to be marching on.

When Mr. Douglass came in, the greeting between the white man and the former slave was very cordial. They had been friends for years. These two men talked freely and I recall only enough of the conversation to have been convinced that in most earnest terms Mr. Douglass entreated his friend to abandon some project. This was several months prior to October 16, 1859, when this same white man, John Brown, was arrested and put to death for his ill-advised raid at Harper's Ferry.

It is a matter of history that only a few weeks before the raid, John Brown urged Douglass to visit him at Chambersburg, and that there, for two days, Douglass tried to convince Brown of the folly of the attempt. On that occasion John Brown said to Mr. Douglass:

> Come with me, Douglass! I will defend you with my life. I want you for a special purpose. When I strike, the bees will begin to swarm and I shall want you to help hive them.

Notwithstanding the refusal of Mr. Douglass to join the John Brown raid, he was an object of suspicion, and so great was the fear of his arrest his friends urged flight. Accordingly Mr. Douglass took refuge in Canada and went from Quebec to England.

Horace McGuire, "Two Episodes of Anti-Slavery Days" [read before the Rochester Historical Society, October 27, 1916], *Publications in the Rochester Historical Society* 4 (1925): 218–220.

From *Frederick Douglass* (1906)

Booker T. Washington

Booker T. Washington was the first black leader to attain a level of national recognition and influence that eclipsed that of Douglass at his prime. Like Douglass, Washington was born into slavery, though much later than Douglass, in 1856. Washington accordingly grew up in a significantly different world than that which Douglass had known through most of his life. Having graduated from Hampton Normal and Agricultural School, and then from Wayland Seminary, Washington was appointed the first leader of Tuskegee Institute in Alabama in 1881. An astute politician, Washington built the school and his own influence, and the "Tuskegee Machine" became the dominant influence on black intellectual and social life into the early twentieth century. Washington's methods and goals during this difficult time for African Americans were not without their critics, and he is often remembered today as an accommodationist, willing to give up too much to acquire only limited rights and opportunity for African Americans, but his successes were significant all the same. The challenges Washington faced in negotiating a violently threatening racial climate while still pressing for African American opportunities make his biography of Douglass, published in 1906, especially revealing. Like many before and after, Washington looks for a Douglass capable of supporting his own views on racial struggle.

Preface

The chance or destiny which brought to this land of ours, and placed in the midst of the most progressive and the most enlightened race that Christian civilization has produced, some three or four millions of primitive black people from Africa and their descendants, has created one of the most interesting and difficult social problems which any modern people has had to face. The effort to solve this problem has put to a crucial test the fundamental principles of our political life and the most widely accepted tenets of our Christian faith. Frederick Douglass's career falls almost wholly within the first period of the struggle in which this problem has involved the people of this country,—the period of revolution and liberation. That period is now closed. We are at present in the period of construction and readjustment. Many of the animosities engendered by the conflicts and controversies of half a century ago still survive to confuse the councils of those who are seeking to live in the present and the future, rather than in the past. But changes are rapidly coming about that will remove, or at least greatly modify, these lingering animosities. This book will have failed of its purpose just so far as anything here said shall serve to revive or keep alive the bitterness of those controversies of which it gives the history; it will have attained its purpose just so far as it aids its readers to comprehend the motives of, and the men who entered with such passionate earnestness into, the struggle of which it gives in part a picture—particularly the one man, the story of whose life is here narrated. [. . .]

I must also acknowledge my sense of gratitude for the opportunity afforded in this work of getting close to the heart and life of this great leader of my race. No Negro can read and study the life of Frederick Douglass without deriving from it courage to look up and forward.

Further Evidences of Popular Esteem, with Glimpses into the Past

The foregoing chapters contain the important incidents and events in the life of Frederick Douglass. He lived in a great transitional period, and, in his struggle to gain his own freedom, he personified the historic events which took place during that time. His life was so wholly under the public eye, and what he did and stood for during more than fifty years, were so much an integral portion of these years, that it is impossible to obtain an estimate of the man apart from the history of slavery. Frederick Douglass and Anti-slavery, are almost interchangeable terms. In himself he was both the argument and demonstration of the things that gave interest and meaning to his life and times. Yet he had another side not exhibited in the history of which he was a part and which he helped to make. Much of a personal nature that would add interest to his life and partly explain the sources of his strength as a leader of men, can be added to the portrait.

The limitations of this volume will permit only a brief outline of some of the things that Frederick Douglass said and did during the last thirty years of his life, which chronologically belonged to previous chapters, but which for the sake of their peculiar significance are reserved for this.

As may be inferred from what has appeared in the course of this narrative, Frederick Douglass was a more than ordinarily interesting personality. He was a figure to attract attention anywhere, and especially so during the last twenty-five years of his life. He was over six feet in height, broad-shouldered, well-proportioned, and his movements had all the directness and grace of a man who had been bred a prince rather than a slave. His features were broad, strong, and impressive. His complexion was that of a mulatto. His head was strikingly large, and crowned with an abundant crop of white hair of almost silken fineness. His eyes were brown and mildly animated. His voice was strong, but of mellow tone. When he was aroused, however, it would fairly thunder with the passionate earnestness of the man. In conversation he was delightful. His manner was graceful and wholly free from personal mannerisms. His mental and moral faculties were well balanced. He was a man without technical education, yet he had more than ordinary learning. All that he knew was acquired outside of schoolrooms and without school teachers. His great library bore witness to his love of books. In the history of governments and of races, and in mental philosophy and poetry, he found special delight. No trained elocutionist could recite verse with better effect. He was especially fond of Byron, Burns, Coleridge, and Pierpont.

He was always quick to recognize ability in one of his race, and so had a peculiar fondness and interest in Paul Laurence Dunbar, who, at his death, was just beginning to be known as a poet, and who received his first real encouragement from Frederick Douglass.

He had an unfailing memory, and consequently a good command of everything he ever saw, heard, or read. He was liked and honoured by men and women, not only because he was interesting, but also because he was singularly free from crotchets, idiosyncrasies, and ill-temper. He was of a lovable disposition, and especially so in the latter days of his life. The all too common character blemishes of selfishness, envy, and jealousy were never charged against him. His whole nature was keyed to high, generous impulses. He loved the right, and hated wrong in any form.

No man of his prominence was freer from vices: he was of temperate habits, clean speech, and personal rectitude. His sense of honour was not partial, but a controlling force in all of his relationships to men and things.

He was also fortunately free from family troubles, except the loss by death of a beloved little daughter, whose few gentle and beautiful years had been his delight, a sorrow which deeply shadowed the earlier period of his public career. His wife, who had helped him to gain his freedom, devoted her life to his comfort and to the happiness of his home. His three stalwart sons, Lewis, Charles, and Frederick, Jr., honoured him by lives of usefulness, and there was always the closest intimacy between him and them. His oldest girl, named Rosa, was very dear to him. She grew up by his side as a faithful helper in his work as well as a devoted daughter. She is widely known and loved for her culture and unselfish disposition. In short, Frederick Douglass's family was worthy of him. If by his deeds he brought to them honour and opportunity, he lived long enough to see his example and precepts honoured again in them.

His home in Cedar Hill, overlooking the Capitol, was a delightful spot. Everything about it bespoke the character of the man. The broad grounds, shaded with trees, the well-cultivated garden, all told of his love of nature. Within the ample house there was a quiet, restful refinement, revealing the taste and habits of the scholar. Books, busts, and pictures all bore witness to that instinctive thirst for culture which no one who knew him well could fail to recognize. He had an extraordinary passion for the violin, and, although he did not place a very high estimate on his own ability, yet he, as well as his nearest friends, received much enjoyment from his knowledge of the use of this instrument.

In later years he found a special delight in the fact that his grandson, Joseph Douglass, exhibited a decided taste and a real genius for the violin. A more affecting picture of the power of music could scarcely be imagined than that of the old man sitting and listening with rapt and tearful attention when this boy played for him some of his favorite tunes.

But perhaps these glimpses of the personality of Frederick Douglass are sufficient to suggest that, behind the great orator, the active politician, the anxious leader in a critical period, there was a real man, whose domestic tastes and disciplined heart give an added value to his public life. It is not at all surprising that one thus gifted should have had many intimates among the best people of his generation. The leading statesmen, educators, and literary men were counted as his close and personal friends. Behind the respect that was felt for his natural talents and his unusual achievements was a sincere admiration and even fondness for the large and warm-hearted nature which could laugh and cry and be touched by the social delights of home and fireside. He was a man of opinions, of ideals, of imagination, and had the gift of adequate expression for every thought and emotion.

After the death of his first wife, Mr. Douglass married again, in 1884, and for this step he was severely criticized. The fact that his second wife, Miss Helen Pitts, was a white woman caused something like a revulsion of feeling throughout the entire country. His own race especially condemned him, and the notion seemed to be quite general that he had made the most serious mistake of his life. Just how deep-seated was the sentiment of white and black people alike against amalgamation has never been so clearly demonstrated as in this case. Douglass was sorely hurt by the many unkind things said about his marriage by members of his own race.

The woman whom he married he had known and admired for many years. She had helped him in various ways in his literary work. She belonged to one of the best families in western New York, and in following the natural impulse of his attachment, he failed to take into consideration the offence his act might give to public feeling. The resentment felt by the people because of his disregard of its unwritten law never entirely died out in his lifetime, but he himself got over the personal discomfiture of it. In addressing a large audience of white and coloured people in Springfield, Mo., in the fall of 1893, he referred to this incident in the following words: "I am strongly of the opinion that you will want me to say something concerning my second marriage. I will tell you: My first wife, you see, was the colour of my mother, and my second wife the colour of my father; you see I wanted to be perfectly fair to both races." This clever bit of raillery on a very delicate subject put him on good terms with his audience and if any were inclined to think the less of him because of his marriage the fact did not then appear.

In the period from 1865 to the Columbian Exposition at Chicago, in 1893, Mr. Douglass was interested in many things. He made various addresses outside of the range of politics, and was busy to the limit of his waning strength. What he wrote found ready acceptance in important publications, and his absence from any great national gathering was a matter of regret. [. . .]

In the matter of religion, Mr. Douglass was not strictly orthodox in his beliefs, although it will be remembered that during his enslavement he found much consolation in the Bible, and was for a time a Methodist exhorter. His religious views, as he grew older, underwent a radical change. He had no patience with hypocrites. He had seen and heard so much that was cruel, unjust, and almost fiendish under the name of religion, that his faith in sectarianism was badly shaken. In his early anti-slavery addresses, he indulged in many absurd parodies of the pious frauds whom he had known. However, he was not an atheist. He had a deep religious sense, but was more fully under the influence of the theological opinions of Theodore Parker than of any other school of religious thought. His best friends and associates were among the Unitarians, the Quakers, and others of liberal faith. His views on religion are finely expressed in a bit of correspondence published by Mr. Holland in his biography. In response to a cordial invitation to speak before the "Free Religious Association" in Boston, in 1874, he wrote:

> I cannot be present at your Free Religious Convention in Boston. This is, of course, of smaller consequence to others than to myself, for I should come more to hear than to be heard. Freedom is a word of charming sound, not only to the tasked and tortured slaves, who toil for an earthly master, but for those who would break the galling chains of darkness and superstition. Regarding the Free Religious movement as one for light, love, and liberty, limited only by reason and human welfare, and opposed to those who convert life and death into enemies of human happiness, who people the invisible world with ghastly taskmasters, I give it hearty welcome. Only the truth can make men free, and I trust that your convention will be guided in all its utterances by its light and feel its power. I know many of its good men and women, who are likely to assemble with you, and I would gladly share with them the burden of reproach which their attacks upon popular error will be sure to bring upon them.

Extracts from letters to friends indicate still more clearly the deeper currents of his thoughts.

> I once had a large stock of hope on hand, but like the sand in the glass, it has about run out. My present solace is in the cultivation of religious submission to the inevitable, in teaching myself that I am but a breath of the infinite, perhaps not so much. I was very sorry not to be able to attend the Free Religious Convention. I shall, hereafter, try to know more of these people. . . . I sometimes, at long intervals, try my old violin; but after all the music of the past and of imagination is sweeter than any my unpracticed and unskilled bow can produce. So I lay my dear old fiddle aside, and listen to the soft, silent, distant music of other days which, in the hush of my spirit, I still find lingering somewhere in the mysterious depths of my soul.

> I do not know that I am an evolutionist, but to this extent, I am one. I certainly have more patience with those who trace mankind upward from a low condition, even from the lower animals, than with those who start him at a point of perfection and conduct him to a level with the brutes. I have no sympa-

thy with a theory that starts man in Heaven, and stops him in Hell. . . . An irrepressible conflict, grander than that described by the late William H. Seward, is perpetually going on. Two hostile and irreconcilable tendencies, broad as the world of man, are in the open field; good and evil, truth and error, enlightenment and superstition. [. . .]

Final Honours to the Living and Tributes to the Dead

With the closing of the Exposition in the autumn of 1893, ended the last chapter in his life as a public official. As office-holding, however, was by no means the most important part of his career, it did not require an office to keep him in view of the people. His prominence outlasted that of many of his contemporaries who were more favoured than he in the matter of public service. He remained, up to the very last hour of his life, one of the few men of the nation of whom it never tired. This was so, largely because he was more a part of the present than of the past. Though he compassed in his life over a half-century of national history, he never got out of touch with current events, retaining to the end his influence on public opinion in all those matters in which he was peculiarly interested, and in regard to which his views had special authority. [. . .]

The last two years of his life seem to have been more free from care and active duties than any previous period. He merited a rest and he had everything about him to contribute to his ease and enjoyment. Among the trees and flowers of his ample grounds on Cedar Hill, and surrounded by his books and the comforts of his classic home, life went on serenely and happily.

One of the interesting sights here was the procession of people of all kinds making pilgrimages every day to the home of "the Sage of Anacostia," as he was fondly called by his friends and neighbours. Thousands of coloured persons visited him to pay their respects to the man whose life had been consecrated to the cause of their emancipation and citizenship. To all he was kindly and considerate. His mind was as alert and keen as ever, and thoroughly alive to passing events. He had a special fondness for the young men of his race, and particularly those who were educated and progressive. It was always an inspiration to him to see the numbers of young coloured men, who were fitting themselves by study and application to pass civil service examinations, and gain for themselves positions of importance in all departments of the government. He frequently invited them to his home to dine with him, and would discuss with them the possibilities for their advancement in all lines of endeavor. He was always hopeful regarding the progress of these young men in business and in the professions.

He was generous, almost to a fault, with his time, money, and services in behalf of any cause that meant a step forward for his people. His health was uniformly good. Every day he was either riding or walking about the streets of Washington, or in conference with those who needed his advice and assistance in all kinds of helpful enterprises. He had a part in every civic event of any importance in the District of Columbia. No one coloured man before or since his death has wielded so much influence in all directions. He had not only won the esteem of the people of Washington, but he knew how to deserve and retain it. In the District government, in the public schools, and at Howard University, his influence was felt and respected.

What he himself was, he had gained by hard work, consecration, temperate habits, and God-fearing conduct toward all his fellows. His life and achievements spoke eloquently to the young men about him and pointed the way to progress. Mr. Douglass had richly earned everything that he had, and those who took him as a model were made to realize that success comes not as a gift, but must be deserved and won as a reward for right thinking and high living. Poor as were his people in all things, Frederick Douglass found enough to be proud of in them and urged continuously upon the younger generation the necessity of cultivating a spirit of race pride,—of setting before themselves and the race of which they were members clear and definite ideals.

In nothing else was the life of Mr. Douglass so important as in the uplifting influence he exerted, directly and indirectly, upon the young men of his time. There were many good leaders worthy of emulation, but none who exercised the authority that he did over the opinions of the other members of his race. His life was an open book. Naturally there were those of his colour who envied him; who sought to discredit his worth and work; who felt that so long as he lived and spoke, none other could be known or heard. The young men of force and intelligence, however, who had it in them to do something large and important looked up to and were inspired by the "old man eloquent" of the Negro race.

It is easily possible to extend observations of this kind concerning the personality and influence of this great man during those restful years when he was happily free from care and public responsibilities. How little he thought of death! Sound of body and sane of mind, and always thinking and planning for what should come after, he lived as if there was no claim upon his future existence which he could not adjust. When death did come on the second day of February, 1895, it found him with no preparation, in the ordinary sense, for its message. And yet it had always been his expressed wish that he should go as he did—"to fall as the leaf in the autumn of life."

On that day he had been attending the Council of Women which was meeting in Metzerott's Hall in the city of Washington, and was much interested in the proceedings. He was an honorary member of that body. They were in quest of larger liberties for themselves, as he so long had been for himself and his people. When Frederick Douglass appeared at the convention in the morning, he was greeted with applause and escorted to the platform by a committee. He remained there nearly the entire day. When he returned to his home on Cedar Hill for dinner, he was in the best of spirits, and with a great deal of animation and pleasure, discussed with Mrs. Douglass the incidents of the meeting.

After the meal he prepared himself to deliver an address in a coloured Baptist church near by. His carriage was at the door. While passing through the hall from the dining-room, he seemed to drop slowly upon his knees, but in such a way that the movement did not excite any alarm in his wife. His face wore a look of surprise as he exclaimed, "Why, what does this mean?" Then, straightening his body upon the floor, he was gone. The men who responded to Mrs. Douglass's agonized cries for help, came hurriedly with physicians, but it was too late. Douglass was dead—without pain, without warning, without fear, and at a time when life was sweet, full, and complete. His last moment of enthusiasm, like his first hours of aspiration when a slave-child, was for liberty; if not for himself, then for some one else.

The announcement that Frederick Douglass was dead came like a shock to every one, especially to those who had seen him about the city during the day, full of animation and apparent physical vigour. The sad news spread rapidly and produced a profound sense of bereavement among all classes of people.

From Booker T. Washington, *Frederick Douglass* (London: Hodder & Stoughton, 1906), 3–6, 302–307, 320–322, 336–341.

From *Race Adjustment: Essays on the Negro in America* (1909)

KELLY MILLER

Born in Winnsboro, South Carolina, in 1863, Kelly Miller eventually became one of the most imposing African American intellectuals of the early twentieth century. After graduating from Howard University in 1886, Miller became the first African American admitted to Johns Hopkins University, where he studied mathematics, physics, and astronomy. He returned to Howard in 1890 to serve as professor of mathematics and, after introducing sociology into the curriculum in 1895, as professor of sociology from 1895 to 1934. Miller was associated with the most prominent black leaders of his time, and his many writings, including a weekly column that appeared in numerous newspapers, offer some of the most cogent views on racial politics and African American civil rights of the time. Miller frequently mentioned Douglass in his writings, not always admiringly, but the following two pieces are his most famous statements on the man who defined black leadership and activism when Miller was coming of age.

From "Radicals and Conservatives"

The radical and conservative tendencies of the Negro race cannot be better described than by comparing, or rather contrasting, the two superlative colored men in whom we find their highest embodiment—Frederick Douglass and Booker Washington, who were both picked out and exploited by white men as the mouthpiece and intermediaries of the black race. The two men are in part products of their times, but are also natural antipodes. Douglass lived in the day of moral giants; Washington lives in the era of merchant princes. The contemporaries of Douglass emphasized the rights of man; those of Washington, his productive capacity. The age of Douglass acknowledged the sanction of the Golden Rule; that of Washington worships the Rule of Gold. The equality of men was constantly dinned into

Douglass's ears; Washington hears nothing but the inferiority of the Negro and the dominance of the Saxon. Douglass could hardly receive a hearing today; Washington would have been hooted off the stage a generation ago. Thus all truly useful men must be, in a measure, time-servers; for unless they serve their time, they can scarcely serve at all. But great as was the diversity of formative influences that shaped these two great lives, there is no less opposability in their innate bias of character. Douglass was like a lion, bold and fearless; Washington is tomblike, meek and submissive. Douglass escaped from personal bondage, which his soul abhorred; but for Lincoln's proclamation, Washington would probably have arisen to esteem and favor in the eyes of his master as a good and faithful servant. Douglass insisted upon rights; Washington insists upon duty. Douglass held up to public scorn the sins of the white man; Washington portrays the faults of his own race. Douglass spoke what he thought the world should hear; Washington speaks only what he feels it is disposed to listen to. Douglass's conduct was actuated by principle; Washington's by prudence. Douglass had no limited, copyrighted programme for his race, but appealed to the Decalogue, the Golden Rule, the Declaration of Independence, the Constitution of the United States; Washington, holding these great principles in the shadowy background, presents a practical expedient applicable to present needs. Douglass was a moralist, insisting upon the application of righteousness to public affairs; Washington is a practical opportunist, accepting the best terms which he thinks it possible to secure.

"Frederick Douglass"

The highest function of a great name is to serve as an example and as a perpetual source of inspiration to the young who are to come after him. By the subtle law known as "consciousness of kind" a commanding personality incites the sharpest stimulus and exerts the deepest intensity of influence among the group from which he springs. We gather inspiration most readily from those of our class who have been touched with the feeling of our infirmities and have been subject to like conditions as ourselves. Every class, every race, every country, and indeed every well-defined group of social interests has its own glorified names whose fame and following are limited to the prescribed sphere of influence. Indeed, human relations are so diverse and human interests and feelings so antagonistic that the names which command even a fanatical following among one class may be despised and rejected by another. He who serves his exclusive class may be great in the positive degree; the man who serves a whole race or country may be considered great in the comparative degree; but it is only the man who breaks the barrier of class and creed and country and serves the human race that is worthy to be accounted great in the superlative degree. We are so far the creatures of local and institutional environment, and so disposed to borrow our modes of thought and feeling from our social medium, that even an appeal to the universal heart must be adapted to the spirit and genius of the time and people to whom it is first made. Even the Savior of the world offered the plan of salvation first to the Jews in the traditional guise of the Hebrew cult.

It is essential that any isolated, proscribed class should honor its illustrious names. They serve not only as a measure of their possibilities, but they possess greater inspirational power by virtue of their close sympathetic and kindly touch. Small wonder that such people are wont to glorify their distinguished men out of proportion to their true historical setting on the scale of human greatness.

Frederick Douglass is the one commanding historic character of the colored race in America. He is the model of emulation of those who are struggling up through the trials and difficulties which he himself suffered and subdued. He is illustrative and exemplary of what they might become—the first fruit of promise of a dormant race. To the aspiring colored youth of this land Mr. Douglass is, at once, the inspiration of their hopes and the justification of their claims.

I do not on this occasion intend to dwell upon the well-known facts and circumstances in the life and career of Mr. Douglass, but deem it more profitable to point out some of the lessons to be derived from that life.

In the first place, Mr. Douglass began life at the lowest possible level. It is only when we understand the personal circumstances of his early environment that we can appreciate the pathos and power with which he was wont to insist upon the true measure of the progress of the American Negro, not by the height already attained, but by the depth from which he came. It has been truly said that it required a greater upward move to bring Mr. Douglass to the status in which the ordinary white child is born than is necessary on the part of the latter to reach the presidency of the United States. The early life of this gifted child of nature was spent amid squalor, deprivation and cruel usage. Like Melchizedek of old, it can be said of him that he sprung into existence without father or mother, or beginning of days. His little body was unprotected from the bitter, biting cold, and his vitals griped with the gnawing pangs of hunger. We are told that he vied with the dogs for the crumbs that fell from his master's table. He tasted the sting of a cruel slavery, and drank the cup to its very dregs. And yet he arose from this lowly and degraded estate and gained for himself a place among the illustrious names of his country.

We hear much in this day and time about the relative force of environment and heredity as factors in the formation of character. But, as the career of Mr. Douglass illustrates, there is a subtle power of personality which, though the product of neither, is more potential than both. God has given to each of us an irrepressible inner something, which, for want of better designation, the old philosophy used to call the freedom of the will, which counts for most in the making of manhood.

In the second place, I would call attention to the tremendous significance of a seemingly trifling incident in his life. When he was about thirteen years of age he came into possession of a copy of the "Columbian Orator," abounding in dramatic outbursts and stirring episodes of liberty. It was the ripened fruit of the choicest spirits, upon which the choicest spirits feed. This book fired his whole soul and kindled an unquenchable love for liberty. It is held by some that at the age of puberty the mind is in a state of unstable equilibrium, and, like a pyramid on its apex, may be thrown in any direction by the slightest impression of force. The instantaneity of religious conversions, which the Methodists used to acclaim with such triumphant outbursts of hallelujah, may rest upon some such psychological foundation. When the child nature stands at the parting of the ways, between youth and adolescence, it yields to some quickening touch, as the fuse to the spark, or as the sensitized plate to the impressions of sunlight. There are "psychological moments" when the revealed idea rises sublimely above the revealing agent. According to the theory of harmonies, if two instruments are tuned in resonant accord the vibrations of the one will wake up the slumbering chords of the other. Young Douglass' soul was in sympathetic resonance with the great truth of human brotherhood and equality, and needed only the psychological suggestion which the "Columbian Orator" supplied. In a moment, in the twinkling of an eye, it burned deep into his soul and made an ineffaceable impression upon his consciousness of the gospel of brotherhood and equality of man. It was the same truth which could only be impressed upon the Apostle Peter in the rhapsodies of a heavenly vision. The age of revelation is not past, and will not pass so long as there remains one soul that yearns for spiritual illumination. There comes at times into our lives some sudden echo of the heavenly harmony from the unseen world, and happy is that soul which beats in vibrant harmony with that supernal sound. When the gospel of liberty first dawned upon the adolescent Douglass, as he perused the pages of the "Columbian Orator," there is no rendition of either the old or the new school of psychology that can analyze the riot of thought and sentiment that swept through his turbulent soul. This was indeed his new birth, his baptism with fire from on high. From that moment he was a possessed man. The love of liberty bound him with its subtle cords and did not release him until the hour of his death on Anacostia's mist-clad height.

Our educational philosophers are ransacking their brains to prescribe wise curricula of study for colored youth. There is not so much need of that which gives information to the mind or cunning to the fingers as that which touches the soul and quickens the spirit. There must be first aroused dormant consciousness of manhood with its inalienable rights, privileges, and dignity. The letter killeth, the spirit maketh alive. The "Columbia Orator" contributed more towards arousing the manhood of Mr. Douglass than all the traditional knowledge of all the schools. Of what avail is the mastery of all branches of technical and refined knowledge unless it touches the hidden springs of manhood? The value of any curriculum of study for a suppressed class that is not pregnant with moral energy, and that does not make insistent and incessant appeal to the half-conscious manhood within is seriously questionable. The revelation to a young man of the dignity, I had almost said the divinity, of his own selfhood is worth more to him in the development of character and power than all the knowledge in all the deluxe volumes in the gilded Carnegie libraries.

In the third place, Negro youth should study Mr. Douglass as a model of manly courage. In order to acquire a clear conception of principles let us discriminate sharply in the use of terms. Courage is that quality which enables one to encounter danger and difficulties with firmness and resolution of spirit. It is the swell of soul which meets outward pressure with inner resistance. Fortitude, on the other hand, is the capacity to endure, the ability to suffer and be strong. It is courage in the passive voice. True courage sets up an ideal and posits a purpose; it calculates the cost and is economic of means, though never faltering in determination to reach that end. Bravery is mere physical daring in the presence of danger, and responds to temporary physical and mental excitation. He who is eager to fight every evil which God allows to exist in society does not display rational courage. Even our Savior selected the evils against which He waged war. The caged eagle which beats his wings into insensibility against the iron bars of his prison-house is accounted a foolish bird. On the other hand, "the linnet void of noble raze" has gained the everlasting seal of poetic disapproval. It is not genuine courage to go through the world like the knight in the tale with sword in hand and challenge on lips to offer mortal combat to every windmill of opposition.

Mr. Douglass was courageous in the broadest and best significance of the term. He set before him as the goal of his ambition his own personal freedom and that of his race, and he permitted neither principalities nor powers, nor height nor depth, nor things present nor things to come, to swerve him from the pursuit of that purpose.

When we speak of moral courage we indulge in tautology of terms; for all courage is essentially moral. It does not require courage to go with your friends or against your enemies; it is a physical impulse to do so. But true moral courage is shown when we say no to our friends.

Mr. Douglass reached the climax of moral courage when he parted with William Lloyd Garrison, his friend and benefactor, because of honest difference of judgment, and when for the same motive he refused to follow John Brown to the scaffold at Harper's Ferry. It required an iron resolution and sublime courage for Douglass to deny the tender, pathetic, paternal appeal of the man who was about to offer up himself as a sacrifice for an alien race. John Brown on the scaffold dying for an alien and defenseless race is the most sublime spectacle that this planet has seen since Christ hung on the cross. That scaffold shall be more hallowed during the ages to come than any throne upon which king ever sat. Who but Douglass would decline a seat on his right hand?

In the fourth place, Mr. Douglass stands out as a model of self-respect. Although he was subject to all of the degradation and humiliation of his race, yet he preserved the integrity of his own soul. It is natural for a class that is despised, rejected and despitefully used to accept the estimate of their contemners, and to conclude that they are good for nothing but to be cast out and trodden under foot. In a civilization whose every feature serves to impress a whole people with a sense of their inferiority, small wonder if the more timid and resigned spirits are crushed beneath the cruel weight. It requires the philosophic calm and poise to stand upright and unperturbed amid such irrational things.

It is imperative that the youth of the colored race have impressed upon them the lesson that it is not the treatment that a man receives that degrades him, but that which he accepts. It does not degrade the soul when the body is swallowed up by the earthquake or overwhelmed by the flood. We are not humiliated by the rebuffs of nature. No more should we feel humiliated and degraded by violence and outrage perpetrated by a powerful and arrogant social scheme. As a man thinketh in his heart, so is he. The inner freedom of soul is not subject to assault and battery. Mr. Douglass understood this principle well. He was never in truth and indeed a slave; for his soul never accepted the gyves that shackled his body.

It is related that Mr. Douglass was once ordered out of a first-class coach into a "Jim Crow" car by a rude and ill-mannered conductor. His white companion followed him to the proscribed department, and asked him how he felt to be humiliated by such a coarse fellow. Mr. Douglass let himself out to the full length of his robust manhood and replied, "I feel as if I had been kicked by an ass." If one will preserve his inner integrity, the ill-usage and despiteful treatment others may heap upon him can never penetrate to the holy of holies, which remains sacred and inviolable to an external assault.

The fifth lesson which should be emphasized in connection with the life of Mr. Douglass is that he possessed a ruling passion outside the narrow circle of self-interest and personal well being. The love of liberty reigned supreme in his soul. All great natures are characterized by a passionate enthusiasm for some altruistic principle. Its highest manifestation is found in the zeal for the salvation of men on the spiritual side. All great religious teachers belong to this class. Patriots and philanthropists are ardently devoted to the present well-being of man. The poet, the painter, and the sculptor indulge in a fine frenzy over contemplative beauty or its formal expression. The philosopher and the scientist go into ecstasy over the abstract pursuit of truth. Minds of smaller caliber get pure delight from empty pleasure, sportsmanship or the collection of curios and bric-à-brac. Even the average man is at his highest level when his whole soul goes out in love for another. The man who lives without altruistic enthusiasm goes through the world wrapped in a shroud.

There have been few members of the human race that have been characterized by so intense and passionate a love for liberty as Frederick Douglass. His love for liberty was not limited by racial, political or geographical boundaries, but included the whole round world. He believed that liberty, like religion, applied to all men "without one plea." He championed liberty for black men, liberty for white men, liberty for Americans, liberty for Europeans, liberty for Asiatics, liberty for the wise, liberty for the simple; liberty for the weak, liberty for the strong; liberty for men, liberty for women; liberty for all the sons and daughters of men. I do not know whether he permitted his thoughts to wander in planetary space or speculated as to the inhabitability of other worlds than ours; but if he did, I am sure that his great soul took them all in his comprehensive scheme of liberty. In this day and time, when the spirit of commercialism and selfish greed command the best energies of the age, the influence of such a life to those who are downtrodden and overborne is doubly significant. Greed for gain has never righted any wrong in the history of the human race. The love of money is the root, and not the remedy of evil.

In the sixth and last place, I would call attention of the young to the danger of forgetting the work and worth of Frederick Douglass and the ministration of his life. We live in a practical age when the things that are seen overshadow the things that are invisible.

What did Douglass do? ask the crass materialists. He built no institutions and laid no material foundations. True, he left us no showy tabernacles of clay. He did not aspire to be the master mechanic of the colored race. The greatest things of this world are not made with hands, but reside in truth and righteousness and love. Douglass was the moral leader and spiritual prophet of his race. Unless all signs of the times are misleading, the time approaches, and is even now at hand, which demands a moral renaissance. Then, O for a Douglass, to arouse the conscience of the white race, to awaken the almost incomprehensible lethargy of his own people, and to call down the righteous wrath of Heaven upon injustice and wrong.

From Kelly Miller, *Race Adjustment: Essays on the Negro in America*, 2nd ed. (New York: Neale Publishing, 1909), 19–20, 213–228.

Index

WRITERS IN THEIR OWN TIME BOOKS

Alcott in Her Own Time
Edited by Daniel Shealy

Douglass in His Own Time
Edited by John Ernest

Emerson in His Own Time
Edited by Ronald A. Bosco and Joel Myerson

Franklin in His Own Time
Edited by Kevin J. Hayes and Isabelle Bour

Fuller in Her Own Time
Edited by Joel Myerson

Garland in His Own Time
Edited by Keith Newlin

Hawthorne in His Own Time
Edited by Ronald A. Bosco and Jillmarie Murphy

Jefferson in His Own Time
Edited by Kevin J. Hayes

Lincoln in His Own Time
Edited by Harold K. Bush, Jr.

Poe in His Own Time
Edited by Benjamin F. Fisher

Stowe in Her Own Time
Edited by Susan Belasco

Thoreau in His Own Time
Edited by Sandra Harbert Petrulionis

Twain in His Own Time
Edited by Gary Scharnhorst

Whitman in His Own Time
Edited by Joel Myerson